HISPANIC
Golden-Age Drama

Pedro Calderón de la Barca

LOVE IS NO LAUGHING MATTER

(No hay burlas con el amor)

Translated with an Introduction & Commentary
by

Don Cruickshank and Seán Page

ARIS & PHILLIPS - WARMINSTER

ISBN (cloth) <u>0 85668 365 5</u>
     (limp) 0 85668 366 3

1000255863

British Library Cataloguing-in-Publication Data
A catalogue record for this book is available from the British Library.

Corrected impression 1994

Printed and published in England by ARIS & PHILLIPS LTD,
Teddington House, Warminster, Wiltshire.

CONTENTS

Introduction

1 Don Pedro Calderón de la Barca (1600–1681)   vii

2 Calderón and the comic conventions of the Golden Age   xiv

3 The *précieuse ridicule* and the *burlador burlado*   xix

4 Staging   xxv

5 Date and textual history of *No hay burlas con el amor*   xxvii

6 Metre   xxx

Select bibliography and abbreviations   xxxv

Play and commentary

Act I   Jornada Primera   2

Act II   Jornada Segunda   66

Act III   Jornada Tercera   132

Editorial emendations   198

Acknowledgements

The only previous translation into English of *No hay burlas con el amor* was published by Kenneth Muir and Ann Mackenzie in 1985. We refrained from consulting this until our own translation had passed through several drafts. When we turned to it to see how certain passages had been handled, we often found its solutions instructive. At the few points where we had come up with identical phrasing, we refrained from introducing changes merely to be different. We made one deliberate borrowing (lines 1675–6).

The body of this book was typeset by the authors on the mainframe computers of University College, Dublin, using Donald E. Knuth's TEX program. We are grateful to the staff of our Computer Centre and of our Department of Computer Science for their assistance. We are especially indebted to our colleague Dr. John Kennedy of the Department of Mathematical Physics for the ingenuity and patience with which he responded to our importunities.

INTRODUCTION

1 Don Pedro Calderón de la Barca (1600–1681)

Calderón was born in Madrid on 17 January 1600. His father was a civil servant belonging to the minor nobility, with enough money to send young Pedro to the best school in Madrid, the Jesuits' new Colegio Imperial, and later to the universities of Alcalá and Salamanca.

Three other legitimate Calderón children survived childhood: Diego (born 1596), Dorotea (born 1598) and José (born 1602). In a fashion typical of the time, it was planned that the eldest brother would inherit the father's job, while Pedro would enter the Church and take up a family chaplaincy endowed by his maternal grandmother. A series of misfortunes conspired to defeat these plans, however.

First of all, Calderón's mother died, in 1610. The father remarried, and the stepmother evidently cared little for her new family. Very few of Calderón's plays portray mothers, a fact which may have some connection with his own mother's early death, or with his uncongenial stepmother. In 1615 the father died unexpectedly, leaving a strange will which revealed that a certain Francisco González who had once lived in the Calderón household, apparently as a servant, was his illegitimate son. Francisco had been thrown out by the father for 'disobedience', but he was to be given a share of the estate if he reappeared, provided he did not marry a certain woman he had been involved with. Diego was threatened with disinheritance if he married a certain unnamed young woman, or any of his cousins. Pedro was enjoined on no account to give up his studies for the Church.[1] Dorotea had already been consigned to a convent in Toledo at the unusually early age of thirteen.[2] Calderón's plays depict a number of fathers who damage the lives of their sons or daughters by attempting to control them in some way: it is easy to believe that this theme derives from the author's personal experience.

Pedro's preparations for an ecclesiastical career did not end immediately with his father's death. He had apparently matriculated at the

University of Alcalá in October 1614 and again in 1615. (This enrolment at university at the age of only fourteen is not the mark of a child prodigy: it was normal in an epoch when life expectation was less and adolescents had the responsibilities and duties of adulthood thrust upon them much earlier.) When his father died in November 1615, Pedro broke off his studies at Alcalá, but resumed them at Salamanca. He enrolled in Canon Law (appropriate for a prospective priest), but he seems to have pursued his studies irregularly. He got into trouble for not paying his rent, and as a result he was excommunicated at the behest of the convent to which he owed it (this was a standard practice at the time) and was lodged in the university prison. This episode seems to have put an end to his university career and, for the time being, to his studies for the Church.

In 1621 Calderón and his two brothers were involved in some kind of affray with one Nicolás de Velasco, son of a servant of the Duke of Frías, Don Bernardino Fernández de Velasco, holder of the important office of Constable of Castile. The young man, who may have been distantly related to the Duke, was killed, possibly in a swordfight, and the Calderón brothers took refuge in the Imperial (i.e. Austrian) Embassy. The case was settled out of court, with the brothers agreeing to pay the dead man's relatives the substantial sum of 600 ducats in compensation. In order to meet this debt, and to pay other money owed to their stepmother, they were forced to sell Diego's title to his father's job. Whatever may have been Pedro's role in the death of Velasco, the Duke bore no grudge against him. Pedro entered the Duke's service as a 'squire' that same year, and fifteen years later he dedicated the first volume of his collected plays to the Duke, who was still his patron.

By this time Calderón's career as a writer had already begun: his first works to appear in print were poems, published in 1620. Much of his poetry was written for specific occasions, including competitions, and his early successes in the latter brought him to the notice of Lope de Vega, then at the height of his career. Lope's praise was somewhat patronising, but Calderón's attitude to Lope was always one of respect. Indeed, Calderón's relations with his fellow-writers seem almost always to have been good ones; there is plenty of evidence, all through his long life, that he sought and enjoyed the company of other writers.

We do not know when Calderón first began writing plays. Moreover, we do not know the dates of many of his plays, which hampers any attempt to study his development as a dramatist. Juan de Vera Tassis, his first biographer, would have us believe that Don Pedro was writing plays as early as 1613, but the first records of performance all date from 1623. A payment was made on 29 June of that year for a performance of *Amor, honor y poder* (*Love, honour and power*); on 21 July and 30 September payments were made for performances of *La selva confusa* (*The confusing forest*) and *Los Macabeos* (*The Maccabees*, otherwise *Judas Macabeo*).[3] These early plays are usually considered to be derivative, modelled on Lope de Vega or Tirso de Molina. Indeed, *La selva confusa* and *Amor, honor y poder* were published under Lope's name in 1633 and 1634 respectively. Such false attributions probably provoked the complaint, first made in Calderón's *Primera parte* of 1636, that his plays were being published under the names of others.

Amor, honor y poder* has been called an 'exemplary play'. It deals (via an Italian source) with Edward III of England and the Countess of Salisbury. This may seem an odd subject for a young Spanish dramatist to choose for what was probably one of his first commissioned court plays, until we remember that the summer of 1623 was the summer of the visit of Charles Stuart, Prince of Wales, who was in Madrid from March until September. *Amor, honor y poder* is the first example of Calderón's ability to choose a subject of some topical interest, and one which would be flattering to his royal patrons while making a moral point, though not in such a way as to embarrass them (young King Edward discovers the strength of love and honour and the limits of his power, and learns self-control). This ability explains Calderón's enduring success as a court dramatist. It also accounts in part for his success as a writer of *autos sacramentales*, particularly those which originate in current events. Some critics have categorised Lope de Vega as an inventor, Calderón as a borrower and synthesiser of the inventions of others. This is true in part, but such criticism has overlooked Calderón's imaginative use of current events, state visits or other royal occasions to provide a starting-point or to add a topical significance to his dramatic productions.

Amor, honor y poder* illustrates another Calderonian trait, in that a ten-line passage describing a fountain recurs in *El príncipe constante* (*The constant prince*, 1629). Inventive Calderón may have been, but he was not above re-using good material, ranging from images and metaphors to jokes and whole passages, usually lyrical ones. Re-using, and also reworking: the more research we do on Calderón texts, the more evidence we find of revision and rewriting of earlier material.

One of the genres for which Calderón is celebrated is the comedy of manners, but the date of his first venture into the genre is not known. Two of the most famous examples, and perhaps the best, *La dama duende* (*The fairy lady*) and *Casa con dos puertas mala es de guardar* (*A house with two doors is a hard one to guard*), were both written in 1629. These are already technical masterpieces in terms of sustained level of humour, handling of complex plot, etc. However, we cannot easily find examples where imperfect technique can confidently be ascribed to inexperience. In *El astrólogo fingido* (*The feigned atrologer*), Calderón's first play to be published (1632), the hero, disappointed in love, says he will go as a soldier to Flanders with Don Vicente Pimentel; and Don Vicente appears as an officer in Flanders in *El sitio de Bredá* (*The siege of Breda*), which was written in the second half of 1625. If this means that *El astrólogo fingido* was written before *El sitio de Bredá*, we can only conclude that it is very good for an early attempt at comedy of manners.

Another genre for which Calderón is noted is the so-called 'wife-murder' play. That is, a play in which a husband kills his wife because he fears she has been or will be unfaithful to him. The fact is that only three plays properly belong to this group, and the date of none of them is certain: *El médico de su honra* (*The surgeon of his honour*, ca. 1633?), *A secreto agravio, secreta venganza* (*Secret vengeance for secret insult*, 1635?) and *El pintor de su deshonra* (*The painter of his own dishonour*, ca. 1645?). A fourth play sometimes included is *La devoción de la cruz* (*Devotion to the cross*, ca. 1630?), which does not really belong, since it deals with the consequences of an attempted wife-murder. The subject clearly interested Calderón, but not as much as the critical attention directed towards these few plays might lead us to suppose. It might be more accurate to say that he was interested in differing attitudes towards worldly honour, or reputation; this interest embraces such different plays as *El príncipe constante* and *El alcalde de Zalamea* (*The mayor of Zalamea*, 1636?), both of which have heroes who realise that 'spiritual' honour takes precedence over worldly honour—and that the two are fundamentally irreconcilable.

Another wide-reaching Calderón theme is the parent-child (usually father-son) relationship, which perhaps appears first in *La devoción de la cruz*. It is the principal motif in *La vida es sueño* (*Life is a dream*, 1635?), and continues to recur regularly in his plays until at least 1661, the year to which *Apolo y Climene* (*Apollo and Clymene*), *El Faetonte* (*Phaeton*), *Eco y Narciso* (*Echo and Narcissus*) and *El monstruo de los jardines* (*The monster of the gardens*) have all been tentatively assigned. Calderón implies that parents who try to exercise too much control over their children's lives often bring about the things they most wish to avoid.

By the age of forty, Calderón had written most of the plays on which his reputation now stands: *El príncipe constante* (1629), *La dama duende* (1629), *Casa con dos puertas mala es de guardar* (1629), *El médico de su honra* (ca. 1633), *La vida es sueño* (1635?), *A secreto agravio, secreta venganza* (1635?), *El alcalde de Zalamea* (1636?), and *El mágico prodigioso* (*The wonder-working magician*, 1637).

Although Calderón came to be much admired and respected by his contemporaries, he has not been well served by his biographers. Vera Tassis, writing the year after the dramatist's death, claimed that Calderón had served as a soldier in Milan and Flanders from 1625 until, possibly, 1636. However, there is no evidence for any such service; on the contrary, there is evidence that Calderón was in Madrid for much of this period. Part of this evidence involves another scrape. In January 1629 one of Calderón's brothers was attacked and wounded by an actor, who took refuge in a Trinitarian convent. Pedro alerted the police and accompanied them into the convent, where the officers displayed what was later alleged to be excessive zeal, removing veils from some of the nuns' faces in their search for the fugitive. For his supposed part in this incident, Pedro was criticised by the Trinitarian court preacher, Hortensio Paravicino. He retaliated by adding some lines to *El príncipe constante*, mocking Paravicino's notoriously pompous oratorical style. The preacher was furious, but the inquiry he demanded found that he was making a mountain out of a molehill: Calderón was rebuked for tampering with the text of a play that had already been passed by the censor for performance, but not for any incidents at the convent.

Their treatment of the Paravicino affair illustrates the extent to which some of Calderón's biographers have reached misguided conclusions. Seizing on four events spanning more than ten years—Pedro's abandonment of the career urged on him by his father, his excommunication and imprisonment in Salamanca, the death of Nicolás de Velasco, and the Paravicino affair—together with details from a spurious autobiographical ballad,[4] they have constructed a portrait of a young hothead constantly at odds with authority. The truth is that we have too few facts to come to any firm conclusions on this matter.

The shortage of facts extends to Calderón's relations with women. On the strength of a remark in the 'autobiographical' ballad, it has been deduced that he was a womaniser. All we actually know is that he never married, although he had a liaison which resulted in the birth of a son, probably in 1647. The mother's name is not known, but it has been suggested that she died as a result of, or soon after, the boy's birth. Be that as it may, Calderón acknowledged the child and personally took responsibility for him, in marked contrast to the behaviour of his own father regarding Francisco.

As far as the ultimate Spanish authority, King Philip IV, was concerned, Calderón was treated only with favour. Between the publication in 1636 and 1637 of the first two collected volumes of his plays, Philip created the playwright a knight of the Order of Santiago. In worldly terms, this was the high point of his career. Some of the importance and prestige of the award may be deduced from the fact that Velázquez, who was King Philip's only royal painter from 1623, had to wait until 1660 before the same honour was bestowed on him.

Just when Calderón's success was at its peak, things began to go wrong. In 1640 Catalonia and Portugal revolted against the central Madrid government. As a member of the Order of Santiago, Calderón had to take part in two military campaigns in Catalonia between 1640 and 1642. In the second he was wounded, and he retired from the army. His younger brother was killed in a later campaign (1645), and his elder brother died in 1647. To make matters worse, theatres were shut down in October 1644 because of the death of the queen, and they remained closed until the following Easter. When the crown prince died in 1646 there was another general closure, which dragged on until 1649 because the king, a keen theatregoer, believed his own pleasure-seeking had somehow contributed to the series of disasters Spain was undergoing at the time. The closure created acute economic difficulties for Calderón, and it may have been these, or the death of his son's mother, together perhaps with his despondency over the general sense of national disillusionment, that prompted him to reconsider entering the priesthood. In any event, although he wrote one of his funniest comedies, *El agua mansa* (*Still water* [*runs deep*]) as late as the summer of 1649, he decided shortly afterwards to enter holy orders. He celebrated his first Mass in October 1651.

Many holders of chaplaincies such as Calderón's treated them as sinecures, but we know from documents that Calderón took part, over a period of years, in running a hostel for the destitute in Toledo. So seriously did he take his new vocation, in fact, that after his ordination he intended to give up writing. However, he was persuaded to continue composing *autos sacramentales* for the municipality of Madrid, and secular plays for performance in the royal theatres.

The *auto sacramental* was a one-act play which celebrated and ex-pounded the doctrine of the Eucharist; in Calderón's Madrid, these were performed in the main square on Corpus Christi Thursday. Calderón had written quite a number of them before 1650, although there are few reliable *auto* dates from his early period. His first ones seem to belong to the mid 1630s—*La cena de Baltasar* (*Belshazzar's feast*), *El nuevo palacio del Retiro* (*The new Retiro palace*), *El gran teatro del mundo* (*The great stage of the world*), etc. No date prior to 1630 has been proposed for any of his *autos*. From 1649 until his death, Calderón was the only author commissioned to write *autos* for Madrid. In his hands, the genre reached a peak of ingenuity and sophistication which no successors managed to emulate.

There is no doubt that Calderón's output changed in nature after 1650, although the change was less complete than has been suggested. He continued to write and rewrite comedies of manners; for example, *Cada uno para sí* (*Every man for himself*) was written after the fall of Barcelona (September 1652), printed in 1661, and revised by Calderón in the late 1660s. However, he wrote fewer plays of this kind, and more mythological ones, a genre he had first ventured into as early as the 1630s. Along with this went a growing interest in musical plays, culminating in his two opera libretti, *La púrpura de la rosa* (*The crimson of the rose*, one act, January 1660) and *Celos aun del aire matan* (*Jealousy, even of the air, kills*, three acts, December 1660). The change may, for all we know, reflect Calderón's own differing attitude to life, which is also reflected by his decision to become a priest; but there is little doubt that the mythological play, with its scope for allegorical meanings, was a more suitable vehicle for what he was trying to say to his court audience than the 'realistic' plays he was writing before 1650. We can also be sure that the court liked mythological plays because they enabled the new staging techniques to be used to best advantage, with transformations, elaborate scene-changes and costumes, exotic mechanical creatures, etc. Moreover, the 'unrealistic' genres of opera, or of partly-sung drama, were better matched to mythological plots. Finally, it should be remembered that Calderón's pre-1650 'realism' is only relative: it was composed of a series of dramatic conventions which bore slightly more resemblance to real life than those which operated in the mythological plays. However, although the settings changed, the themes did not: they were still the themes of love, honour and power which had informed his first recorded play in 1623.

Another constant which runs through Calderón's life is his pride in his profession, a pride which manifested itself in a concern for his reputation as a writer and for the accuracy of his texts. Although he referred deprecatingly in his will to some of his manuscripts as being of little value, he bequeathed them to a trusted friend; and although his prefaces also belittle his writings (in the manner of the day), the constant complaints about careless printing from bad copies, or about incorrect attributions, betoken a man who cared—perhaps to the point of being touchy—about his literary reputation. He wanted posterity to have at least the chance to judge him fairly, by what he had actually written: the lists of his plays which he prepared in his old age, the constant rewriting and revising of his work throughout his life, the preparation of fair copies (which still survive) of many of his *auto* texts, all support this view of him.

During Calderón's lifetime there appeared five collected volumes of his plays and one of his *autos*. The first and second volumes (1636 and 1637) were nominally edited by his younger brother José; the third and fourth (1664 and 1672) by friends of varying competence. Volume V, unauthorised, appeared in 1677, and Calderón angrily repudiated it in the preface to the volume of *autos* he published that same year. Other plays appeared singly, or in miscellaneous collections.

Calderón died on 25 May 1681, while still working on the *autos sacramentales* for that year. His output was considerable: more than 120 plays (of which about a dozen were written in collaboration with various other authors); over 70 *autos sacramentales*; at least two dozen minor humorous pieces of various kinds; and a modest amount of verse, much of it occasional. Calderón criticism has tended to concentrate on a handful of plays, neglecting most of the comedies and mythological works. His editors have done him similarly little justice: numbers of autograph manuscripts, including fair copies, remain unedited. It is hardly surprising that the full extent of his contribution to European drama is still being assessed.

2   Calderón and the comic conventions of the Golden Age

Comedy probably had its origins in the primitive Greek fertility-rites or revels (*komoi*) organised to celebrate the arrival of spring and its triumph over winter. Spring brought the birth of new livestock, the germination of seed, the budding of fruit-trees, and many primitive societies felt a need to promote and assist these processes with appropriate rites of their own. The primitive Greek rites almost certainly involved ceremonies of sexual initiation for the young members of the tribe who had just reached puberty. As ceremonies became more formalised, special 'revel-songs' (*komoidia*) were composed for them, and these developed into Greek comedy.

Spanish Golden-Age comedy is quite different from classical Greek comedy, but some of its conventions derive from the same beginnings. Spanish comedies nearly always deal with the love affairs of young adults (that is, with their sexual initiation) and culminate in marriage (that is, a fertility-rite). Love affairs are seldom conducted with the full knowledge and approval of the older generation, the parents; sometimes there is strong parental opposition. The marriages agreed in the closing scene represent the victory of youth over age; they are symbolic re-enactments of the triumph of spring over winter.

Paradoxically, the younger generation defeats the older one by joining it. As in the primitive Greek fertility-rites, the passage from the freedom of childhood leads to the restraints of adulthood. Thus, classical Spanish comedy is about growing up, about the tension between the desire to be free and the need to conform; and the tension is resolved in laughter.

There has been considerable discussion about the nature of Spanish tragedy in the light of the views expressed by Aristotle in his *Poetics*. Educated Spaniards of Calderón's time were familiar with Aristotle through his commentators. However, since Aristotle's detailed study of comedy had not survived, they had to go elsewhere for views on the theory of comedy. Traditionally important views such as those of Horace (65–8 B.C.), who argued that 'poetry' (i.e. imaginative literature) should aim to combine the giving of pleasure with the inculcation of useful precepts, were supported by the conclusions of the Council of Trent (1545–63), which insisted on the need for moral content in works of art. The aim of comedy came to be seen as 'castigare ridendo mores', to censure (undesirable) behaviour by means of laughter.[5]

Spanish Golden-Age comedy was either comedy of manners or comedy of intrigue, although by the date of Calderón's first plays (1623) Ruiz de Alarcón had already introduced early versions of what was later to be known as the *comedia de figurón* (character comedy). A refinement of the comedy of manners, this genre depicted eccentric or anti-social behaviour carried to sometimes ridiculous lengths. Beatriz and, to a lesser extent, Don Alonso display some *figurón* characteristics.

Even when classical Spanish comedy veered towards comedy of manners or of character, it seldom ignored the importance conceded to action, which is the hallmark of comedy of intrigue or of situation. There is rarely any attempt at profound examination of character, and most personages are presented in a thoroughly conventional way. Thus the setting is usually a city, most frequently Madrid. The young lovers almost always belong to the upper class, where young men behave like gentlemen, and young women behave like ladies. These young aristocrats are frequently five in number: two couples and an odd one out to permit some flexibility, or to threaten established relationships. This is essentially the situation in *No hay burlas con el amor*: the pairing of Don Juan and Leonor, and of Don Alonso and Beatriz, is threatened by Don Luis, who is a genuine rival to Don Alonso and an imagined rival to Don Juan. (Don Diego takes no part in the action; he is merely a *confidant* for Don Luis.)

Authority is represented by parents, almost invariably the father of the young ladies. Fathers are conventionally obsessed by the possibility that their daughters will be seduced and family honour ruined. They make it hard for the young lovers to meet or even to communicate, and threaten not only the smooth progress of courtship, but even (at least according to convention) the lives of any daughters who they may believe are misbehaving. Don Pedro, the father of Leonor and Beatriz, follows all these conventions.

Servants, being from the lower classes, use less elevated language than their masters. If there are dirty jokes, it is usually they who will tell them. They also display the vices 'typical' of the lower orders: cowardice, lying, gossip, self-interest, cynicism. Their cynicism is particularly noticeable in relations with the opposite sex: married servants are at loggerheads with their spouses; single servants (the norm in comedies) reveal a very cynical attitude to marriage.

Spanish Golden-Age comedy generally follows conventions closely, but conventions are also its subject-matter. The comedy of manners laughs at social conventions, while character comedy laughs at eccentrics, that is, people who flout conventions. Going a step further, comedy can laugh at its own conventions, and this is what Calderón does in our play, although he does not neglect the targets of the eccentric individual and the absurd conventions of society.

The eccentric character in our play is clearly Beatriz, with her vanity, her ostensible prudery and her extravagant language. According to seventeenth-century conventions, women should be 'feminine', marriage-orientated, non-intellectual. This view is upheld by Don Diego (465–8, 470–4), Don Pedro (1435–63) and Don Alonso (1643–56, 2305–7). An alternative view is stated by Don Luis (469, 475–7), who admires Beatriz for precisely those qualities which antagonise her father and Don Diego. Don Alonso, of course, has a change of heart, and ends up falling for Beatriz.

Although less obviously than Beatriz, Don Alonso is also an 'unconventional' character. Despite his elevated social rank, he displays many of the characteristics associated with the 'lower orders' of society: he is cynical, especially with regard to women (1059–88); he is not at all eager to put himself out for the sake of a lady's reputation (1924, 1931–3, 1937–40, 1941–2);[6] though not precisely a coward, he has none of the conventional young gallant's taste for such escapades as leaping from balconies (2027–9, 2033); and he is more than a little lukewarm in his reaction to jealousy inspired by rivals (2316–19, 2566–75). (Don Juan and Don Luis, with their prompt respective rejections of Leonor and Beatriz because of the suspicion of rivals, are 'conventional' in this regard.) Finally, although Don Alonso does not actually tell 'dirty' jokes as such, his various funny remarks about women, such as his likening them to fruit (1071–84), and his story about Clara's skirt (1515-34), are more appropriate to servants than to masters.

If Don Alonso possesses some of the conventional characteristics of comic servants, his servant Moscatel possesses some we associate with aristocrats. This reversal of roles is drawn to our attention as early as lines 56–64. Contrary to convention, Moscatel is in love, while his master is a cynic. As the play progresses, Moscatel describes his feelings, and expresses them to his beloved, in the elevated language of the upper classes. He talks about 'adoring Inés's presence' and 'winning her favour' (697–704); describes her as a 'cherub' (1089-92), and says that he has 'happy expectations' that his courtship will be looked on with favour (1094–6). When Inés is annoyed with him, he can quote the words of Don Gutierre, the protagonist of *The surgeon of his honour* (1275–6; see note on these lines). When he conveys Inés's rejection of Don Alonso's advances, he paraphrases the words used by Mencía, the heroine of the same play (1482–5; see note on these lines). His remarks about honour and jealousy (prompted by his master's interest in Inés) echo those of his social superiors in other plays (1123–4, 1143, 1203, 1228–30, 1240, 2456–9). He also reveals a concern over conflicting loyalties—to his master and to his beloved—that is typical of the stage nobleman, but quite uncharacteristic of the stage servant (1211–14, 1216–50). Finally, while Moscatel does not quite approach the typical young nobleman's reckless boldness in the conduct of his love-affair, he at least calls on love to inspire him with courage (402–6).

Some of these 'noble' characteristics of Moscatel's are also found in his beloved, Inés. She talks about being 'less uncaring' than she seems (705-11); she uses the vocabulary a young noblewoman might use to reject unwelcome advances, including the especially characteristic 'I am who I am' (1251–66), and even gets some revenge on Beatriz with a metaphor about 'dawn's white pearls' (2122–4).

This is not to say, however, that there is a complete reversal of roles. Moscatel displays the 'typical' comic servant's fear for his own skin when caught by Don Pedro (716–68), and a 'typical' reluctance to confront a sexual rival (2016–20, 2402–3). He tells a 'typically' scatological joke (2325–57) about a bullfight, and, despite his gallantry towards Inés, his proposal to her at the end of the play is far from romantic. Likewise Inés, despite her moral principles vis-à-vis Don Alonso, and her occasionally elevated language, is a completely conventional stage servant-wench in her gossiping, her fibbing and her inability to keep a secret. At the end of the play, despite accepting Moscatel's proposal, she joins him in referring to marriage as the 'worst of all disasters' (3106; cf. 3112): a typical piece of stage-servant cynicism. Moreover, although Don Alonso and Beatriz flout, respectively, the conventions of their rank and of their sex, they end up apparently reconciled to them. With a certain amount of resistance, they have undergone the initiation ceremony and joined the adult members of society.

Are we to conclude, then, that the play upholds the conventional view of society presented by so many other plays? The answer, to quote Moscatel, is yes and no (672). Both Don Alonso and Beatriz are depicted as antisocial and immature. If comedy is about growing up, it is they who need to do it. The conventions they flout are not presented as particularly valuable, but their reasons for flouting them are reprehensible. The couple are rebels, but they have no cause.

The silliness and pretentiousness of the upper-class characters is to some extent exposed by their servants. Lope de Vega said in his *Arte nuevo de hacer comedias en este tiempo* (*New art of writing plays in our time*, 1609) that 'servants should not deal with lofty matters'. Given this convention, there is no doubt that we are meant to be amused by the servant who apes the posturing and apostrophising of his 'betters'. At the same time, Moscatel makes it harder for us to take such posturing seriously in its usual context. In addition, both he and Inés expose at least some of it for what it is: Moscatel accuses Don Juan and Don Alonso of 'beating about the bush' when they cannot admit plainly that they want to see Leonor and Beatriz (2616–18); Don Juan cannot admit it because he is 'jealous', while Don Alonso cannot bring himself to admit that he is no longer fancy-free (cf. also 2293–5). Later, Inés also mocks Don Juan's 'jealousy', and Leonor's inability to see through it (2792–6).

What is being made fun of here is one of the most important 'noble' conventions: that one must not lose face. Seen in this light, the play has a number of 'losers', although no one suffers very much. Don Pedro, the zealous and jealous father, so concerned about the loss of face he would suffer through flighty daughters, and so anxious to control their lives, has lost control over them. He has not even kept his paternal prerogative of choosing husbands for them. Moreover, not only do his daughters marry men of their own choice; they do so precisely because their behaviour has been, by Don Pedro's exacting standards, flighty (i.e. they engaged in courtship). As for Don Juan, he suffers the indignity of having to admit that the suspicions he entertained about Leonor were baseless (3089–91), and Don Alonso suffers the indignity of having to admit not only that he pretended to love Beatriz for a joke, but that the joke backfired on him (2904–54); in addition his plan to deceive and seduce Inés ends with her deceiving him with a pretence of affection. It may be added that the same pretence of affection completely deceives Moscatel, who had earlier made the anti-feminist claim that there was nothing so easy as fooling a woman (1873–4). Lastly, although Don Luis has not lost face, his insistence on not doing so has lost him Beatriz. We may well suspect, from his extravagant language and his extravagant views about honour and jealousy (486–500, 1175–80, 2654–6), that Calderón wished

to present him as carrying the conventional 'noble' views on these topics
to extreme lengths, and to indicate that these were responsible for his
failure.

Among the female characters, Beatriz undergoes a certain amount
of suffering, but it is self-inflicted. She is neither a real prude nor a
real intellectual, and the process of discovering this is a little painful.
Finally, it is worth noting that of all the play's characters (discounting
the insignificant Don Diego) it is two of the women, Leonor and Inés,
who emerge most unscathed from the events. Even they have occasion
to regret the attempted deception of Beatriz; and their expression of
regret is entirely in keeping with the theme of the play, that one should
not fool around with love. Thus Inés agrees with Moscatel that the
introduction of Don Alonso as Beatriz's pretended lover is 'a very bad
joke' (1926); and Leonor, wishing that she had never thought of the idea
in the first place, admits that 'what began as a joke is turning out to be
deadly serious' (1959–60).

That Calderón's intention in writing the play was at least partly to
promote a moral awareness in his audience is obvious from remarks made
directly to the audience, especially by Don Alonso. The most significant
of these is his closing one, 'Take a lesson from me; let everyone beware
of love' (3117–18), but there are others (e.g. 2034–8). As one critic has
noted, direct address of this kind 'emphasizes for us the distance between
the dramatized world and our world outside the play; yet, paradoxically
enough, it serves at the same time to draw us deeper inside the make-
believe society inhabited by...the...characters'.[7] The process of distancing
is seen most clearly in Calderón's references to other plays (963, 1232,
1245, 1919–22), or in his references to the performing of plays (56–64,
104–5, 1062–4). This playing with dramatic convention is done partly
to amuse, but the reminders to the audience that they are watching a
play must also inhibit any tendency to identify with the characters. In
theory, this should promote Brechtian 'alienation', leaving the audience
sufficiently detached to form dispassionate moral judgements about the
action and the characters.[8] In a relatively light-hearted play such as
the present one, alienation does not go very far, and the moral lesson,
though present, takes second place to entertainment. The intention is
to promote laughter rather than to censure.

3   The *précieuse ridicule* and the *burlaᴅor burlado*

Beatriz: the *précieuse ridicule*

When Molière's *Les précieuses ridicules* was performed on 18 November
1659, it created something of a storm. The target of Molière's satire was
those people, particularly women, whose pursuit of delicacy in taste, in

sentiment and in language had degenerated (as he saw it) into affectation and narrowness. That his satire had legitimate targets is certain; the storm arose because Molière seemed also to be attacking those who were sincerely and genuinely striving to refine the literary taste and language of the time. Inevitably, the controversy aroused prejudices which had a long history: prejudices involving the whole question of the education of women, and their status as arbiters of literary taste and as authors.

There were women writers at least as far back as Sappho, the Greek poetess of the seventh century B.C. The question of giving women the same education as men was raised by Cleobolus of Rhodes (6th century B.C.) and Plato. In practice only the Spartans took the education of women seriously; but, as Spartan education was largely physical, this had no effect on literature. The proportion of women attaining literacy remained extremely low throughout the Classical and medieval periods. In the Middle Ages education was dominated by the Church, which allotted only a subordinate role to women, and ensured that their education ran along strictly devotional lines.   There were relatively few (and only partial) exceptions, such as Hrotsvitha (tenth century), the Saxon abbess who adapted the comedies of Terence for her nuns, or Marie de France (twelfth century), France's first poetess, who was possibly also an abbess.

The coming of the Renaissance and the invention of printing heralded slow but eventually enormous changes.   The study of letters (as opposed to arms) became respectable among the aristocracy, while printing brought the written word within reach of a whole new range of social groups.   There was a positive change in attitude to the education of women,[9] and the considerable growth of general literacy had a corresponding effect on literacy among women. In Spain, where the policies of Ferdinand and Isabella (1474–1516) encouraged perhaps the highest rate of urban literacy in Europe in the sixteenth and seventeenth centuries,[10] the growth in female literacy is hard to measure accurately, but the effects in terms of women's writing became very apparent in the course of the seventeenth century.[11]

The spread of literature to new social groups, including women, prompted a number of reactions. The first was alarm at the potentially harmful effects of imaginative literature on those considered ill-prepared for it, including women.[12] The second, arising from a wish to endow modern European vernaculars with the range and sophistication of expression enjoyed by Greek and Latin, was a movement towards the refinement of language, often by means of increased use of Classical style, allusion or vocabulary. This allegedly led to 'Euphuism' in English, *marinismo* in Italian, *préciosité* in French, and *culteranismo* in Spanish.

In turn these literary movements prompted reactions when they were carried—or were felt by some to be carried—to excess. Mingled with the reaction, and disguised in it, was a certain amount of male alarm at the growing involvement of women in the largely male preserve of literature.[13]

The apostle of *culteranismo* is Luis de Góngora (1561–1627), but he was by no means the first to try to raise the literary standard of the Castilian (i.e. Spanish) language. However, with his Latin vocabulary, latinised (and occasionally even hellenised) syntax, no one tried harder to increase the flexibility of the language or to enlarge its range.[14] No one attracted more hostility, more parody—or more imitation.

Góngora's great *culto* poems, the *Polifemo* and the *Soledades* (*Polyphemus* and *Solitudes*), were not printed until 1627, but they had circulated in manuscript from 1613, and had soon provoked hostile reaction. Juan de Jáuregui, another poet, probably wrote his *Antídoto contra la pestilente poesía de las 'Soledades'* (*Antidote against the pestilent poetry of the 'Solitudes'*) in 1614, and Quevedo satirised Góngora's latinate vocabulary and syntax in the cruel sonnet beginning

> He who would be *culto* in only a day,
> the following jar-(must learn)gon.[15]

Góngora was a poet with an exceptional ear and an outstanding poetic sensibility, but, as Quevedo indicated, tortured syntax and Latin words could easily be used to produce verse that bore a superficial resemblance to his poetry. Góngora's professed indifference or even hostility to the uneducated reader who might find his poetry impenetrable could easily be turned into literary snobbery, or obscurity for its own sake. Such attitudes were by no means unknown in the preceding generation; they observed the tradition of Horace's 'odi profanum vulgus et arceo'.[16]

Apart from antipathy to Góngora's style, Quevedo's satirical works reveal a dislike of what he perceived as humbug, and a strong streak of antifeminism. All three feelings coincide in *La culta latiniparla*, a 'catechism of terms for the instruction of learned women and latinifemales', published in 1631, just four years before *No hay burlas con el amor* was performed. With a few trivial exceptions, Calderón's Beatriz does not use the precise vocabulary recommended by Quevedo; but the advice about vocabulary and syntax, and about the name-dropping of Classical authors, probably provided a blueprint for the character.

Beatriz, in fact, seems to have no precedent in other plays. Those which are mentioned in the context of *No hay burlas con el amor* are Lope de Vega's *La discreta enamorada* (*Discreet in her love*, ?written 1606, published 1653), *Los melindres de Belisa* (*The fastidiousness of Belisa*, 1606–8, published 1617), *El mayor imposible* (*The most impossible thing*, 1615, published 1647) and *El desprecio agradecido* (*Grateful for scorn*, ca. 1633, published 1637); Tirso de Molina's *La celosa de sí misma* (*Jealous of herself*, published 1627); and Antonio Hurtado de Mendoza's *El marido hace mujer y el trato muda costumbre* (*Husbands form wives and attitudes shape behaviour*, 1631–32, published 1636). These may present heroines who are literate, who have intellectual aspirations, or who reject men, but there is no sign of Beatriz's most striking characteristic, her pedantic mode of speech.[17] The only 'Spanish' precedent for this characteristic appears to be Don Armado de Adriano, the 'fantastical Spaniard' in Shakespeare's *Love's labour's lost* (printed in 1598, though perhaps written in 1595). Don Armado's nationality is indicative of the poor Hispano-English relations of the 1590s rather than of a Spanish source. It has frequently been claimed that Don Armado was meant to satirise the Euphuism of Lyly, but his language is more akin to that of Sidney's *Arcadia* (published 1590). If there is any connection between *Love's labour's lost* and *No hay burlas con el amor*, it is a very remote and indirect one, in a common Italian source such as The Pedant, one of the stock figures of Italian *commedia dell'arte*.

Even if *La culta latiniparla* is not the blueprint for Beatriz, it implies the existence of a type in sufficient numbers for satire or caricature to be viable; and it prompts the question, to what extent did Calderón share the attitudes of Quevedo, as expressed in *La culta latiniparla*?

Calderón's attitude to Góngora is well known: he quotes him, refers to him with respect, imitates his style. We cannot suppose that Beatriz was created with the intention of satirising Góngora or his language. If there is mockery here, it is at least partly at Calderón's own expense. The most obvious example of Calderón's self-mockery in the play is a remark of Don Alonso's:

> Is this one of those plays by Don Pedro Calderón,
> where there's bound to be a hidden lover or a
> veiled lady? (1919–22)

However, the fact is that much of Beatriz's extravagant vocabulary is used elsewhere by Calderón in serious circumstances: e.g. the verb *abstraer* ('abstract', 577, 903), *diestra* ('dexter', 578, 1708), *nocturno* ('nocturnal', 612), *víbora humana* ('human viper', 615), *eclipse* (1355), *epiciclo* ('epicycle', 1358), *crinita* ('planet-stricken', 1433), *escrúpulo* ('proclivity', 1709), *lúgubre* ('lugubrious', 1713), *paroxismo* ('paroxysm', 1719), *trágico coturno* ('tragic buskin', 1746), *antonomasia* (1779), etc. As Arellano has pointed out, such words or expressions had been satirised or criticised by purists of this period.[18] Calderón is only following Lope de Vega, who in *La dama boba* (*The foolish lady*) held up for mockery one of his own sonnets, which was published elsewhere as a serious piece of poetry.[19]

As for the possibility of antifeminism or reaction against the education of women, there are some clues in another, similar Calderón play, *El agua mansa* (*Still water runs deep*, 1649), where Eugenia, one of a pair of sisters, has much in common with Beatriz. Eugenia's father, Don Alonso, plans to unite one of his daughters in marriage with a cousin, Don Toribio, an absurd and extravagant figure. In Don Alonso's eyes, all that matters is that Don Toribio has blue blood. He has no concern for the wishes or feelings of his daughters: indeed, he thinks that the best way to cure the wilful Eugenia of her interest in literature is to marry her off and have her raising a family as quickly as possible. By the end of the play, some lessons have been learned: Clara, the 'quiet' sister, manages by her determination to marry the man of her own choice, thus illustrating the point of the play's title. Eugenia is cured of her pedantry and her wilfulness, but her father acknowledges that she deserves 'more consideration' than to be given to 'such a boorish husband'. She is allowed to marry Don Juan, who has proved himself a considerate and loving suitor. Don Toribio is sent home in disgrace, but his closing words state unequivocally that the play is an 'exemplary' one, with a moral. Eugenia's defect was not that she professed an interest in literature, but that her interest was pedantic, merely an excuse for acting in a snobbish, wilful and contemptuous way.

This play enables us to understand Calderón's attitude to Beatriz more clearly. His character Don Diego believes that women should learn to sew and mend, not to study stylistics and write verse (470–4); but it is pedantry, the misuse of education, that Calderón regards as a fault. We can see this from the way Beatriz's pedantries are flung back in her face (1405–6, 1409–10, 1411–12, 1414–16). A different attitude towards women's literacy is suggested when Inés has to admit that her illiteracy prevents her from distinguishing the title of one book from another, or even from reading a playbill (593–6).

Alonso: the *burlador burlado*

The key word where Don Alonso is concerned is *burlar*, 'to deceive, mock, ridicule, trick': the word is constantly applied to him by others or by himself (e.g. 39, 1549–50, 1667–70, 1685–91, 1695). *Burlas* ('joking, deception') are regularly contrasted with *veras* ('truth, earnestness') (e.g. 187, 385–6). The point about Don Alonso is that he never takes love seriously, and never takes women seriously. While boasting that he has never fallen in love himself, he laughs at those who do; however, since women are a source of amusement for him, he is quite happy to pretend to be in love if this will increase the enjoyment and the chances of making a conquest. In the end, of course, it is he who is the most deceived. What began in jest ends in earnest when he falls in love with Beatriz, whose pedantry, intellectual pretentions and apparent prudishness do not make her an obviously suitable partner for such a man of the world as Don Alonso.

As the deceiver who ends up deceived, Don Alonso must remind us of Don Juan Tenorio, the protagonist of *The trickster of Seville*. There are differences, of course: the deceptions of the prototype trickster are altogether grander—and also crueller, because their perpetrator seems to consider them successful only if they result in suffering. (Don Alonso's conversation with Moscatel and Don Juan in lines 1684–96 suggests that it simply never occurs to him that anyone may be hurt by his behaviour.) Moreover, one cannot imagine Tirso de Molina's Don Juan ever falling in love, whatever some of his literary descendants may have done. When he is finally deceived, his deception must be commensurate whith those he practised himself: it results in his death. Don Alonso is a much more amiable deceiver than Don Juan, and his confession of his foolishness (2904–54) undoubtedly has a disarming effect, but it should not be forgotten that he is a thorough snob. He laughs at members of his own social class who fall in love, but when servants do so, his laughter becomes mingled with scorn, sarcasm and disbelief.

Don Alonso's snobbishness is an important feature of his character. He and Beatriz actually have a great deal in common. Their contempt for the opposite sex is due to fear, and their fear springs from emotional immaturity and lack of self-confidence. Both are afraid of genuine emotional involvement, so both try to avoid it, affecting a superior contempt for those who do fall in love. Thus Don Alonso, pretending to help Don Juan's love affair to prosper, laughs at him behind his back (409–20), and Beatriz can prudishly scold her 'libidinous' sister for having a boyfriend (603–36). This allows both of them to feel superior.

The sense of superiority is increased when it is possible to rebuke a member of the lower class; specifically, a servant. Don Alonso finds it bad enough when his social equals take love seriously, but when a servant, male or female, does so, it provokes him to anger (181, 1493–5); evidently the ability of the 'lower orders' to feel emotions he is afraid of is even more alarming. As for Beatriz, her attempts to be intellectually superior seem considerably more successful when measured against an uneducated servant, on whom scorn can be heaped (581–3, 593–9).

Calderón's view of the behaviour of Don Alonso and Beatriz is clear from the closing speeches of the play, when Moscatel and Inés remind us of the moral lessons to be drawn from their master and mistress respectively (3103–6, 3107–12). Calderón comically reinforces his point by making the servants, whenever they talk of love, use the high-flown language of the upper-class lovers. Moscatel's vocabulary when Don Alonso threatens his 'honour' by making advances to Inés belongs not merely to his social superiors, but to the protagonists of such plays as *The surgeon of his honour*, Don Gutierre and Mencía. Thus Moscatel's remark about 'love and honour' (1211) echoes Don Gutierre's obsession (e.g. line 2068 of *The surgeon of his honour*); the parenthetical remark about words failing him, and being struck dumb (1228–30) is Gutierre's too (2850–1); Inés's 'I am who I am' (1258) is parallelled in dozens of plays, so it is not surprising to find Mencía use it (1649–50); we have seen that Moscatel's quotation from a ballad ('eyes, well may you weep! Be not of tears ashamed': 1275–6) is also used by Gutierre (1599–1600), and so on.

The use of such language by the servants has a threefold effect. First, it helps to raise their love affair to the same serious level as that of the major characters like Don Juan and Leonor. Second, since Moscatel and Inés retain many characteristics typical of 'comic servants' (telling jokes, making funny remarks about serious matters, uttering witty asides), their use of a pompous style sometimes has a comic effect (e.g. in lines 1484–5); but it is the style we laugh at, not the user of it. Third, the amusement provoked by Moscatel and Inés extends, as previously suggested, to the people who normally speak in this way: the Gutierres and the Mencías. Certainly it is not easy to take Gutierre's utterances quite as seriously when one has heard them from the lips of Moscatel. If recent criticism is correct in suggesting that plays such as *The surgeon of his honour* are designed to provoke a critical response in the spectator or reader, then such apparently lighthearted pieces as *Love is no laughing matter* may be seen to have a comparable purpose.

4   Staging

Before the opening of the Coliseo del Buen Retiro in 1640, there were only three permanent theatres in Madrid. Two, the Corral de la Cruz and the Corral del Príncipe, were ordinary public theatres; the third, the so-called *Salón de Palacio*, was a private royal theatre in the old palace. Unlike the Coliseo, none of them was built as a theatre. The two *corrales* were just what that term suggests: open yards surrounded by buildings. The *salón* was a large rectangular hall in the palace. The *corrales* had some simple stage-machinery and an apron-stage. The *Salón de Palacio* was a little more like the conventional modern theatre, with proscenium arch and front curtain, behind which there was perspective scenery which could be changed mechanically. We do not know where our play was first performed, but as it contains no references to scenery changes, it was probably played in one of the *corrales*.

The open *corral* stage was surrounded on three sides by spectators, some of them in the pit, some on balconies. A balcony above the stage was part of the performance area, but it is not used in our play. Hanging from the balcony was a curtain which could be pulled aside to show another small performance area, the inner stage. This too is unnecessary for the staging of our play, although the curtain itself is occasionally used by characters who have to hide from others without actually leaving the stage (e.g. 1392+, 2781+).

Only four sets are needed: an interior representing Don Alonso's house; an exterior representing the street outside Don Pedro's house; an interior representing Don Pedro's house; and an exterior representing a street some way from Don Pedro's house. Together these four sets accommodate eleven separate *cuadros*, or scenic divisions. Most of the play takes place in Don Pedro's house. At a pinch, two sets would suffice; the two interiors could be distinguished by the presence, in Don Pedro's house, of the only essential piece of furniture, a china-cupboard (1935–6).

Lines	Inside Don Alonso's house	Inside Don Pedro's house	In the street	Outside Don Pedro's house
1– 420	⊗			
421– 500				⊗
501–1022		⊗		
1023–1286			⊗	
1287–1477		⊗		
1478–16˘8	⊗			
1699–2038		⊗		
2039–2263		⊗		
2264–2637	⊗			
2638–2741				⊗
2742–3120		⊗		

The costume used would have been contemporary. Some of the items worn are actually mentioned in the text. Gentlemen wore swords (required in the closing scene) and daggers (2389), and hats when out of doors (423+). Ladies (and servants-girls) wore hooped skirts (1280–1), with shawls (1277) and veils (1104+) when out of doors. It should perhaps be remembered that female roles were played by actresses, not by boys as on the contemporary English stage.

The only other props specified by the text are two love-letters (363, torn after a struggle, 897; and 1104+), a mirror (575+), a pair of gloves

(585), a candlestick (1985+, 1985–6), a ribbon (2441) and a diamond (2510). Something has to represent the sound of breaking china (1944+, 1945), although this does not have to be seen; and although Inés is told to fetch a copy of Ovid (587–92), and Don Pedro goes off to fetch a buckler (3047), neither article is brought on stage.[20]

5   Date and textual history of *No hay burlas con el amor*

No early manuscript of the play has survived. The earliest printed version is in the form of a *suelta* (a play published singly) included with eleven other plays by various authors in the one-volume *Parte quarenta y dos de comedias de diferentes autores* (*Part forty-two of plays by different authors*), Zaragoza, Juan de Ybar, 1650. Doubt has been cast on the authenticity of the date, place and printer's name shown on this volume, but recent investigation, especially of typographical features, shows that most of the contents, including our play, were indeed printed by Juan de Ybar in Zaragoza, probably in 1650.[21] However, the play was certainly in existence long before this. It was mentioned in print five years earlier in the *Loa que representó Antonio de Prado* (*Prologue performed by Antonio de Prado*), a short comic piece written by Luis Quiñones de Benavente and published in his *Jocoseria* (*Comicoserious*), Madrid, 1645. Additional evidence enables us to push the date back another ten years. The Prado in question was one of the period's leading actor-managers, whose career ran from at least 1614 until his death in April 1651; he was an *autor* (manager of his own company) as early as 1622. The *loa* was obviously written specifically for him and his company, since it mentions himself, his wife (the *autora*, Mariana Vaca de Morales), and other actors and actresses. It was written to be performed when the theatres re-opened at Easter, with the new season's plays rehearsed during the traditional Lenten closure. In the *loa* we find the following:

Prado	Tres comedias tengo nuevas de Don Pedro Calderón.	I have three new plays by Don Pedro Calderón.
Autora	Y es la primera que hacemos *No hay burlas con el amor*.	And the first we're performing is *Love is no laughing matter*.

This suggests that the play, like the *loa*, was written specifically for Prado's troupe, and that it was performed soon after Easter in some unspecified year. On the basis of references to certain persons and plays mentioned in the *loa*, the year appears to be 1634 or 1635.[22] We know that Prado was in Madrid from November 1634 until June 1635 (Lent 1635 was 21 February to 8 April), and that he was apparently on tour in early 1634, so we can be fairly sure that the play was written and first performed in 1635.[23] This conclusion is partly supported by Moscatel's reference in line 1232 to Prado's playing of the king of Sweden: we know that Prado performed a play entitled *El rey de Suecia* (*The king of Sweden*) in the presence of King Philip IV on 1 February 1633, and that the same play was still creating a stir in March 1634.[24]

Although we can identify most of the actors and actresses who were with Prado at this time, it is perhaps idle to speculate in any detail on which players would take which parts in *No hay burlas con el amor*. Prado himself normally took male leads, but in 1635 he was probably over forty and rather stout, and so the part of Don Alonso was most likely played by another member of the company. We can be pretty sure that Moscatel was played by José Frutos Bravo, who took the comic roles every year from 1632 to 1644. Prado may very well have played Beatriz's father, Don Pedro, although the company then did include Juan de Escorihuela y Ariño, who played 'barbas' (literally, 'beards'); that is, old men.[25]

Prado kept *No hay burlas con el amor* in his repertoire for many years: his company performed it on 10 April 1651, just before he died. The title was not included in a list of eleven plays offered by his son Sebastián in November 1651, but it continued to be performed by other companies.[26]

By this time, as we have seen, the play was already in print. At some time between this printing and the year 1677 the play was cut and its title was changed to *La crítica del amor*. The effect of the cuts was to diminish the importance of Don Alonso and to increase the stature of Beatriz. We cannot tell whether these changes were made by a publisher or by an actor, as the doctored copy has been lost. We can be sure, however, that they were not made by Calderón himself, for he apparently failed to recognise the altered version of the text as his own when it was published in the spurious *Quinta parte* of 1677.

In 1682 Don Juan de Vera Tassis published his edition of Calderón's *Verdadera quinta parte de comedias* (*True fifth part of plays*): this restored the original title of the play and a handful of the cut lines. In 1694 Vera published a second edition of this *parte*, restoring a few more lines, but also making some unauthorised changes. Vera's main source for his text was the spurious *Quinta parte* of 1677. He must have had another source for the few lines he restored, but if this source was *Diferentes 42*, he used it very unsystematically. He cannot have had access to Calderón's original manuscript. All modern editions derive from Vera Tassis, most of them from his second edition. As a consequence, they all omit some three hundred authentic lines which Calderón had no part in cutting. The relationship between these various versions of the text is expressed in the diagram opposite.[27]

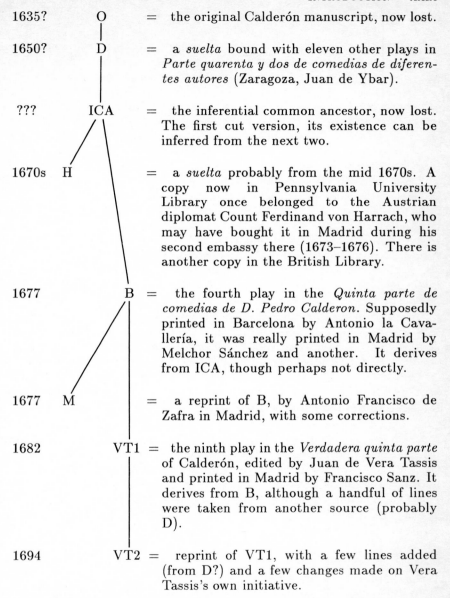

1635?   O   =   the original Calderón manuscript, now lost.

1650?   D   =   a *suelta* bound with eleven other plays in
                       *Parte quarenta y dos de comedias de diferen-
                       tes autores* (Zaragoza, Juan de Ybar).

???   ICA   =   the inferential common ancestor, now lost.
                       The first cut version, its existence can be
                       inferred from the next two.

1670s   H   =   a *suelta* probably from the mid 1670s. A
                       copy   now   in   Pennsylvania   University
                       Library   once   belonged   to   the   Austrian
                       diplomat Count Ferdinand von Harrach, who
                       may have bought it in Madrid during his
                       second embassy there (1673–1676). There is
                       another copy in the British Library.

1677   B   =   the fourth play in the *Quinta parte de
                       comedias de D. Pedro Calderon*. Supposedly
                       printed in Barcelona by Antonio la Cava-
                       llería, it was really printed in Madrid by
                       Melchor Sánchez and another.   It derives
                       from ICA, though perhaps not directly.

1677   M   =   a reprint of B, by Antonio Francisco de
                       Zafra in Madrid, with some corrections.

1682   VT1   =   the ninth play in the *Verdadera quinta parte*
                       of Calderón, edited by Juan de Vera Tassis
                       and printed in Madrid by Francisco Sanz. It
                       derives from B, although a handful of lines
                       were taken from another source (probably
                       D).

1694   VT2   =   reprint of VT1, with a few lines added
                       (from D?) and a few changes made on Vera
                       Tassis's own initiative.

A number of other *sueltas* of the late seventeenth and early eighteenth
centuries survive, but they derive from Vera Tassis, mostly from VT2,
and have no new authoritative readings. The very small possible debt

of VT1 and VT2 to D is not indicated. Our diagram, showing D deriving straight from Calderón's original, simplifies the relationship. Undoubtedly there were intervening versions, which introduced numerous corruptions and 'corrections'. D is a poor copy-text, carelessly set and horrendously punctuated, and it has so many gaps and so many errors of rhyme and metre that it cannot possibly have been taken directly from Calderón's original manuscript. Most likely it was based on a spare prompt copy sold by Prado or by someone in his company to the bookseller Pedro Escuer, who financed Juan de Ybar's printing of *Diferentes 42*. However, in spite of its shortcomings, it is clearly the most authoritative surviving version, and its status is further enhanced by its possession of over 300 clearly authentic lines found nowhere else. We have therefore based our edition on it. As it has not been edited critically before, all substantive departures from it are listed in an appendix. We have as a matter of course modernised capitalisation, punctuation, accentuation, lineation and (except where rhyme or metre would be damaged) spelling. The correction of misprints is noted only when the supposed error could involve a variant reading. Added stage directions are enclosed in square brackets, but they are not otherwise noted.

In attempting to establish our text, we have taken the view that our task was to produce a version that made sense on stage. When D's sense is defective, we have tried to avoid leaving blanks or merely referring to the defects in footnotes: we have adopted the inventions of other editors or devised our own. In some cases these probably restore the original reading, but they do not claim to be authoritative: in important cases the sources are indicated in the notes.

The only other critical edition of the play is by Ignacio Arellano (Pamplona, 1981). It has many virtues, but it suffers from the disadvantage of being based on VT1. However, it contains lists of variants from all the texts consulted by Arellano. These do not include D or H, but they include the version published by J.E. Hartzenbusch in volume IX of the Biblioteca de Autores Españoles series (Madrid, 1849),which is also based on Vera Tassis. We have found some of Hartzenbusch's solutions of editorial problems helpful.

6   Metre

The greater part of the play is written in 'romance', the free-moving verse form used in traditional ballads. Each line has eight syllables (a stressed final syllable counts as two), and alternate lines assonate: e.g. 'siendo' assonates with 'ruego', 'chanza' with 'mata', 'calle' with 'tarde'. About a sixth of the play uses the 'redondilla', which consists of 'romance' lines in quatrains with the rhyme-scheme abba. The other forms used are 'décimas', ten-line stanzas of 'romance' lines with the rhyme-scheme abbaaccddc; 'quintillas', somewhat freer five-line stanzas of 'romance' lines which can rhyme aabab, aabba, abaab, ababa or abbab; and 'silva', a free mixture of seven-syllable and eleven-syllable lines, often alternating and usually rhymed in pairs.

The metre table below shows the pattern of usage throughout the play. This will mainly be of interest to scholars, but one may note in passing that the analysis of verse forms often provides editors with a very useful aid for establishing the best version of a corrupt text such as the D printing.

Lines	Romance	Redondillas	Décimas	Silva	Quintillas	All
1- 192		192				
193- 500	308					
501- 820		320				
821-1022	202					
Act I totals	510	512				1022
1023-1286	264					
1287-1346				60		
1347-1473			127			
1474-1477		4				
1478-1527	50					
1528-1532					5	
1533-1698	166					
1699-1770				72		
1771-2038	268					
Act II totals	748	4	127	132	5	1016
2039-2263			225			
2264-2637	374					
2638-2741					104	
2742-2798				57		
2799-2904	105					
2905-2954			50			
2955-3120	166					
Act III totals	646		275	57	104	1082
Overall totals	1904	516	402	189	108	3120
Percentages	61.03	16.54	12.88	6.06	3.46	99.97

Notes

1 The will was published by Narciso Alonso Cortés in 'Algunos datos relativos a D. Pedro Calderón', *Revista de Filología Española*, 2 (1915), 41–51. The only complete attempt at a Calderón biography is Emilio Cotarelo y Mori's *Ensayo sobre la vida y obras de D. Pedro Calderón de la Barca* (Madrid, 1924), which is still useful, but badly in need of revision.

2 It is not unreasonable to suppose, from what we know of other cases, that Dorotea had committed some sexual indiscretion. For one interpretation of the scanty evidence available, see A.A. Parker, 'The father-son conflict in the drama of Calderón', *Forum for Modern Language Studies*, 2 (1966), 99–113.

3 See N.D. Shergold and J.E. Varey, 'Some early Calderón dates', *Bulletin of Hispanic Studies*, 38 (1961), 276, 284, 280. It should be remembered that the dates are dates on which payments were made; performance dates were probably earlier. However, contemporary accounts of the festivities organised to entertain Prince Charles, which included many plays, suggest that these three plays represent Calderón's contribution to the occasion.

4 The ballad refers to an injury received in a fight over a woman, but E.M. Wilson has shown that Calderón was not the author: '¿Escribió Calderón el romance *Curiosísima señora?*', *Anuario de Letras*, 2 (1962), 99–118. For the Paravicino affair, see Wilson's 'Fray Hortensio Paravicino's protest against *El príncipe constante*', *Ibérida: Revista de Filología*, 6 (1961), 245–66.

5 The expression is attributed to Jean-Baptiste de Santeuil (1630–1697), who belonged to the generation after Calderón, but this view of comedy can be found in theorists whom Calderón could have consulted, notably Alonso López Pinciano, *Filosofía antigua poética* (Madrid, 1596), Epístola IX: see the edition of A. Carballo Picazo, 3 vols (Madrid, 1953), III, 17.

6 To an audience already familiar with Don Alonso's lack of gallantry, Beatriz's subsequent interpretation of his motives would clearly illustrate her naiveté where men are concerned. Perhaps Calderón is also suggesting that she is being blinded by her first experience of love.

7 Calderón, *Three comedies*, trans. Kenneth Muir and Ann L. Mackenzie (Lexington, 1985), p. 203.

8 See, for example, C.A. Jones, 'Some ways of looking at Spanish Golden-Age comedy', in *Homenaje a William L. Fichter*, ed. A.D. Kossoff and J. Amor y Vázquez (Madrid, 1971), pp. 329–39.

9 The change in attitude took a long time to translate itself into practice. Fray Martín de Córdoba's *Jardín de nobles doncellas* (written about 1467, printed in Valladolid, 1500) has been called a milestone in the history of women's education, but only Chapter 1 of Part III deals (briefly) with *literary* education. In any case, the author considers education appropriate only for women destined to rule, like the Infanta Isabella, for whom his work was written. It was common for writers whose ideas on education were otherwise revolutionary to be affected by the strong tradition of antifeminism. Rabelais is one example. Another is Juan Huarte de San Juan, whose *Examen de ingenios para las ciencias* (Baeza, 1575) has long been accepted as a major innovation in educational theory, although his view of the role of women is summed up by Chapter XX: 'In which it is declared what steps must be taken so that males and not females are conceived'. However, see Otis H. Green, *Spain and the Western tradition*, 4 vols (Madison, 1965), III, 134–6,

where he observes 'that Spanish humanism was democratic, that it extended to women'.

10 See D.W. Cruickshank, '"Literature" and the book trade in Golden-Age Spain', *Modern Language Review*, 73 (1978), 812; and C. Larquié, 'L'Alphabétisation à Madrid en 1650', *Revue d'Histoire Moderne et Contemporaine*, 28 (1981), 132–57. Larquié puts the literacy rate in Madrid in 1650 at over 40%, in Toledo at over 50%.

11 The first major figure in female education in Spain is Beatriz Galindo (?1474–1534), 'La Latina', who taught Latin to Queen Isabella and produced a commentary on Aristotle. Her reputation survived in Calderón's time, and Lope de Vega referred to her in his *Jerusalén conquistada* (1609; canto XIX) and in his *Laurel de Apolo* (1630; silva V). For women writers in Spain, see M. Serrano y Sanz, *Apuntes para una biblioteca de escritoras españolas desde 1401 a 1833*, 2 vols (Madrid, 1893–95). Serrano includes writers of historical, devotional and other non-literary works, but it is noticeable how the numbers pick up towards the end of the sixteenth century and increase markedly in the early seventeenth. See also Melveena McKendrick, *Women and society in the Spanish drama of the Golden Age* (Cambridge, 1974), pp. 18–24, 218–41.

12 For example, an appeal by the Cortes of 1555 to Charles V claimed that 'men, boys and girls and other kinds of people' were being corrupted by chivalresque novels; writing her autobiography in the 1560s, St Teresa admitted that when young she had spent 'many hours of the day and of the night' in the 'fruitless exercise' of reading these novels: Cruickshank, '"Literature" and the book trade', pp. 806, 810.

13 Dr McKendrick points out that women writers 'seem outwardly to have aroused in their male counterparts nothing but respect and admiration' (*Women and society*, p. 219), but that in some cases at least (e.g. Lope de Vega) this was quite at variance with their inner feelings (p. 241).

14 In a letter written in 1613 or 1614 Góngora argued that thanks to his efforts Spanish had 'reached the perfection and height of Latin': *Obras completas*, ed. J. and I. Millé y Giménez (Madrid, 1961), p. 896.

15 'Quien quisiere ser culto en solo un día, / la jeri-(aprenderá)gonza siguiente': Francisco de Quevedo, *Obra poética*, ed. J.M. Blecua, vol. III (Madrid, 1971), p. 227.

16 'I hate and shun the uninitiated rabble': *Odes*, III, i.

17 Near the start of Act III of *El desprecio agradecido*, the servant Inés speaks mockingly of her mistress's squeamishness in circumlocutory and grandiloquent fashion; but the speech is only seven lines and the style, without Latinisms, is quite different from Beatriz's. As Muir and Mackenzie note (*Three comedies*, p. xl), Calderón may owe a slight debt to Lope's *La dama boba* (*The foolish lady*), written in 1613 and published in 1617, which presents two sisters, Nise and Finea, the former witty, well-read and intelligent, the latter extraordinarily naive and silly, and apparently ineducable. Finea is transformed by her love for Laurencio, and becomes quite as clever as her sister: that is, she is a little like Beatriz, in reverse. Nise has some of Beatriz's characteristics, including a father who disapproves of her taste in literature, of which he provides a list of examples (lines 2117–32); but she lacks Beatriz's syntax and vocabulary.
One of the characters of Cervantes's play *El laberinto de amor* (*Love's labyrinth*), published in 1615, is a student named Tácito. He sometimes uses Latinate vocabulary, but he does so to amuse, and he does not share Beatriz's pedantry,

prudery or Latin syntax. There is no evidence that Calderón had him in mind when creating Beatriz.

18 Ignacio Arellano, 'El sentido cómico de *No hay burlas con el amor*', in *Actas del Congreso Internacional sobre Calderón y el Teatro Español del Siglo de Oro (Madrid, 8–13 de junio de 1981)* (Madrid, 1983), I, 370.

19 See the edition prepared by A. Zamora Vicente (Madrid, 1963), pp. 167–8 and note. It may be added that when Lope published the sonnet in *La Circe* (1624), he supplied it with a prose commentary, i.e. 'footnotes' (see line 308 of our text, and its note).

20 The best general work on the history of the stage and staging in Spain is N.D. Shergold, *A history of the Spanish stage from medieval times until the end of the seventeenth century* (Oxford, 1967). For a detailed study of one of Madrid's two public theatres during the Golden Age, see J.J. Allen, *El Corral del Príncipe (1583–1744). The reconstruction of a Spanish Golden Age playhouse* (Gainesville, Florida, 1983). See also J.E. Varey, 'Staging and stage directions', in *Editing the comedia*, ed. F.P. Casa and M.D. McGaha (Ann Arbor, 1985), pp. 146–61.

21 D.W. Cruickshank, 'The second part of *La hija del aire*', in *Golden-Age studies in honour of A.A. Parker*, BHS, 61 (1984), 286–94.

22 Hannah E. Bergman, *Luis Quiñones de Benavente y sus entremeses* (Madrid, 1965), pp. 332–41.

23 Information compiled from Bergman, *Luis Quiñones*, pp. 526–8, and from N.D. Shergold and J.E. Varey, 'Some palace performances of seventeenth-century plays', BHS, 40 (1963), 212–44.

24 See lines 1231–2 and the corresponding note.

25 See Bergman, *Luis Quiñones*, pp. 336, 476–7, 485.

26 For the performance in April 1651, see Bergman, *Luis Quiñones*, p. 341; for plays owned by Sebastián de Prado on 25 November 1651 (seven months after his father's death), see C. Pérez Pastor, *Documentos para la biografía de D. Pedro Calderón de la Barca* (Madrid, 1905), pp. 189–90; for a performance in 1660, see p. 276.

27 D.W. Cruickshank, 'El texto de *No hay burlas con el amor*', to appear in *El mundo del teatro español en su Siglo de Oro: estudios dedicados a John E. Varey*. Although the number of editions of our play published in the first century and a half of its existence is considerable, and points to a high degree of popularity, it has since fallen into comparative neglect. The only English translation published prior to the present one is included in the volume referred to above in note 7.

Select bibliography and abbreviations

Modern editions / translations of *No hay burlas con el amor*

Don Pedro Calderón de la Barca, *Obras*, ed. Juan Eugenio Hartzenbusch, 4 vols (Biblioteca de Autores Españoles, vols VII, IX, XII, XIV), II (Madrid, 1849, and reprints), pp. 309–28.

Don Pedro Calderón de la Barca, *Obras completas. Tomo II: comedias*. Ed. A. Valbuena Briones (Madrid, 1956, and later editions), pp. 491–525. Brief introduction, pp. 491–3.

Pedro Calderón de la Barca, *No hay burlas con el amor*, ed. Ignacio Arellano (Pamplona, 1981). Critical edition with lengthy introduction and numerous notes.

Pedro Calderón de la Barca, *Three comedies*, trans. Kenneth Muir and Ann L. Mackenzie (Lexington, Kentucky, 1985), pp. 131–190. Translation, part verse, part prose, with introduction (pp. xxxvi–xli) and notes (pp. 201–6).

On *No hay burlas con el amor*

Anon., '*No hay burlas con el amor*', in *Comedias escogidas de Don Pedro Calderón de la Barca*, 4 vols (Madrid, 1826–33); I, pp. 117–19. A brief but favourable study which refers to Molière's *Les femmes savantes* and Quevedo's *La culta latiniparla*.

Arellano, Ignacio: 'El sentido cómico de *No hay burlas con el amor*', in *Actas del 'Congreso Internacional sobre Calderón y el Teatro Español del Siglo de Oro', (Madrid, 8-13 de junio de 1981)*, ed. Luciano García Lorenzo, 3 vols (Madrid, 1983), I, pp. 365–80. The only critical study devoted wholly to our play.

Atkinson, W.C.: 'Studies in literary decadence: II. La comedia de capa y espada', *Bulletin of Spanish Studies*, 4 (1927), 80–9. Includes a brief but favourable study of our play.

Humbert, C.: 'Das Urteil des Herrn von Schack über Molière's *Femmes savantes*', *Archiv für das Studium der neuern Sprachen und Literatur*, 23 (1858), 63–99. A comparison of our play with Molière, *Les femmes savantes*, based on the assumption that Molière knew and was influenced by Calderón's play.

On Calderonian comedy

Bergman, Hannah E.: 'Auto-definition of the *comedia de capa y espada*', *Hispanófila*, Special No. 1 (1974), 3–27.

Jones, C.A.: 'Some ways of looking at Golden-Age comedy', in *Homenaje a William L. Fichter. Estudios sobre el teatro antiguo hispánico y otros ensayos*, ed. A.D. Kossoff & J. Amor y Vázquez (Madrid, 1971), 329–39.

Mason, T.R.A.: 'Los recursos cómicos de Calderón', in *Hacia Calderón. Tercer Coloquio Anglogermano, Londres 1973*, ed. Hans Flasche (Berlin/New York, 1976), 99–109.

Muir, Kenneth: 'The comedies of Calderón', in *The drama of the Renaissance: essays for Leicester Bradner* (Providence, 1970), 123–33.

Navarro González, A.: 'Comicidad del lenguaje en el teatro de Calderón', *Iberoromania*, 14 (1981), 116–32.

ter Horst, Robert: 'The origin and meaning of comedy in Calderón', in *Studies in honour of Everett W. Hesse*, ed. W.C. McCrary & J.A. Madrigal (Lincoln, Nebraska, 1981), 143–54.

Varey, J.E.: '*Casa con dos puertas*: towards a definition of Calderón's view of comedy', *Modern Language Review*, 67 (1972), 83–94.

Wade, Gerald E.: 'Elements of a philosophical basis for the interpretation of Spain's Golden-Age comedy', in *Estudios literarios de hispanistas norteamericanos dedi-*

cados a Helmut Hatzfeld con motivo de su 80 aniversario, ed. J.M. Solá-Solé, A. Crisafulli & B. Damiani (Barcelona, 1974), 323–47.

Wardropper, B.W.: 'Calderón's comedy and his serious sense of life', in *Hispanic studies in honour of Nicholson B. Adams*, ed. J.E. Keller & K.-L. Selig (Chapel Hill, 1966), 179–93.

— : 'El problema de la responsabilidad en la comedia de capa y espada de Calderón', in *Actas del Segundo Congreso Internacional de Hispanistas*, ed. J. Sánchez Romeralo & N. Poulussen (Nijmegen, 1967), 689–94.

Wilson, E.M.: 'The cloak and sword plays', in his *Spanish & English literature of the 16th & 17th centuries*, (Cambridge, 1981), pp. 90–104.

General bibliography

Blue, William R.: *The development of imagery in Calderón's comedias* (York, S. Carolina, 1983).

Bryans, John V.: *Calderón de la Barca: imagery, rhetoric and drama* (London, 1977).

Cascardi, Anthony J.: *The limits of illusion: a critical study of Calderón* (Cambridge, 1984).

Cotarelo y Mori, Emilio: *Ensayo sobre la vida y obras de D. Pedro Calderón de la Barca* (Madrid, 1924).

Edwards, Gwynne: *The prison and the labyrinth: studies on Calderonian tragedy* (Cardiff, 1978).

Hesse, Everett W.: *Calderón de la Barca* (New York, 1967).

Honig, Edwin: *Calderón and the seizures of honour* (Cambridge, Massachusetts, 1972).

Maraniss, James E.: *On Calderón* (Columbia & London, 1978).

Mujica, Barbara Louise: *Calderón's characters: an existential point of view* (Barcelona, 1980).

Parker, A.A.: *The allegorical drama of Calderón* (Oxford, 1943); translated and partially revised as *Los autos sacramentales de Calderón de la Barca* (Barcelona, 1983).

—: *The approach to the Spanish drama of the Golden Age* (London, 1957); revised version entitled 'The Spanish drama of the Golden Age: a method of analysis and interpretation', in *The great playwrights*, ed. Eric Bentley (Garden City, New York, 1970), I, 679–707.

—: 'Towards a definition of Calderonian tragedy', *BHS*, 39 (1962), 223–37.

Reichenberger, K. & R.: *Bibliographisches Handbuch der Calderón-Forschung / Manual bibliográfico calderoniano*. 3 vols: I (Kassel, 1979); III (Kassel, 1981); II in preparation. Until Volume II appears, readers can consult Warren T. McCready, *Bibliografía temática de estudios sobre el teatro español antiguo* (Toronto, 1966), pp.214–59, complete until 1950; Jack H. Parker & Arthur M. Fox, *Calderón de la Barca Studies 1951-69* (Toronto, 1971); and the Calderón section of the bibliography published annually in the periodical *Bulletin of the Comediantes* (ed. James A. Parr, University of Southern California).

Sloman, A.E.: *The dramatic craftsmanship of Calderón* (Oxford, 1958).

ter Horst, Robert: *Calderón: the secular plays* (Lexington, Kentucky, 1982).

Tyler, Richard W. & Elizondo, Sergio G.: *The characters, plots and settings of Calderón's comedias* (Lincoln, Nebraska, 1981).

Valbuena Prat, A.: *Calderón, su personalidad, su arte dramático, su estilo y sus obras* (Madrid, 1941).

Varey, J.E. (ed.): *Critical studies of Calderón's comedias* (Farnborough & London, 1973).

Wardropper, Bruce (ed.): *Critical essays on the theatre of Calderón* (New York, 1965).

Wilson, Edward M. & Moir, Duncan: *The Golden Age: drama 1492–1700* (London & New York, 1971), pp. 99–119.

Wilson, Margaret: *Spanish drama of the Golden Age* (Oxford, 1969), pp. 149–86.

Abbreviations used in explanatory notes

Aguilar I: Don Pedro Calderón de la Barca, *Obras completas*, vol. I, 5th ed., ed. A. Valbuena Briones (Madrid, 1966).

Aguilar II: Don Pedro Calderón de la Barca, *Obras completas*, vol. II, 1st ed., ed. A. Valbuena Briones (Madrid, 1956).

Aguilar III: Don Pedro Calderón de la Barca, *Obras completas*, vol. III, 1st ed., ed. A. Valbuena Prat (Madrid, 1952). Unless otherwise stated, all Calderón references are to these particular editions; plays quoted without name of author are by Calderón.

Arellano: the edition of Ignacio Arellano (Pamplona, 1981) listed above.

Autoridades: Real Academia Española, *Diccionario de la lengua castellana* (Madrid, 1726–39). Facsimile ed., 3 vols (Madrid, 1963).

BAE: Biblioteca de Autores Españoles.

BHS: *Bulletin of Hispanic Studies*.

Cejador, *Refranero castellano*: Julio Cejador y Frauca, *Refranero castellano*, 3 vols (Madrid, 1928–29).

Correas: Gonzalo Correas, *Vocabulario de refranes y frases proverbiales (1627)*, ed. Louis Combet (Bordeaux, 1967).

Covarrubias: Sebastián de Covarrubias Horozco, *Tesoro de la lengua castellana o española* (Madrid, 1611).

DLE: Real Academia Española, *Diccionario de la lengua española*, 19th ed. (Madrid, 1970).

Hartzenbusch: the edition of J.E. Hartzenbusch (Madrid, 1849) listed above.

María Moliner: *Diccionario de uso del español*, 2 vols (Madrid, 1970).

Martínez Kleiser: L. Martínez Kleiser, *Refranero ideológico español* (Madrid, 1953).

Millé: Luis de Góngora y Argote, *Obras completas*, ed. Juan and Isabel Millé y Giménez (Madrid, 1961).

OED: *The Oxford English Dictionary*, 12 vols (Oxford, 1933, and reprints).

Sbarbi: José María Sbarbi, *Diccionario de refranes, adagios, proverbios, modismos, locuciones y frases proverbiales de la lengua española*, 2 vols (Madrid, 1922–23).

Vera Tassis: the edition by Juan de Vera Tassis y Villarroel of Calderón's *Verdadera quinta parte de comedias* referred to in Section 5 of this Introduction.

NO AY BVRLAS CON EL AMOR.

COMEDIA FAMOSA.

DE DON PEDRO CALDERON.

Hablan en ella las personas siguientes.

Don Alonso de Luna.
Don Iuan de Mendoza.
Moscatel gracioso.
Don Luis. Don Diego.

Don Pedro Enriquez viejo.
Doña Beatriz Dama.
Doña Leonor Dama.
Ynes Criada.

IORNADA PRIMERA.

Salen Don Alonso de Luna, y Moscatel,
muy tristes.

D. Al. Valgate el diablo, que tienes,
que andas todos estos dias
con mil necias fantasias;
ni a tiempo a seruir me vienes,
ni a proposito respondes,
y por errarlo dos vezes
sino te llamo, pareces,
y si te llamo te escondes.
Que es esto? dilo.

Mos. Ay de mi,
suspiros que al alma deue.

D. Al. Pues vn Picaro se atreue,
a suspir s?ay de mi.

Mos. Los picaros no tenemos alma.

D. Al. Si para sentir,
y con rudeza dezir
de su pena sus estremos,
mas no para suspirar,
que suspirar es accion
digna de noble passion.

Mos. Y quien me puede quitar,
la noble passion a mi.

D. Al. Que locuras.

Mos. Ay señor,
mas noble passion que amor.

D. Al. Pudiera dezir que si,
mas para aorrar la question
que no digo.

Mos. Que no luego
si yo a tener amor llego,
noble sera mi passion.

D. Al. Tu amor.

Mos. Yo amor.

D. Al. Bien podia,
si aqui tu locura empieza,
reyrme oy de tu tristeza,
mas que ayer de tu alegria.

Mos. Como tu nunca has sabido,
que es estar enamorado,
como siempre has estimado,
la libertad que has tenido.
Tanto que en los dulces nombres

A

NO HAY BURLAS CON EL AMOR

COMEDIA FAMOSA

DE DON PEDRO CALDERÓN

Hablan en ella las personas siguientes

Don Alonso de Luna
Don Juan de Mendoza
Moscatel, gracioso
Don Luis

Don Pedro Enríquez, viejo
Doña Beatriz, dama
Doña Leonor, dama
Inés, criada

Don Diego

LOVE IS NO LAUGHING MATTER

A FAMOUS PLAY

BY DON PEDRO CALDERÓN

The following characters speak

Don Alonso de Luna
Don Juan de Mendoza
Moscatel, a comic servant
Don Luis

Don Pedro Enríquez, an old man
Doña Beatriz, a lady
Doña Leonor, a lady
Inés, a maidservant

Don Diego

J O R N A D A   P R I M E R A

Salen Don Alonso de Luna y Moscatel muy triste

DON ALONSO	¡Válgate el diablo! ¿Qué tienes, que andas todos estos días con mil necias fantasías? Ni a tiempo a servirme vienes, ni a propósito respondes; y, por errarlo dos veces, si no te llamo, pareces, y si te llamo, te escondes. ¿Qué es esto? Dilo.	5
MOSCATEL	¡Ay de mí! Suspiros que el alma debe.	10
DON ALONSO	Pues ¿un pícaro se atreve a suspirar hoy así?	
MOSCATEL	Los pícaros, ¿no tenemos alma?	
DON ALONSO	Sí, para sentir, y con rudeza decir de su pena los extremos; mas no para suspirar, que suspirar es acción digna de noble pasión.	15
MOSCATEL	Y ¿quién me puede quitar la noble pasión a mí?	20
DON ALONSO	¡Qué locuras!	
MOSCATEL	¿Hay, señor, más noble pasión que amor?	
DON ALONSO	Pudiera decir que sí; mas, para ahorrar la cuestión, que no, digo.	25
MOSCATEL	¿Que no? Luego, si yo a tener amor llego, noble será mi pasión.	
DON ALONSO	¿Tú, amor?	
MOSCATEL	Yo amor.	

Moscatel: Calderón usually chooses absurd names, often punning ones, for his comic servants. Spanish *moscatel* is English 'muscatel', i.e. a type of grape and a type of wine (comic servants are often fond of wine); but *moscatel* also means 'bore', 'pest',

ACT I

Enter Don Alonso de Luna and Moscatel; the latter looks very dejected

DON ALONSO	The Devil take you! What's the matter? For days now you've talked nothing but nonsense. You're late with everything, and you give some silly answer whenever I ask a question. To make matters worse, you appear out of nowhere when I haven't called; and, when I *do* call, you're not to be found. What's going on? Answer me.
MOSCATEL	Alas! These are sighs that spring from the soul.
DON ALONSO	So, do rogues nowadays presume to sigh like that?
MOSCATEL	We rogues have souls, don't we?
DON ALONSO	Yes, for feeling your coarse sorrows and talking about them, but not for sighing. Sighing is more proper to noble passions.
MOSCATEL	And who's to say I don't feel a noble passion?
DON ALONSO	What rubbish!
MOSCATEL	Sir, is there a nobler passion than love?
DON ALONSO	I could say there is; but, to avoid an argument, I'll say there's not.
MOSCATEL	There's not? Well then, if it's love I feel, surely my passion must be a noble one.
DON ALONSO	You, feel love?
MOSCATEL	Yes; I, feel love.

---

or 'fool', 'simpleton' (*DLE*). See for example Tirso de Molina, *La celosa de sí misma* (*Jealous of herself*), in his *Obras dramáticas completas*, ed. B. de los Ríos, 3 vols (Madrid, 1962), II, 1445b.

Don Alonso	Bien podía,
	si aquí tu locura empieza, 30
	reírme hoy de tu tristeza
	más que ayer de tu alegría.
Moscatel	Como tú nunca has sabido
	qué es estar enamorado;
	como siempre has estimado 35
	la libertad que has tenido,
	tanto, que en los dulces nombres
	de amor fueron tus placeres
	burlarte de las mujeres
	y reírte de los hombres; 40
	como jamás a ninguna
	quisiste, y más te acomodas
	a engañar, señor, a todas
	que hacer elección de una;
	como eres (en el abismo 45
	de amor jugando a dos manos,
	potente rey de romanos)
	mal vencedor de ti mismo,
	de mí te ríes, que estoy
	de veras enamorado. 50
Don Alonso	Pues yo no quiero crïado
	tan afectüoso. Hoy
	de casa te has de ir.
Moscatel	Advierte...
Don Alonso	No hay para qué advertir.
Moscatel	Mira...
Don Alonso	¿Qué querrás decir? 55
Moscatel	Que se ha trocado la suerte
	al paso, pues siempre dio
	el teatro enamorado
	el amo, libre el crïado.

---

39 **cheating women** (*burlarte de las mujeres*): deception of women is the trade-mark of Don Juan Tenorio in *El burlador de Sevilla* (*The trickster of Seville*). The Spanish word has a wider range of meanings than can be conveyed by any one word in English (e.g. *burla*, '[practical] joke', *burlar*, 'to seduce', *burlarse de*, 'to laugh at, to mock'). Not surprisingly, the word is used frequently in our play, especially in association with Don Alonso, who is presented as a less ruthless, more happy-go-lucky Don Juan figure. Calderón's audience, familiar with the story of Don Juan, would very soon come to expect Don Alonso's downfall. Moreover, they were probably familiar with the proverb, recorded by Correas (1627), 'con la mujer y el frío, no te burles, compañero' ('don't take chances with women or the cold, my friend').

| DON ALONSO | Now I know what has driven you crazy! If that's your trouble, I find it even more laughable to see you pining today than I did to see you so self-satisfied yesterday. |

MOSCATEL   Just because you've never known what it's like to be in love; because you've always been so obsessed with freedom, that the only pleasure you've enjoyed in Love's sweet name has lain in cheating women and scoffing at men; because you've never really loved a woman, but preferred to fool around with lots of them rather than settle on one; because you always play a totally selfish double game and always have one eye on the main chance; you make fun of me, when I'm truly in love.

DON ALONSO   I cannot put up with such a lovestruck servant. You must leave this house at once!

MOSCATEL   Just think...

DON ALONSO   There's nothing to think about.

MOSCATEL   Just look...

DON ALONSO   What are you saying?

MOSCATEL   Look how things have been turned upside-down. In the theatre it's always the master who's in love, the servant who's fancy-free.

46–7 **one eye on the main chance**: a literal translation is impossible. The title *rey de romanos* ('king of the Romans') was given to the emperor-elect of the Holy Roman Empire. In a figurative sense (as here) it was applied to any person who was expected to occupy a post as soon as it fell vacant (*DLE*, María Moliner). Don Alonso is forever on the point of taking over a newly-vacated position as some available lady's 'escort'.

56–64 As Moscatel says, most of Calderón's comedies present a gentleman besotted by a lady, while his more cynical servant aids and abets him (and also makes fun of him). Such self-reference (and self-parody) is typical of Calderón; this is the first example of many in our play. It has been seen as a forerunner of Brecht's *Verfremdungseffekt* ('alienation-technique'), but its aim in such plays as this is primarily comic.

	No tengo la culpa yo	60
	de esta mudanza, y así
	deja que hoy el mundo vea
	esta novedad, y sea
	yo el galán, tú el libre.

DON ALONSO   Aquí
hoy no has de quedar.

MOSCATEL   ¿Tan presto,   65
que aun de buscar no me das
otro amo tiempo?

DON ALONSO   No hay más
de irte al instante.

Sale Don Juan

DON JUAN   ¿Qué es esto?

MOSCATEL   Es pagarme mi señor
el tiempo que le he servido   70
con haberme despedido.

DON JUAN   ¿Con Moscatel tal rigor?

DON ALONSO   Es un pícaro, y ha hecho
la mayor bellaquería,
bajeza y alevosía   75
que cupo en humano pecho,
la más enorme traición
que haber pudo imaginado.

DON JUAN   ¿Qué ha sido?

DON ALONSO   ¡Hase enamorado!
Mirad si tengo razón   80
de darle tan bajo nombre,
pues no hace alevosía,
traición ni bellaquería,
como enamorarse, un hombre.

DON JUAN   Antes pienso que por eso   85
le debierais estimar,
que diz que es dicha alcanzar,
y yo por tal lo confieso.
¿Criados enamorados?
Un hombre que se servía   90

85–103 This topic, the ability of love to ennoble the lover, is typical of Renaissance
neoplatonism, but it is also part of the medieval courtly-love tradition. Juan Ruiz
explains in the *Libro de buen amor* (*Book of good love*), 1343: 'muchas noblezas
ha el que a las dueñas sirve' ('he who serves the ladies has many noble qualities',

It's not my fault our roles have been re-
versed, but why not give the world a chance
to observe this novel situation? Let me be
the gallant and you be free.

DON ALONSO   You shan't stay here another day.

MOSCATEL   You mean I have to leave right away?
Won't you even give me time to find a new
master?

DON ALONSO   No. You must go at once.

Enter Don Juan

DON JUAN   What's all this about?

MOSCATEL   As a reward for the time I've served him,
my master has just sacked me.

DON JUAN   Such harshness with Moscatel?

DON ALONSO   He's a rogue, and he has gone and committed the worst, the lowest, the slyest villainy
ever conceived in human heart, the most
monstrous treachery imaginable.

DON JUAN   What has he done?

DON ALONSO   He has fallen in love! Tell me now if I
haven't got a right to blacken his name!
Surely there's nothing quite so perfidious,
so treacherous, so villainous as for a man
to fall in love.

DON JUAN   I'm more inclined to think you should
congratulate him. They say that to find
love is to find happiness, and I agree.

Why shouldn't servants fall in love? A

---

155); or 'fázele fablar fermoso al que antes es mudo, / al omne que es covarde fázele
muy atrevudo' ('[love] makes him who is silent speak fair, it makes the coward very
daring', 156).

87 **they say** (*diz*): modern Spanish would be *dicen* or *se dice*; *diz* was a handy means
of losing one or two syllables to fit the metre.

de dos mozos, y los veía
necios y desaliñados,
nada en su enmienda buscaba
como es decirles a ratos:
'¡Enamoraos, mentecatos!';   95
que, estándolo, imaginaba
que cuerdos fuesen después,
y aliñados; y, en efecto,
¿qué acción, qué pasión, qué afecto,
decid, si no es amor, es   100
el que al hombre da valor,
el que le hace liberal,
cuerdo y galán?

DON ALONSO   ¡Pesia tal!
De los milagros de amor
la comedia me habéis hecho,   105
que fue un engaño culpable,
pues nadie hizo miserable,
de avaro y cobarde pecho
al hombre, si no es amor.

DON JUAN   ¿Qué es lo que decís?

DON ALONSO   Oíd,   110
y este discurso advertid:
veréis cuál prueba mejor.
El hombre que enamorado
está, todo cuanto adquiere
para su dama lo quiere,   115
sin que a amigo ni a crïado
acuda, por acudir
a su gusto; luego es
miserable amando, pues
no es, ni se puede decir   120
virtud, lo que no es igual,
y miserable no ha habido
mayor, que el que sólo ha sido
con su gusto liberal.
Que hace osados es error,   125
pues nadie contra su fama

104–5 **paint a pretty picture of the miracles of love**: literally, 'you have performed the
play of the miracles of love'. This might be taken to refer to a real play, although
Sbarbi notes that the phrase *hacer la comedia* ('to perform the play') means 'to
feign for some purpose what one does not really feel' (II, 231). In any case, no play
of precisely this title is recorded. Arellano (p. 193) quotes Antonio Mira de Amescua's

man with two servants, observing that they
had become foolish and slovenly, made no
attempt to correct them other than to say
from time to time:

'Fall in love, you dolts!'; for he believed
that, if they did, they would come to their
senses and spruce themselves up again; and,
indeed, what action, what passion, what
feeling other than love can fill men with
courage and make them generous, wise and
chivalrous?

DON ALONSO   I'll be damned! You certainly paint a pretty
picture of the miracles of love, but you
cheat outrageously, for there has never been
anything half so effective as love for turning
men into mean, cowardly wretches.

DON JUAN   What do you mean?
DON ALONSO   Listen to me, and mark my words, and
you'll soon see how right I am.

A man in love wants nothing better than
to give all he owns to his beloved, and so
he neglects his friends and servants while
he chases after his own pleasure. And then,
of course, he feels thoroughly miserable in
love, because such extravagant behaviour
can never be regarded as virtuous; and
there is no man more miserly than one who
is liberal only towards his own desires.

It is not true that love makes men bold,
for no man can help feeling afraid when he

Cuatro milagros de amor (*Four miracles of love*) and Cotarelo's suggestion that it was
written about 1629 (i.e. only six years or so before our play); but Calderón might
equally well be coining a title by analogy with the more famous *Los milagros del
desprecio* (*The miraculous effects of scorn*), attributed to Lope de Vega in *Diferentes
XXVII*, 'Barcelona, 1633'.
126 **jeopardises his honour**: Don Alonso is apparently referring to the prevalent view

entra en casa de su dama
que no entre con temor.
¡Cuántos cobardes han sido
de miedo de no perdellas;   130
cuántos, mirando por ellas,
mil desaires han sufrido!
Luego, si gusto u honor
hacen sufrir y callar,
nadie me podrá negar   135
que hace cobardes amor.
Pues si privan los sentidos
los favores o desprecios,
bien claro está que hace necios,
puesto que hace divertidos;   140
pues que si se llega a ver
o desdeñado o celoso
el hombre más cuidadoso
de lucir y parecer,
desde aquel punto se deja   145
descaecer, sin acudir
al parecer y al lucir,
y sólo aliña su queja.
Luego amor en sus cuidados
hace, con causas mudables,   150
cobardes y miserables,
necios y desaliñados.
Y en fin, sea así o no sea así,
no quiero mozo que ama
y que, por servir su dama,   155
deje de servirme a mí.

DON JUAN   A vuestra sofistería
nada quiero responder,
Don Alonso, por no hacer
agravio a la pena mía   160
del amor; y si en su historia
discurro, temo quedar
vencido, y no quiero dar
yo contra mí la victoria.

---

that a woman-friend (or a wife) represented a powerful threat to a man's honour.
He had to defend her from the predatory attentions of other men, and, because all
women were weak and fickle, she might at any moment dishonour him by getting
involved with some other man. Don Alonso never commits himself to any woman in
particular, and so he feels his honour is safe.

jeopardises his honour by entering the house of a lady friend.

How many men have turned coward through fear of losing a woman? How many, in pursuing one, have put up with a thousand insults? Well then, if love and honour oblige a man to suffer in silence, surely nobody can deny that love makes men cowards!

If the bestowing or withholding of favours makes them lose their senses, then obviously love drives men to distraction and makes fools of them.

Even a man most eager to stay in fashion and make a good impression will, as soon as he finds himself spurned or starts to feel jealous, fall into a decline and abandon the effort to keep up appearances or to stay in fashion, and will devote himself exclusively to preening his injured feelings.

Thus worries caused by the inconstancy of love create only cowards, wretches, fools and slovens.

Besides, whether all this is true or not, I do not wish to have a servant who is in love, and who serves his beloved instead of serving me.

DON JUAN   I shall make no attempt to rebut your sophistry, Don Alonso, lest I should only exacerbate the pangs of love I suffer. Were I to recount the story of my own woes, I fear I should be routed, and I have no wish to be the author of my own downfall.

---

130 **losing a woman**: the Spanish *perdellas* (i.e. modern *perderlas*) is a seventeenth-century form required by the rhyme with *ellas*.

154–6 This curious mixture of indicative and subjunctive moods in the Spanish (*ama*, 154, and *deje*, 156) results from the need to rhyme *ama* with *dama* (155). We would expect to find two subjunctives.

	A buscaros he venido	165
	para consultar con vos	
	un pesar; mas viendo, ¡ay Dios!,	
	que de mi amor ha nacido,	
	le callaré, porque quien	
	da a un crïado tal castigo,	170
	mal escuchará a un amigo.	
DON ALONSO	No escuchará sino bien;	
	que no es todo uno, Don Juan,	
	ser vos el enamorado,	
	o el bergante de un crïado;	175
	que vos sois noble, galán,	
	rico, discreto y, en fin,	
	vuestro es amar y querer;	
	mas ¿por qué ha de encarecer	
	el amor la gente ruin,	180
	y a quién no da enojo y risa	
	que haya en el mundo (¡qué errores!)	
	quien diga con hambre amores,	
	y requiebre sin camisa?	
	Y porque sepáis de mí	185
	que trato de un mismo modo	
	burlas y veras, a todo	
	me tenéis, Don Juan, aquí.	
	—Salte allá fuera.	
DON JUAN	Dejad	
	que me escuche Moscatel,	190
	porque a vos os busco y a él.	
DON ALONSO	Pues proseguid.	
DON JUAN	Escuchad.	
	Ya, Don Alonso, sabéis	
	cuán rendido prisionero	
	de la coyunda de amor,	195
	el carro tiré de Venus,	
	tan fácil victoria suya	
	que no sé cuál fue primero,	
	querer vencer o vencerme,	
	que un tiempo sobró a otro tiempo.	200

172–84 This attitude, which may seem like mere snobbishness, formed a serious part of medieval medical belief; but the attitude had been undermined (as it is here, subtly) by the likes of Lope de Vega, who contrasted the simple and sincere eloquence of peasants with the grandiloquence of their masters (thus Peribáñez's declaration

I came to see you because I wanted your advice about a difficulty. But since it is from love my problem springs, I shall hold my tongue; someone who castigates a servant as you have done is unlikely to lend a willing ear to a friend.

DON ALONSO   On the contrary, he will lend a very willing ear indeed. It is not at all the same thing, Don Juan, for you to be in love as it is for a rascal of a servant.

You are a nobleman, gallant and rich, a man of taste and discernment. It is entirely proper for *you* to be in love.

But what business have lowbred persons waxing lyrical about love? Who could help being angered or amused by the amorous declarations of a man with an empty belly, or the pretty compliments of one who hasn't even got a shirt to his back?

But I want you to know, Don Juan, that true love and false love are all the same to me; therefore I place myself entirely at your service. You, wait outside!

DON JUAN   Please let Moscatel hear what I have to say. I don't need just you, but him as well.

DON ALONSO   Very well. Proceed.

DON JUAN   Hear me out. You already know, Don Alonso, how, captive beneath the yoke of love, I came to draw the chariot of Venus. Her triumph was so swift that I cannot tell which came first, my attempt to vanquish or my own capitulation, for one trod hard upon the other's heels.

---

of love for Casilda compares favourably with the high-sounding metaphors of the Commander of Ocaña).

194–6 At the end of Calderón's mythological play *Fieras afemina Amor* (*Love tames wild beasts*) Venus comes on stage in her chariot, which is propelled by a group of 'captives', i.e. those who have fallen under her sway.

Ya sabéis que la disculpa
de tan noble rendimiento
fue la beldad soberana,
fue el soberano sujeto
de Doña Leonor Enríquez,   205
hija del noble Don Pedro
Enríquez, de quien mi padre
amigo fue muy estrecho.
Este, pues, milagro hermoso,
este, pues, prodigio bello   210
es la dicha que conquisto,
es la gloria que deseo.
No os digo que venturoso
amante, ¡ay de mí!, merezco
favores suyos, que fuera   215
descortés atrevimiento
que los merezco decir;
que aunque es verdad que los tengo,
tenerlos es una cosa,
y otra cosa merecerlos.   220
Y así, que los tengo, digo;
que los merezco, no puedo,
que es conseguir lo imposible
dicha, y no merecimiento.
Con este engaño, llevado   225
en las alas del deseo,
lisonjeado de la noche,
aplaudido del silencio,
festejado de las sombras,
a quien más favores debo   230
que al sol, que a la luz, que al día,
vivo de saber que muero,
hasta que más declarado
pueda a rostro descubierto

213–24 The unworthiness of the lover vis-à-vis his beloved is an important motif of
courtly love: she may show him some favour or encouragement, but he never deserves
this. For a discussion of the survival of courtly-love traditions into the seventeenth
century, see O.H. Green, *Spain and the Western tradition*, 4 vols (Madison, 1963),
I, 207–63.
227–31 Courtship was conducted after dark, Romeo-and-Juliet style; i.e. the young
gentleman would stand in the deserted street at night and chat to the young lady on
her balcony. See below, 335–6.
232 **dying of love**: another courtly-love motif: love as suffering, even death. If anything could make a lover worthy of his lady, it was suffering. Cf. such plays as Lope de

As you know, this noble overthrow was
wrought by the sovereign beauty of that
most sovereign lady Doña Leonor Enríquez,
daughter of the noble Don Pedro Enríquez,
a close friend of my late father.

This miracle of loveliness, this prodigy
of beauty, is the prize I covet, the glory I
aspire to.

Alas! I cannot say I have been fortunate
enough to deserve her favour, for it would
be gross arrogance to claim I was worthy of
it.

Though I do indeed enjoy her favour,
enjoying it is one thing, deserving it is quite
another.
Therefore I can say I have it, but not that
I deserve it. To achieve the impossible is
bliss, but we cannot aspire to this condition
as of right.
Thus dazzled, borne on the wings of desire, aided by darkness, abetted by silence,
wooed by shadows (to which I owe more
than to the sunlight of the day), I thrive on
the knowledge that I shall be dying of love
until I can openly declare myself and ask

Vega's *El sufrimiento premiado* (*Suffering rewarded*), and see Green, *Spain and the Western tradition*, I, 175, 180, 224; II, 327, etc.

233–62 Don Juan's late father and Don Pedro were friends, so Don Juan has access to Don Pedro's house. Normally Don Juan's father would have approached Don Pedro to ask, on his son's behalf, for the hand of one of Don Pedro's two daughters, but since the father is dead and Don Juan has taken his place as a family friend, it would not be out of place for Don Juan to make the request himself. What would be out of place would be to 'abuse Don Pedro's hospitality' by courting one of his daughters; or even to imply, by asking for the hand of one in particular, that he had had his eye on her (this, at least, is the convention under which the play operates; its relation to real life is a matter for debate). So, although Don Juan's intentions with regard to Leonor are perfectly honourable, he cannot ask for her hand, or ask Don Pedro for the hand of *one* of his daughters, since the latter course would land him with the frightful Beatriz.

pedirla a su noble padre,   235
de quien no dudo ni temo
que me la dé, porque iguales
haciendas y nacimientos,
no hay que esperar, donde amor
tiene hechos los conciertos.   240
La causa de no pedirla
y casarme desde luego
con ella, es (aquí entra agora
la pensión de este contento,
el subsidio de esta dicha,   245
y el azar de aqueste encuentro)
tener Leonor una hermana
mayor, y como no es cuerdo
discurso querer que case
a la segunda primero,   250
no me declaro con él,
porque si a pedirle llego
alguna de sus dos hijas
(que claro está que no tengo
de decir a la que adoro),   255
por ser la mayor, es cierto
que me ha de dar a Beatriz;
y si digo que no quiero
sino a Leonor, es hacer
sospechoso mi deseo,   260
despertando la malicia
que hoy yace en profundo sueño,
y quizá perder la entrada
que agora en su casa tengo,
si no es ya que está perdida   265
con el más triste suceso
de amor, que me pasó anoche,
pues la pena con que vengo
buscándoos... Oídme, que aquí
os he menester atento.   270
Beatriz, de Leonor hermana,
es el más raro sujeto
que vio Madrid, porque en él,

---

243 Calderón used the old spelling *agora* when he wanted three syllables, and *aora*
(modern *ahora*) when he wanted two. We preserve this distinction.
244–6 **obstacle/impediment/'miss'**: *pensión*, metaphorically, was roughly equivalent
to English 'snag', 'drawback', 'obstacle', e.g. *De una causa dos efectos*: 'La dicha

her noble father for her hand. And I have
no reason to believe he will refuse me, because no one could expect a couple bound
by love to be better matched than we are
in social station and in birth.

The only reason I do not seek her hand
and marry her straight away (here we en-
counter the obstacle to such happiness, the
impediment to such bliss, the 'miss' of this
match) is that Leonor has an older sister;
and, since it is not to be expected that the
younger one should be married off first, I
am afraid to approach the father; because,
if I ask him for one of his two daughters
(and obviously I cannot say which of them
I adore), he is certain to give me Beatriz,
as she is the elder.

And if I say I want only Leonor, that is
bound to make him suspect my intentions
and to arouse his watchfulness from its
present slumber, and I may well forfeit
the ready access I now have to his house:
assuming, of course, that I have not already
lost it as a result of a most unfortunate
incident that took place last night. Indeed,
the very reason why I've come to see you…

Listen carefully. Beatriz, Leonor's sister,
is the oddest creature ever seen in Madrid.

---

y la fortuna sólo es mía; / si bien por pensión tengo / della el **grande** cuidado con
que vengo' ('The happiness and good fortune are mine alone; though the snag about
them [literally, 'it'] is, I believe, the worry I bring with me': *Two effects from a
single cause*), Aguilar II, 480a. *subsidio* is similar, but Don Juan uses *azar* here
in the gaming sense of 'bad luck'. In preserving some notion of 'game', we have
introduced an extra pun.

siendo bellísima, y siendo
entendida, están echados   275
a perder, por los extremos
de una extraña condición,
belleza y entendimiento.
Es Doña Beatriz tan vana
de su persona, que creo   280
que en su vida a ningún hombre
miró a la cara, teniendo
por cierto que allí no hay más
que verle ella y caerse muerto;
de su ingenio es tan amante   285
que, por galantear su ingenio,
estudió latinidad
e hizo en castellano versos;
tan afectada en vestirse
que en todos los usos nuevos   290
entra, y de ninguno sale.
Cada día por lo menos
se riza dos o tres veces,
y ninguna a su contento.
Los melindres de Belisa,   295
que fingió con tanto acierto
Lope de Vega, con ella
son melindres muy pequeños;
y con ser tan enfadosa
en estas cosas, no es esto   300
lo peor, sino es hablar
con tan estudiado afecto
que, crítica impertinente,
varios poetas leyendo,
no habla palabra jamás   305
sin frases y sin rodeos;
tanto, que ninguno puede
entenderla sin comento.

---

287 According to proverbial tradition ('mujer que sabe latín, no tendrá buen fin':
Sbarbi, II, 110: 'any woman who Latin knows, to a bad end surely goes'), it was a
bad thing for women to be too well educated.

288 **verses in Castilian**: at the time when our play was written (1635), women poets
were becoming slightly less rare. The *Anfiteatro de Felipe el grande* (1631), an an-
thology of 100 poems (mostly sonnets) collected by Joseph Pellicer de Salas y Tovar to commemorate a minor exploit of the king's, contained six pieces by women,
three of them anonymous. However, the only poetess of this period whose reputation
is at all considerable is María de Zayas y Sotomayor (1590-?1660). She was praised

She is extremely lovely and very clever, but her beauty and her brains are utterly ruined by her strange and extravagant nature.

Doña Beatriz is so conceited about her appearance that I believe she has never looked a man straight in the face because she is convinced that, if she did so, he would instantly fall down dead.

She is so besotted with her own cleverness that, in order to enhance it, she has studied Latin and has written verses in Castilian.

Her affectation in dress is so extravagant that she adopts every new fashion and abandons none.
Each day she curls her hair two or three times at least, but never gets it quite to her liking.
The fastidiousness of Belisa, so well portrayed by Lope de Vega, is nothing by comparison with hers.

But these things pale to insignificance beside the mannered affectation of her speech. Peevish and pedantic, thanks to her reading of a handful of poets, she never utters a word except in long and convoluted sentences that nobody could possibly understand without the aid of footnotes.

---

by Lope de Vega in his *Laurel de Apolo* (1630), *silva* VIII, and by Castillo Solórzano. Some of her verse had been printed by this time, and two volumes of stories came later (1637, 1647). In the stories she argues that women should be allowed to develop their intelligence, and that they should be respected for it and for their education.
295 **the fastidiousness of Belisa:** *Los melindres de Belisa* is the title of a play by Lope de Vega, written 1606–1608, printed 1617. *melindres* are both 'prudishness' and 'affectedness', and Belisa, like Beatriz, rejects men; she is also absurdly squeamish about insects, frogs, or the sight of blood.
303 **pedantic:** *crítica* is used here in the particular sense of a person given to speaking or writing in an affected manner (*Autoridades*).
308 **without the aid of footnotes:** in Calderón's time the work of contemporary as well

La lisonja y el aplauso
que la dan algunos necios,   310
tan soberbia, tan ufana
la tienen que, en un desprecio
de la deidad del amor,
comunera es de su imperio.
Esta tema a todas horas,   315
este enfado a todos tiempos
aborrecible la hacen
tanto, que no hay dos opuestos
tan contrarios como son
las dos hermanas, haciendo   320
por instantes el estrado
la campaña de su duelo.
Ha dado, pues (yo no sé
si es necia envidia o si celo),
en asistir a Leonor,   325
de suerte que no hay momento
que no ande al alcance suyo,
sus acciones inquiriendo
tanto que al sol de sus ojos
es la sombra de su cuerpo.   330
Anoche, pues, en su calle
entré embozado y secreto,
y, haciendo al balcón la seña
donde hablar con Leonor suelo,
la ventana abrió Leonor,   335
y yo a la ocasión atento
llegué a hablarla; pero apenas

---

as Classical poets was sometimes published with commentaries. The audience here
would think primarily of *El Polifemo de Don Luis de Góngora, comentado por Don
García de Salcedo Coronel* (Madrid, 1629), and Joseph Pellicer de Salas y Tovar's
Lecciones solemnes a las obras de Don Luis de Góngora y Argote (Madrid, 1630).
Calderón admired and imitated Góngora, but he was obviously not above using for
a humorous purpose the controversy which still surrounded the poet's style.

314 **rebelled:** *comunera* is used here in the sense of 'rebel' (specifically of the commons
against the sovereign: *Autoridades*). In *El mayor encanto amor* (*Love the greatest
enchantment*), performed in the summer of 1635, a few months after our play, the
giant Brutamonte, who rebels against Circe, is described to her in the almost identical
terms 'comunero de tu imperio' (Aguilar I, 1531b).

315 **unceasing obsession:** *tema* was one of a number of words, neuter in the original
Greek but masculine in modern Spanish, which were sometimes regarded as feminine
in the Golden Age. Here it means 'mania', 'obsession', as in the proverbial phrase
'cada loco con su tema' ('every madman with his mania'), which is the title of several
dramatic works (e.g. by Antonio Hurtado de Mendoza). *Tema* is feminine in line 1044

The flattery and applause she receives
from certain foolish people have made her
so proud and haughty that she has scorn-
fully rebelled against the god of love.

This unceasing obsession with her own appearance, and the unrelenting bizarreness
of her speech, have made her so insufferable
that it is difficult to imagine two poles as far
apart as these two sisters continually pitted
against each other on the battleground of
their own drawing-room.

Lately (I don't know whether out of envy
or suspicion) Beatriz has begun to follow
her sister's every step so closely that there
is never a moment when she is not at her
elbow, scrutinising her every move, clinging
to her like a bodily shadow cast by the
sunlight of Leonor's eyes.

Last night I entered Leonor's street steal-
thily, with my face concealed. When I made
the usual signal towards the balcony where
we talk together, the window was opened
by Leonor, and I promptly went to speak
to her.

---

and masculine in 1733.

321 **drawing-room:** the *estrado* was a dais where ladies sat on cushions to receive
visitors (Covarrubias). This eastern custom was one of many that survived the
eight centuries (711–1492) of Moorish presence in the Iberian peninsula. The correct
English word in the circumstances was 'divan': 'A continued step, or raised part of
the floor, against the wall of a room, so as to form a sofa or couch' (*OED*); cf. 1634–
40. For an illustration, see J. Deleito y Piñuela, *La mujer, la casa y la moda en la
España del rey poeta*, 3rd ed. (Madrid, 1966), f.p. 33. Although Calderón wrote a
play *También hay duelo en las damas* (*Among the ladies too there's duelling*), this
is unlikely to be even a veiled reference to it. It was not published until 1664, and
was probably written some time after 1635.

333–7 This form of courtship (talking to the beloved via a window or balcony of her
house) was still the norm in parts of Spain in the early part of the twentieth century,
although it had become fully ritualised by then: see G. Brenan, *South from Granada*
(Harmondsworth, 1963), Chapter XIX, 'Courtship and marriage'. It also plays an
important part in Lorca's *La casa de Bernarda Alba* (*The house of Bernarda Alba*),
written in 1936.

la voz explicó el concepto
que estudiado y no sabido
no me cabía en el pecho,   340
cuando tras ella Beatriz
salió, y con notable estruendo
la quitó de la ventana,
dos mil locuras diciendo,
que si yo entendí el estilo   345
con que las dijo, sospecho
que fueron que ella a su padre
diría el atrevimiento.
No sé si me conoció,
y así cuidadoso temo   350
el saber o no saber
en qué ha parado el suceso,
por cuya causa no voy
a visitarle, temiendo
su enojo; pero tampoco   355
a dejar de ir me resuelvo,
porque si acaso ha llegado
a su noticia mi intento,
la vida del dueño mío
no dudo que corra riesgo.   360
Y así, porque en irme o estarme
hay peligro, elijo un medio,
que es enviar este papel
disimulado y secreto,
que aun no va de letra mía,   365
para cuyo efecto quiero
a Moscatel que le lleve,
valiéndose de su ingenio,
y se le dé a Inés, crïada
de Leonor, porque no siendo   370
conocido por crïado
mío, no hay que tener miedo.
Y así que le deis licencia,

---

359 **my beloved**: the Spanish masculine form *dueño mío* was applicable to either sex
as a term of endearment since (as *Autoridades* explains) the feminine *dueña* meant
'female chaperone' at that time.

359–60 Another dramatic convention: the male members of a family were supposedly
responsible for the 'honour' (i.e. sexual virtue) of the female members (brother for
sister, husband for wife, father for daughter). Some husbands did kill their wives
for committing adultery, but nothing like as many as the honour plays (and some
of their critics) might lead us to believe; and the numbers of girls killed by brothers or

Scarcely had I begun to recite the well-rehearsed expressions that overflowed my heart when Beatriz emerged behind her and loudly removed her from the window, mouthing absurdities whose meaning, to judge by the tone in which they were uttered, was that she intended to inform their father of this misdemeanour.

I don't know if she recognised me, and therefore I am torn between a desire to know and a desire not to know how the matter ended. For this reason I have refrained from visiting the house, out of fear of their father's anger. And yet I cannot make up my mind to stay away; because, if my behaviour has indeed come to his notice, then I have no doubt but that the life of my beloved is in danger.

Since it is just as hazardous for me to go as to stay, I have decided to dispatch this secret letter, which is written in another hand. If I sent one of my own servants he would be recognised; so, to avoid this risk, I want Moscatel to use his ingenuity to get the letter into the hands of Leonor's maidservant, Inés.

I'm asking you, Don Alonso, to give him

---

fathers for chatting to boy-friends from a balcony (or even for anticipating their wedding-night) was certainly very small. Killing, however, was not the only sanction. As noted in our Introduction, Calderón's elder sister Dorotea was sent to a convent in Toledo (i.e. not Madrid, where the family lived) in 1611, when she was only thirteen (three years short of the canonical age of consent); she remained there for the rest of her life, another seventy years. We do not *know* what Dorotea had done, but since thirteen was then a marriageable age, it is possible that she had committed some sexual offence. Neither do we know how often such things happened in real life, although Don Juan had plenty of *literary* precedents for being concerned about Leonor.

	Don Alonso, es lo que os ruego,	
	y que conmigo en la calle	375
	os halléis, porque si llego	
	a saber que está Leonor	
	en peligro, estoy resuelto	
	a sacarla de su casa	
	aunque todo el mundo entero	380
	lo estorbe; y para esta acción	
	he elegido el valor vuestro.	
	Mi amigo sois, Don Alonso,	
	y bien conocido tengo	
	que las burlas del buen gusto	385
	son las veras del acero.	
	No como amante os obligo,	
	no como amigo os pretendo;	
	como caballero, sí,	
	pues basta ser caballero	390
	para que a un hombre valgáis	
	que está a vuestras plantas puesto.	

DON ALONSO   Moscatel, ese papel
toma; en casa de Don Pedro
Enríquez, con la invención   395
que te ofreciere tu ingenio,
entra, y dale a esa cri̇ada
que ha dicho Don Juan.

DON JUAN   ¿Tan presto
lo disponéis?

DON ALONSO   Si ha de ser,
¿cuánto es mejor que sea luego?   400
—Toma el papel; con nosotros
ven.

MOSCATEL [ap.]   Aunque aquí temer puedo
el peligro, pues Inés
(que es de mis sentidos dueño)
es la que voy a buscar,   405
amor me dé atrevimiento.

DON ALONSO   Guiad agora hacia la calle.

DON JUAN [ap.]   ¡Qué amigo tan verdadero!

DON ALONSO [ap.]   ¡Qué amores tan enfadosos!
'Sí me oyeron, no me oyeron.'   410

379–81 Another dramatic convention with some foundation in real life. Lope de Vega,
   for example, eloped with his first wife Isabel de Urbina in 1588; many years later his

permission to do this, and I want you yourself to accompany me to Leonor's street;
because, should I learn that Leonor is in
any danger, I mean to snatch her from the
house though the whole world tries to stop
me. In case the need arises, I want you to
assist me.

You are my brave and loyal friend, Don
Alonso, and I know full well that the
frivolity of your pleasure-seeking is soon
replaced by the seriousness of your steel.
It is not as a lover that I turn to you,
nor as a friend that I call on you; it is as a
gentleman that I appeal to you; and, as a
gentleman, you will surely help a man who
throws himself at your feet.

DON ALONSO   Moscatel, take that letter. Use any trick
your wits suggest, but see that you get into
the house of Don Pedro Enríquez and give it
to the maidservant mentioned by Don Juan.

DON JUAN   Such alacrity!

DON ALONSO   If something has to be done, then isn't it
better it should be done at once? —Take
the letter and come with us.

MOSCATEL (*aside*)   I think I might be walking into trouble
here. But, since it's Inés (mistress of my
affections) that I've to look for, Love, make
me bold.

DON ALONSO   Lead us to her street.
DON JUAN (*aside*)   What a true friend!
DON ALONSO (*aside*) What a nuisance this love business is! 'They

daughter Antonia ran off with a young nobleman (who did not, however, marry her).
Elopements in broad daylight could, of course, lead to hot pursuit, and the young
gentleman of the day conventionally expected his friends to help.

¡Bien haya yo, que en mi vida
he enamorado con riesgo,
sino dama a todo trance,
sino moza a todo ruedo,
que a la primera visita   415
llamo recio y hablo recio!
Y el haber en mí o no haber
o temor o atrevimiento
no consiste en más razón
que haber o no haber dinero.   420

[Vanse por una puerta y salen por otra]

DON JUAN   Ésta es la calle. Porque
no nos vean, estaremos
en algún portal mejor.

Salen Don Luis y Don Diego, y pasan quitándose los sombreros

DON ALONSO   Decís bien. Mas ¿quién son éstos
que parece que la casa   425
de Leonor miran atentos?

DON JUAN   Éste es un Don Luis Osorio,
a quien muy continuo veo
en la calle aquestos días,
y ha dado, ¡viven los cielos!,   430
en cansarme.

DON ALONSO   Pues ¿hay más
de que también le cansemos
nosotros a él?

DON JUAN   Dejadle,
que no es de estas cosas tiempo.
Pasemos de largo, y no   435
demos que decir.

DON ALONSO   Pasemos,
aunque con tantas figuras
pueda ser hombre.

[Vanse Don Luis y Don Diego]

DON JUAN *[a Moscatel]*   Tú luego

---

420 **I have:** the Spanish is ambiguous: '...depends only on whether there is money or
not'. However, since Don Alonso is never interested in marriage, it cannot matter to
him whether his lady friends have money or not.

420+ Exit and re-entry was the standard way of indicating, on the classical Spanish stage, a change of scene: in this case from the interior of Don Alonso's house to
the street outside Leonor's. If any scenery or props were used, the stage-hands would

heard me, they heard me not!' Fortunately for me, I never took the slightest risk in courting a woman, no matter what her social rank, but always spoke out bluntly at the very first visit, not caring whether I won or lost!

With me, being timid or bold depends only on whether I have money or not.

They go off on one side and re-enter on the other

DON JUAN   This is the street. We had better stay out of sight in one of these doorways.

Enter Don Luis and Don Diego. They raise their hats while crossing the stage.

DON ALONSO   You're right. But who are these men who seem to be keeping such a close watch on Leonor's house?

DON JUAN   The nearer one is Don Luis Osorio, whom I have seen repeatedly in the street these last few days, something I find extremely irksome.

DON ALONSO   Then, can you think of any reason why we shouldn't irk him back?

DON JUAN   Ignore him. This is no time for such matters. Let us just pass by without making any trouble.

DON ALONSO   Very well, though I must say it's hard to believe a clown like that could be much of a man.

Exeunt Don Luis and Don Diego

DON JUAN (*to Moscatel*)   You turn back now and give that

---

come on and change them while the stage was vacant. It will be noticed, though, that Don Juan sets the scene with line 421.

421–2 **we had better**: literally, 'so that they do not see us': *porque* could be used in classical Castilian like modern *para que.*

423 **who are...?**: the plural (and now correct) form *quienes* did exist in the seventeenth century, but it was considered inelegant, and the singular *quien* was used, as here.

436 **clown**: in the singular, a *figura* was a ridiculous-looking person; thus Eugenia,

	darás la vuelta, y darás	
	el papel a Inés.	
MOSCATEL	Me temo...	440
DON JUAN	No hay qué temer, que aquí estamos	
	a la vista. Éntrate presto.	

Vanse Don Juan, [Moscatel] y Don Alonso, y salen Don Luis
y Don Diego por la otra puerta, mirando a las ventanas

DON LUIS	Ésta es la capaz esfera,	
	éste el abreviado cielo	
	de la más bella deidad	445
	y del planeta más bello	
	que vio el sol desde que nace	
	en joven golfo de fuego	
	hasta que abrasado muere	
	en cana hoguera de hielo;	450
	y con ser tal su hermosura,	
	en ella ha sido lo menos,	
	porque pudiera ser fea	
	en fe de su entendimiento.	
DON DIEGO	Y en fin, ¿mujer tan discreta	455
	servís para casamiento?	
DON LUIS	Por conveniencia y amor	
	la sirvo y la galanteo,	
	para cuyo efecto ya	
	han de tratarlo mis deudos.	460
DON DIEGO	Pues no sé si lo acertáis.	
DON LUIS	¿Por qué no, si en ella veo	
	virtud, hacienda y nobleza,	
	gran beldad y gran ingenio?	
DON DIEGO	Porque el ingenio la sobra;	465

---

in *El agua mansa* (*Still water runs deep*), announces her first sight of her 'noble' cousin Don Toribio with the comment '¡Jesús! ¡Qué rara figura!' ('Goodness! What a scarecrow!'), Aguilar II, 1299b. Cf. also *La cisma de Ingalaterra* (*The schism of England*), Aguilar I, 153. In the plural, as here, the word meant 'ridiculous gestures or movements' (*Autoridades*). It is perhaps interesting that Beatriz's admirer is portrayed as some kind of eccentric.

443–50 The earlier hint (437) at Don Luis's eccentricity is reinforced by this metaphor, extravagant but at the same time typical of Calderonian lovers. In the geocentric system of the universe, each of the major heavenly bodies (moon, sun and the five planets then known) had its own sphere, or heaven, which revolved around the earth; all the planets bore the names of Classical deities, with Saturn the most distant. In metaphorical terms, Beatriz is the planet/deity and her house is the minor sphere/heaven in which she revolves. Sometimes Calderón's metaphors make

letter to Inés.

MOSCATEL	I'm afraid...
DON JUAN	There's nothing to be afraid of. We'll stay here within sight of the house. Go on in!

Exeunt Don Juan, Moscatel and Don Alonso. Enter Don Luis and Don Diego from the other side, looking at the windows.

DON LUIS	This is the capacious sphere, this the abbreviated heaven of the most beauteous deity and the most beauteous planet ever beheld by the sun from that moment when it rises newborn from the blazing gulf until it dies amid the flames of the hoary pyre.
	Yet, great though her beauty be, it matters naught, for ugliness itself would fade before the brilliance of her mind.
DON DIEGO	Are you wooing this accomplished woman with a view to marriage?
DON LUIS	I woo and court her out of self-interest and out of love. Of course, the arrangements will be handled by my family.
DON DIEGO	I don't know if you're doing the right thing.
DON LUIS	Why not, if she is virtuous, rich, noble, beautiful and clever?
DON DIEGO	Because she's *too* clever!

---

the lady the sun, but here the sun is imagined as seeing no more lovely planet in the course of its day's travel from sunrise until it sinks into the sea in the evening.

451–4 The notion of the 'dumb blonde' (and conversely, of the ugliness of the intelligent woman) is not at all modern. Beauty and intellect were often held to be mutually exclusive, or at least opposed, as in proverbs such as 'tonta y hermosa, son una misma cosa' ('pretty and no brain, they're one and the same'), Martínez Kleiser 44.011, or 'talentosa y fea, van por una misma *verea*' ('talented and plain, they go down the same lane'), Martínez Kleiser, 44.228. Of course there were frequent exceptions, of whom Beatriz (at least in Don Luis's eyes) is one.

456 **wooing**: no English verb adequately renders *servís*, the standard courtly-love term: see Green, *Spain and the Western tradition*, I, 72–122. It need not imply marriage as an aim, hence Don Diego's question.

465–74 Although the conversation has a modern ring about it, the topic of women's

	que yo no quisiera, es cierto,	
	que supiera más que yo	
	mi mujer, sino antes menos.	
DON LUIS	Pues ¿cuándo el saber es malo?	
DON DIEGO	Cuando fue el saber sin tiempo.	470
	Sepa una mujer hilar,	
	coser y echar un remiendo,	
	que no ha menester saber	
	gramática, ni hacer versos.	
DON LUIS	No es ejercicio culpable	475
	donde es tan noble el exceso	
	que no tiene inconveniente.	
DON DIEGO	Ni yo que le tenga pienso,	
	pues antes sé lo contrario	
	del rigor y del desprecio	480
	con que os trata.	
DON LUIS	Ese desdén	
	adoro. La vuelta demos	
	a la calle; no otra vez	
	pasen esos caballeros	
	que ya miro con cuidado.	485
DON DIEGO	Vamos, pues.	
DON LUIS	¡Hermoso centro	
	de la ingratitud que adoro!	
	Presto a tus umbrales vuelvo,	
	porque el galán que en la calle	
	de su dama a todos tiempos	490
	no vive, violento vive,	
	bien como vive violento	
	el pez fuera de las ondas,	
	el ave fuera del viento,	
	fuera de la tierra el bruto,	495
	el rayo fuera del fuego,	
	la flor fuera de la rama,	
	la voz fuera del aliento,	

education also preoccupied the seventeenth century, when male chauvinists were even more numerous. In *El agua mansa* (*Still water runs deep*), the younger sister, Eugenia, is addicted to writing verse, and the father actually plans to marry her off first on the grounds that a husband and children will put a stop to such nonsense: 'el marido y la familia / son los médicos más sabios / para curar lozanías' ('a husband and family are the best cure for exuberance'), Aguilar II, 1291b. A few lines later he echoes Don Diego: '¿Versos? ¡Gentil cañamazo! / ¿No fuera mucho mejor / un remiendo y un hilado?' ('Verse? A pretty frippery! Wouldn't mending and spinning

I myself would certainly not want a wife who knew more than I did.

DON LUIS	But, can knowledge ever be a bad thing?
DON DIEGO	Certainly, when it is out of place. A woman should know how to spin and sew and put on patches. There's no need for her to study ancient authors and be able to write verse.
DON LUIS	One cannot find fault with a practice in which excess is such a virtue that it could not possibly do harm.
DON DIEGO	I'm not suggesting one should. But, judging from the cruelty and scorn with which she treats you, I don't think this applies in her case.
DON LUIS	Oh, how I adore that disdain! Let's go back along the street, just in case those bothersome gentlemen pass this way again.
DON DIEGO	Very well.
DON LUIS	Oh! Beauteous abode of the ingratitude I adore!

Soon I shall return to your threshold; for the lover who cannot linger outside his lady's house is as much out of his element as a fish out of water, as a bird without air or a beast without land, as a flame where there is no fire or a blossom where there is no bough or a voice where there is no

---

be much better?').

474 **ancient authors**: literally, 'grammar', which meant what we would now call stylistics, using Classical texts.

482–3 **I adore that disdain**: the true courtly lover adores the disdain or ingratitude (487) with which his beloved responds to his 'service'.

486–500 Another eccentric—but typical—speech from Don Luis. Every element, and by extension every creature or created thing, had its abode (or, more precisely, 'centre', cf. *centro*, 486) to which it aspired or 'gravitated'. If a creature left its centre it was 'out of its element', *violento*. Naturally, the elements referred to here are the four traditional ones: earth, air, fire and water.

| | fuera del alma la vida,
y el alma fuera del cielo. | 500 |

Vanse, y salen Leonor e Inés, criada

LEONOR	¿Está mi hermana vestida?	
INÉS	Tocándose ahora quedó, y por no pudrirme yo de ver cuán desvanecida pide uno y otro consejo, a su espejo la dejé.	505
LEONOR	¡Qué necio con ella fue, a todas horas, su espejo!	
INÉS	¿Cómo necio?	
LEONOR	¿No lo es quien a gusto en un pesar no sabe un consejo dar a quien se le pide, Inés? Pues si Beatriz le ha pedido mil consejos cada día, y a tan continua porfía nunca a gusto ha respondido, muy necio es.	510 515
INÉS	Ahora reparo la causa.	
LEONOR	¿Cuál puede ser?	
INÉS	No se deben de entender, porque ella habla culto, él claro; y así se están todo el día porfiando los dos.	520
LEONOR	¡Quién fuera tan feliz que no tuviera más cuidado! ¡Ay, Inés mía, con cuánto temor estoy de que aquesta melindrosa, esta crítica enfadosa, a mi padre cuente hoy	525

500+ ***Exeunt, and enter...*** : once again the empty stage indicates a change of scene.
The stage-hands could take advantage of the opportunity to bring on a few items
of furniture, suggesting an interior. As usual, the text is in no hurry to be precise:
Inés's remarks about her master leaving home (531–2) imply that we are in Don
Pedro's house, but we have to wait until 667 ('this room') for complete confirmation.

504   **conceited**: the D reading, *descodocida*, is not a word, and the *desconocida*
('unknown') of the other early editions makes no sense. We favour *descomedida*

breath, as a life without a soul and a soul without a heaven.

Exeunt, and enter Leonor and her maid Inés

LEONOR   Has my sister finished dressing?

INÉS   She's still doing her hair. I couldn't stand any more of the conceited way she keeps asking her mirror what it thinks, so I left her.

LEONOR   Her mirror is always so silly!

INÉS   How do you mean, silly?

LEONOR   If a person cannot give good advice to someone with a problem, surely that person is silly, Inés?

Well then, if Beatriz has asked her mirror for advice a thousand times a day, and if, in spite of so much nagging, it has never given her a satisfactory answer, surely it must be a very silly mirror indeed?

INÉS   I know why that is.

LEONOR   Why?

INÉS   Because they can't understand each other. Beatriz is obscure and the mirror is clear, so they spend the whole day at odds.

LEONOR   Oh! My dear Inés! How wonderful it must be to have so little to worry about! I'm terrified this affected, tiresome, pedantic creature will go to Father and report

---

'excessive, rude'), but have found no record of the word in Calderón, so we have opted for the more ordinary *desvanecida*.

507–20 The joke employs a pun on *clear*. Beatriz spends the whole day seeking advice from her mirror, but it never gives the right answers because she and it do not understand each other: Beatriz's speech is *culto*, 'learned', with obscurity implied (see p. xxi), while the mirror, being made of glass, 'speaks clear'. Vera Tassis and later editions make Leonor ask Beatriz for advice, and refer to a mutual misunderstanding between the sisters, rather than between Beatriz and her mirror. This loses the pun.

lo que anoche me escuchó
al balcón hablar!

INÉS   Supuesto   530
que haber salido hoy tan presto
mi señor de casa, dio
lugar para prevenir
el lance, y que no ha tenido
tiempo de haberlo sabido,   535
procuremos desmentir
su malicia con alguna
invención.

LEONOR   Ya he imaginado
y digo que no he hallado
a propósito ninguna,   540
porque ¿cómo la he de hallar,
si ella misma quien vio fue
a Don Juan?

INÉS   Lo que se ve
es lo que se ha de negar,
con brío y con desenfado,   545
procurando deshacerlo;
lo que no llegan a verlo,
señora, se está negado.

LEONOR   El medio (¡ay de mí!) mejor
que me ofrece el pensamiento   550
es, Inés, con rendimiento,
dueño hacerla de mi amor,
de mi empleo y mi esperanza,
pues es hacer en efeto
puerta de hierro a un secreto   555
el hacer de él confïanza.

INÉS   Y eso es lo que sucedió
a un galán que enamoraba
una dama donde estaba
un clérigo que los vio.   560

---

553 **my suitor:** *empleo* is used here in the special sense of 'person one is courting' (*Autoridades*); it usually implied intent to marry, and could be used as an equivalent of the English noun 'intended' in this context. Thus *DLE* lists *emplearse* as formerly meaning 'to marry'; and in Lope de Vega's *Fuenteovejuna* (*Sheepwell*) Esteban tells his daughter Laurencia 'que harto mejor se emplea / Frondoso, Laurencia, en ti', i.e. that Frondoso would be better married to her: lines 1419–20 of F. López Estrada's edition (Madrid, 1969).

554 The spelling *efeto* (for modern *efecto*) is required by the rhyme with *secreto* (555).

what she heard me say last night on the
balcony!

INÉS · My master left home so early this morning
that he hasn't yet had time to find out
anything. Let's concoct some way to stop
her by giving the lie to her story.

LEONOR · I've racked my brains, but I cannot come up
with anything suitable. Besides, how could
I, when she saw Don Juan with her own
eyes?

INÉS · It's precisely when something has been seen
that it must be most emphatically denied!
What has *not* been seen, madam, is denied
as a matter of course.

LEONOR · The best solution I can think of, Inés, is
humbly to tell her all about my feelings,
about my suitor and my hopes; the surest
way to lock a secret behind iron doors is to
reveal it in confidence.

INÉS · That's what a young man once did when a
priest caught him courting a woman.

557–68 Priests, of course, cannot disclose what they are told in the confessional. *hacer del ladrón fiel* ('appoint the poacher gamekeeper' in our rendering) is a proverbial expression, meaning 'to take a person of doubtful reliability into one's confidence'. The expression occurs in various Calderón plays, e.g. *El médico de su honra* (*The surgeon of his honour*), Aguilar I, 331a. The company-manager Roque de Figueroa was paid on 28 March 1631 for a performance of a play entitled *El ladrón fiel*: N.D. Shergold and J.E. Varey, 'Some palace performances of seventeenth-century plays', *BHS*, 40 (1963), 228.

	El clérigo no tenía	
	en materia del callar	
	buena fama en el lugar,	
	y viendo el riesgo que había	
	de que a todos lo dijese,	565
	haciendo del ladrón fiel,	
	se fue a confesar con él,	
	porque hablarlo no pudiese.	

LEONOR   Eso mismo intento yo.

INÉS   Sí, pero esta santa liga   570
           a los clérigos obliga,
           pero a las clérigas no.

LEONOR   Pues ¿qué he de hacer, ¡ay de mí!,
           Inés, si esta industria sola
           es la que me queda?

           Sale Beatriz con un espejo, mirándose en él

BEATRIZ   ¡Hola!   575
           ¿No hay una fámula aquí?

INÉS   ¿Qué es lo que mandas?

BEATRIZ   Que abstraigas
           de mi diestra liberal
           este hechizo de cristal
           y las quirotecas traigas.   580

INÉS   ¿Qué son quirotecas?

BEATRIZ   ¿Qué?
           Los guantes. ¡Que haya de hablar
           por fuerza en frase vulgar!

INÉS   Para otra vez lo sabré.
           Ya están aquí.

BEATRIZ   ¡Cuánto lidio   585
           con la ignorancia que hay!
           ¡Hola, Inés!

INÉS   ¿Señora?

BEATRIZ   Tray
           de mi biblioteca a Ovidio,

---

576 **handmaiden**: *fámula* is one of the Latin words for 'servant', 'used in the affected, *culto* style' (*Autoridades*).

580 **chiroteques**: Greek (although borrowed late into Latin), meaning 'containers for the hands'. Arellano (pp. 216–17) quotes another example from Calderón's *El escondido y la tapada* (*The hidden lover and the veiled lady*), Aguilar II, 688a.

587 The spelling *tray* (for modern *trae*) was admissible in classical Spanish for the

The priest was not renowned in the district for his ability to hold his tongue. The young man realised there was a danger the affair would become common knowledge, so he decided to appoint the poacher gamekeeper, and went to the priest in confession, to prevent him from saying anything.

LEONOR   I'll try and do the same.

INÉS   Yes, but priests are bound by sacred vows; priestesses are not.

LEONOR   But what else can I do, Inés? That's the only chance I have.

Enter Beatriz with a mirror, in which she gazes at herself

BEATRIZ   Hello! Is there no handmaiden about?

INÉS   What is it you want?

BEATRIZ   I desire you to abstract this bewitching crystal from my unretentive dexter and to fetch my chiroteques.

INÉS   What are chiroteques?

BEATRIZ   What! My gloves! Oh, that one should be obliged to employ such vulgar expressions!

INÉS   Next time I'll know what you mean. Here they are.

BEATRIZ   Oh, how one must constantly struggle against ignorance! Inés!

INÉS   Yes, madam?

BEATRIZ   Bring Ovid from my library; not the

---

sake of a rhyme (here, with *hay*, 586).

587–92 Three of the best-known works of the Latin poet Ovid (43 B.C.–A.D. 18). Her choice of reading matter is perhaps the best indication that Beatriz's 'erudition' is half-baked and a pose. She rejects the *Ars amandi* (or *Ars amatoria*, *The art of love*, which might have been written as a handbook for Don Alonso) and the *Metamorphoses* (which deal with mythological transformations, some of which involve love-affairs—e.g. Acis and Galatea, the subject of Góngora's *Polifemo*), and settles on the *Remedia amoris* (*Remedies for love*). The title is in keeping with her rejection

      no el *Metamorfosis*, no,
      ni el *Arte amandi* pedí,   590
      el *Remedio amoris*, sí,
      que ése le investigo yo.

INÉS   Pues ¿cómo he de conocer
      libro, si es que eso has pedido,
      si aun el cartel no he sabido   595
      de una comedia leer?

BEATRIZ   Oscura, idiota y lega,
      ¿no te medra cada día
      la concomitancia mía?

LEONOR   ([*Ap.*] Agora mi papel llega.)   600
      Hermana...

BEATRIZ   ¿Quién me habla así?

LEONOR   Quien a tus pies obediente
      viene a arrojarse.

BEATRIZ   Deténte;
      no te apropincues a mí,
      que empañarás el candor   605
      de mi castísimo bulto,
      y profanarás el culto
      de las aras de mi honor;
      porque mujer que fïó
      del caos de la sombra fría   610
      y, en descrédito del día,
      nocturno amor aceptó,
      no mirar consiga atento
      mi semblante a voz profana,
      pues víbora será humana   615
      que con su, inficione, aliento.

LEONOR   Beatriz discreta y hermosa,

---

of the 'noble passion', but she seems unaware that Ovid was writing with his tongue firmly in his cheek. It may be noted that Jacinta, the heroine of Ruiz de Alarcón's *La verdad sospechosa* (*Suspect truth*, published 1630) refers to the reading of Ovid as a pastime (lines 2135–9). She does not actually say that she does this herself.

592 **conduct my research**: the Spanish verb *investigar* is not listed by Covarrubias (1611), but Góngora uses it in line 379 of the first *Soledad* (1613).

604 **seek not such propinquity**: the Spanish verb *apropincuar* is a pure Latinism, recorded by *Autoridaaes* only in a jocular context. This passage is quoted as an example.

605 **purity**: the Spanish *candor* (literally, 'whiteness') is another Latinism, but one used by Góngora (e.g. *Soledad* I, 897). It is also one of the words recommended by Quevedo to those who would 'become cultured in only a day' (see p. xxi).

606 **bosom**: the 1650 edition reads *bulto* here and at 1410, which in the context we have

Metamorphoses, no; nor the *Ars amandi* either; but the *Remedia amoris*, for it is there that I conduct my research.

INÉS
How do you expect me to recognise a book, if that's what you're asking for, when I can't even read a playbill?

BEATRIZ
Benighted creature, unlettered and un-schooled! Does my daily concomitance avail you naught?

LEONOR
(*Aside.* Here's my chance.) Sister...

BEATRIZ
Who addresses me thus?

LEONOR
One who throws herself obediently at your feet.

BEATRIZ
Desist! Seek not such propinquity with me, for you will sully the purity of my most chaste bosom and desecrate the altar of my honour.

A woman who boldly strays amid the dark confusion of cold shadows and, shun-ning daylight, accepts nocturnal love, must not expect me to grant attentive audience to her profane speech, for such a one must be a human viper which with its breath envenoms.

LEONOR
Wise and beautiful Beatriz, you are my

rendered as 'bosom'. Arellano suggests (p. 219) that Beatriz is using the Latinism *vulto* (from *vultus*, 'face'); since *vulto* has the same pronunciation as *bulto*, the audi-ence could not have distinguished. Cf. Góngora's sonnet 'Hurtas mi vulto/bulto...' (Millé 359, 'bulto'; B. Ciplijauskaité ed. [Madrid, 1969], p. 100 and n. 1, 'vulto'). The sonnet is addressed to the artist who did a head-and-shoulders likeness of Góngora, and 'Hurtas mi vulto' would mean 'You steal my face', while the other would mean 'You steal my form/bust' (in the sense of 'statue'). It seems likely that Góngora meant *vulto*, and so this would be likely to be favoured by Beatriz; but what is *chaste* about a face?

613–16 A textual crux. D here reads '...consiga atenta...que con su inficion se alienta', the main effect of which would be to create 'a human viper which thrives on its own poison'. Our reading, first suggested by Hartzenbusch, makes much better sense in the context, and although it involves a violent hyperbaton, it is less violent than Quevedo's 'jeri-(aprenderá)gonza' (see p. xxxiii, n. 15).

mi hermana eres.

BEATRIZ   Eso no,
que tener no puedo yo
hermana libidinosa.   620

LEONOR   ¿Qué es libidinosa, hermana?

BEATRIZ   Una hermana que al farol
trémulo, virrey del sol,
osa abrir una ventana,
y, susurrando por ella   625
a voz media y labio entero,
da que decir a un lucero,
da que callar a una estrella.
Pero yo minoraré
el escándalo que has hecho,   630
diciendo al paterno pecho
sacrilegios de tu fe.
Un devoto anoche vi...

LEONOR   Y ¿conocístele?

BEATRIZ   No,
ni pudo ser, porque yo,   635
¿qué másculo conocí?

LEONOR   Pues yo te quiero decir
quién era, y con el intento
que me habló.

BEATRIZ   ¡Qué atrevimiento!
¿Tal insulto había de oír?   640

LEONOR   Pues aunque oírlo no quieras,
lo has de oír, porque también
no está a mi decoro bien
que tú con locas quimeras
te persuadas a que ha sido   645
liviandad lo que honor fue.

BEATRIZ   ¿Honor?

LEONOR   Oye.

BEATRIZ   No daré
direto a tu voz mi oído.

LEONOR   Pues direto o no direto,
todo has de escucharlo ya.   650

---

636 **known a male:** Beatriz's word *másculo* is another Latinism, and more outlandish than can be rendered in English. The English verb 'know' and Spanish *conocer* both have the sense 'to have carnal knowledge of'. We are not certain that this ambiguity

	sister.
BEATRIZ	I am no such thing! I cannot have a libidinous sister!

LEONOR	Sister, what does 'libidinous' mean?
BEATRIZ	It means a sister who dares to ope a casement neath the uncertain light of that lamp which is viceroy to the sun, and, whispering in low, immodest tones, sets the planets talking and strikes the stars dumb.
	But I shall minify your scandalous behaviour by disclosing to the paternal bosom the sacrilegious nature of your faith. Last night I saw a worshipper...

LEONOR	And did you recognise him?
BEATRIZ	No. How could I possibly have done so, if I have never known a male?

LEONOR	Well, I want to tell you who he was, and his purpose in speaking to me.

BEATRIZ	What effrontery! Must I listen to such insolence!
LEONOR	Even if you do not wish to listen, you shall do so, because you damage my good name by entertaining the outlandish notion that there was some levity on my part where in reality there was only honour.

BEATRIZ	Honour?
LEONOR	Listen.
BEATRIZ	I shall not willingly lend my ear to your voice.
LEONOR	Willingly or unwillingly, you shall listen.

---

was intended, but we have preserved it.
648–9 The spelling *direto* (for modern *directo*) is required by the rhyme with *secreto* (652).

Beatriz	Oído por fuerza, será clandestino tu secreto, y no puedo error tan mucho cometer.
Leonor	Si hablando estoy...
Beatriz	Áspid al conjuro soy; 655 no lo escucho, no lo escucho.

Vase Beatriz

Leonor	¡Oye!... Mas ¿quién ahí ha entrado?
Inés	A mi señor buscará.
Leonor	Mira quién es, mientras va mi desdicha y mi cuidado 660 siguiendo una fiera.

[*Vase Leonor y*] *sale Moscatel*

Moscatel [*ap.*]	Amor, ¡qué cobarde eres conmigo, pues aun no valen contigo las leyes de embajador!
Inés	¿Es posible que has tenido, 665 Moscatel, atrevimiento de entrar hasta este aposento?
Moscatel	Sin saber qué me ha movido a haber entrado hasta aquí, rigor es anticipado... 670
Inés	Pues ¿no basta haber entrado?
Moscatel	Sí y no.
Inés	Pues ¿cómo no y sí?
Moscatel	No, pues no sabes a qué; sí, pues enojada estás; no, pues presto lo sabrás; 675 sí, pues tarde lo diré; y aunque pude haber venido de tu hermosura llamado, traído de mi cuidado y del tuyo distraído, 680 a darte aqueste papel vengo, que Don Juan me envía,

655 **more deaf than adders'**: various snakes, having no obvious ears, were thought to
be deaf. Beatriz here recalls *Troilus and Cressida*, II, ii, 170–2, which echoes Psalm
58, 4–5 (Authorised Version). The *New English Bible* and the Vulgate (Septuagint,

BEATRIZ	If I listen under duress, the secret I learn will be clandestine. I cannot commit such a grievous fault as that.
LEONOR	But what I'm saying is...
BEATRIZ	My ears are more deaf than adders' to your entreaties. I will not listen, I will not listen.

Exit Beatriz

LEONOR	Please hear me! But, who has just come in?
INÉS	It must be someone looking for my master.
LEONOR	Go and see who it is, while I in pain and anguish follow this shrew.

Exit Leonor and enter Moscatel

MOSCATEL (*aside*)	Oh, Love! You certainly don't make *me* feel brave! And I suppose you won't get me diplomatic immunity either!
INÉS	Is it possible, Moscatel, that you have had the brazenness to enter this room?
MOSCATEL	Until you know why I'm here, don't be too hasty to condemn...
INÉS	Isn't your mere presence bad enough?
MOSCATEL	Yes and no.
INÉS	How do you mean, no and yes?
MOSCATEL	No, because you don't know why I'm here; yes, because you are annoyed; no, because you shall learn soon enough; yes, because I shall delay the telling.
	And, though I might have come here lured by your beauty, attracted by my own longings and distracted by yours, I have actually come to give you this letter from

---

Psalm 57, 5–6) both refer to an *asp*, as Beatriz does in the Spanish, rather than to an adder. Beatriz, with her knowledge of Latin, may be remembering the Vulgate text.

664 **diplomatic immunity** (i.e. from prosecution): that is, Moscatel has come on an 'embassy', but this does not remove his fear of being discovered by Leonor's father.

ya que a mi cuidado fía
lo que a Leonor dice en él;
que por no ser conocido   685
por crïado suyo yo,
con el papel me envió,
si ya la causa no ha sido
conocer de mi dolor,
saber de mi mal severo,   690
que de amor no es buen tercero
el que no sabe de amor.

INÉS Pues di que el papel me diste
y que a Leonor le daré;
y vete presto, porque   695
temerosa, ¡ay de mí triste!,
de que Beatriz...

MOSCATEL   Yo me iré;
que aunque adoro tu presencia,
las leyes de tu obediencia
tan constante observaré   700
que a precio de su rigor
compraré el desprecio mío,
y a costa de tu desvío
mereceré tu favor.

INÉS Bien pudiera responderte   705
que tan ingrata no he sido
como te habré parecido;
pero tiéneme de suerte
el temor de verte aquí
que dejo para después   710
la respuesta. Vete pues,
que tiempo... Mas ¡ay de mí!,
mi señor por la escalera
sube. Aquí no me ha de hallar,
viéndote conmigo hablar.   715

Vase corriendo Inés, y sale Don Pedro, viejo

MOSCATEL Oye, aguarda, escucha, espera.
DON PEDRO ¿Quién ha de esperar y oír?
¿Quién aguardar y escuchar?
MOSCATEL Quien me tuviere que hablar
o yo tenga que decir.   720
DON PEDRO ¿Qué hacéis aquí?

Don Juan, who has entrusted to my care
the things he says here to Leonor.

He asked *me* to bring the letter because
I wouldn't be recognised as one of his servants, and maybe also because he knew I
was head-over-heels in love, and felt that
someone unacquainted with love wouldn't
make a very good go-between.

INÉS

Tell him you've given me the letter, and
that I'll give it to Leonor. Now leave at
once. I'm terrified Beatriz...

MOSCATEL

I'll go. Much as I adore your presence, I'll
obey you so exactly that I'll redeem myself
from your displeasure, and bear your scorn
in order to win your favour.

INÉS

I could easily tell you I've been less uncaring
than I seem; but the sight of you here makes
me so afraid, that I shall leave my explanations until later. Go now; it's time... But,
oh! what dreadful luck! My master is on
his way up the stairs! He mustn't catch me
here talking to you!

Exit Inés running, and enter Don Pedro, an old man

MOSCATEL

Look here! Wait! Listen! Hold on!

DON PEDRO

Who has to wait and listen? Who has to
hold on and look here?

MOSCATEL

Someone who has something to tell me, or
to whom I have something to say.

DON PEDRO

What are you doing here?

MOSCATEL [*ap.*]   ¿Qué he de hacer?
                                   ¿Ya vos no lo estáis mirando?

DON PEDRO   ¿Que no habláis?

MOSCATEL   Estoy pensando
                      lo que os he de responder.

DON PEDRO   ¿Qué buscáis?

MOSCATEL   ([*Ap.*] ¡Que aquesto pase!)   725
                      A quien sea mi homicida.

DON PEDRO   ¿Por qué?

MOSCATEL   Porque yo en mi vida
                      hallé cosa que buscase.

DON PEDRO   ¿Quién sois?

MOSCATEL   Habéis preguntado
                      en propios términos. Hoy   730
                      un crïado honrado soy,
                      si hay un honrado crïado.

DON PEDRO   ¿A quién servís?

MOSCATEL   No serví,
                      aunque crïado me llamo.

DON PEDRO   ¿Cómo no?

MOSCATEL   Como mi amo   735
                      es el que me sirve a mí.

DON PEDRO   Ya es mucha bellaquería
                      hablarme de esa manera,
                      y ya más plazo no espera
                      la justa cólera mía.   740

MOSCATEL [*ap.*]   Malo va esto, ¡vive Dios!
                      Si me da con algo aquí,
                      ¡miren qué se me da a mí
                      que en la calle estén los dos!

DON PEDRO   Quién sois me habéis de decir,   745
                      qué queréis y qué buscáis,
                      y a qué en esta casa entráis,
                      o en ella habéis de morir
                      a mis manos.

MOSCATEL   Si firmado
                      habéis la sentencia ciego   750

730–2 The dishonesty of servants was proverbial, and Calderón more than once refers
to a proverb which calls them 'enemigos no excusados', that is, 'enemies that can't
be done without': see for example *De un castigo tres venganzas* (*Three vengeances*

MOSCATEL (*aside*)	What do you think I'm doing? Can't you see for yourself?
DON PEDRO	Why don't you answer?
MOSCATEL	I'm trying to decide what to say.
DON PEDRO	What are you looking for?
MOSCATEL	(*Aside*. Why did this have to happen?) I'm looking for someone to murder me.
DON PEDRO	Why so?
MOSCATEL	Because I've never in my life found anything I looked for.
DON PEDRO	Who are you?
MOSCATEL	Now that's a fair question! Today I am an honest servant, if there's such a thing as an honest servant.
DON PEDRO	Whom do you serve?
MOSCATEL	I've never served anyone, though I call myself a servant.
DON PEDRO	How is that?
MOSCATEL	It's my master who serves me.
DON PEDRO	Such downright insolence! How dare you answer me like this? My righteous anger will tolerate no more of it.
MOSCATEL (*aside*)	Oh, my God! This is going very badly! If he attacks me now, having those two out there in the street won't be much help to me in here!
DON PEDRO	You shall tell me who you are and what you want and what you are looking for, and why you have come to this house, or else you shall die at my hands here and now.
MOSCATEL	If, without even knowing who I am, you

---

from a single punishment), Aguilar I, 52b. Muir and Mackenzie (p. 202) suggest an extra target: *criado honrado* means 'honest servant', but *honrado criado* could also mean 'born gentleman' (i.e. the implication is not only that there are no honest servants any more, but also no proper gentlemen).

> con 'ejecútese luego',
> yo soy Moscatel, crïado
> de un Don Alonso de Luna.

Salen Don Juan y Don Alonso

DON JUAN
Pues está allí Moscatel,
y vimos entrar tras él   755
a Don Pedro, mi fortuna
no espera más.

DON ALONSO
                                    Yo dispuesto
a cuanto suceda estoy.
A tomar la puerta voy.

DON PEDRO [*a* Proseguid.
Moscatel]

Llega Don Juan

DON JUAN
                        Señor, ¿qué es esto?   760

MOSCATEL [*ap.*]   Eso sí.

DON PEDRO
                    ([*Ap.*] Forzoso es ya
reportarme.) Este hombre hallé
aquí. Qué busca, no sé.

DON JUAN
¿No? Pues él nos lo dirá,
o a aqueste acero rendido   765
morirá.

MOSCATEL [*ap. a él*]   ¡Bueno!

DON JUAN [*ap. a Moscatel*]   Algo di,
Moscatel, que importa así.

MOSCATEL
([*Ap.*] ¡Buen socorro me ha venido!)
Un hombre busco, y no hallando
nadie que me respondiera,   770
de escalera en escalera
me fui poco a poco entrando,
sin ver a quién preguntar;
hasta esta parte llegué,
donde una doncella hallé   775
([*ap.*] la verdad en su lugar);
pensando que era ladrón,

753+ Don Juan and Don Alonso come on stage here, but they are clearly not meant
    to be seen by Don Pedro and Moscatel; nor is there any indication that the latter are
    visible to the former. We may suppose that the two young men have come into Don
    Pedro's house without reaching the room where Don Pedro is interviewing Moscatel.
    The two pairs would be at opposite ends of the stage, and at 760+ Don Juan would
    cross to the other side of it.

have ordered the immediate execution of
the sentence, let me tell you I am Moscatel,
servant of Don Alonso de Luna.

Enter Don Juan and Don Alonso

DON JUAN   Moscatel is in there somewhere, and we've
                    seen Don Pedro enter after him. My fate
                    must be settled this instant.

DON ALONSO   I'm ready for anything. I'll watch the door.

DON PEDRO (*to Moscatel*) Proceed.

Don Juan comes up to them

DON JUAN   What is going on, sir?
MOSCATEL (*aside*) That's more like it!
DON PEDRO   (*Aside.* I must pull myself together.) I
                    found this man inside my house. What he
                    wants, I do not know.
DON JUAN   No? Then let him tell us, unless he wants
                    to perish on this blade.

MOSCATEL (*aside to Don Juan*) Charming!
DON JUAN (*aside to Moscatel*) Say something, Moscatel! You
                    must think up something!
MOSCATEL   (*Aside.* A fine help you are!) I was look-
                    ing for a man, and, when nobody answered
                    my call, I gradually came up along the
                    stairs without meeting anyone I could ask,
                    until I got as far as this room, where I
                    found a maid (*Aside.* The truth where the
                    truth fits!), and she, thinking I was a thief,

---

761–2 **I must pull myself together:** for a gentleman to be seen to fear that his honour
   might be threatened was the first step towards being dishonoured—according to
   dramatic convention, at least. So Don Pedro pretends to be casual.
776 **The truth where the truth fits:** a proverb in Spanish; see Martínez Kleiser,
   63.102, and Sbarbi, II, 439. It is used by Calabazas in *Casa con dos puertas mala es
   de guardar* (*A house with two doors is a hard one to guard*), Aguilar II, 275a.

	huyó de mí, y a ella era	
	el 'escucha, aguarda, espera'.	
DON JUAN	Bien puede tener razón.	780
DON PEDRO	([*Ap.*] Aunque no estoy satisfecho	
	de que me diga verdad,	
	fuera necia liviandad	
	de mi espada y de mi pecho	
	saber Don Juan que he tenido	785
	otra sospecha; y así	
	fingir me conviene aquí	
	que su disculpa he creído,	
	porque menos recatado	
	le pueda después seguir,	790
	saber quién es, y salir	
	de una vez de este cuidado.)	
	Pues, si venís a buscar	
	un hombre, ¿por qué os turbó	
	el verme a mí?	
MOSCATEL	Porque yo	795
	soy muy fácil de turbar.	
DON JUAN	Ea, id con Dios.	
MOSCATEL	Que a los dos	
	guarde.	
DON JUAN [*ap. a él*]	A Don Alonso di	
	que se quite luego de ahí.	
	[*Vase Moscatel*]	
DON PEDRO	Don Juan, luego vuelvo. Adiós.	800
DON JUAN	¿Dónde vais?	
DON PEDRO	Vuelvo a buscar	
	unas cartas que perdí.	
DON JUAN	No habéis de salir de aquí,	
	u os tengo de acompañar.	
DON PEDRO	([*Ap.*] Algo, sin duda, ha entendido	805
	de mi enojo; fuerza es	
	deslumbrarle.) Venid, pues.	
DON JUAN [*ap.*]	Bien hasta aquí ha sucedido,	
	pues sin sospechar en mí,	
	asistirle a todo puedo.	810

Vanse. Sale Inés, y Leonor.

781–92 See note 761–2. The 'otherwise' (786) that Don Pedro suspects is, of course,

fled from me, and it was to her I was calling
'Listen! Wait! Hold on!'

DON JUAN   He may well be telling the truth.

DON PEDRO   (*Aside.* I'm not convinced he is, but it
would be foolish of me to let my sword or
my heart reveal to Don Juan that I suspect
otherwise.

Therefore I had better pretend to believe
his excuse, so that later, when his guard is
down, I can follow him and find out who he
is, and resolve this doubt once and for all.)

But, if you came here looking for a man,
why did you get so upset when you saw me?

MOSCATEL   Because I'm very easily upset.

DON JUAN   Be off with you. May God go with you.

MOSCATEL   May He protect you both.

DON JUAN (*aside to him*) Tell Don Alonso to move off.

Exit Moscatel

DON PEDRO   Don Juan, I shall be back shortly. Farewell.

DON JUAN   Where are you going?

DON PEDRO   I'm going out again to look for some papers
I lost.

DON JUAN   I wouldn't dream of letting you leave here
without me.

DON PEDRO   (*Aside.* No doubt he has somehow sensed
my anger. I must throw him off the scent.)
Come along, then.

DON JUAN (*aside*)   So far, so good. Since he doesn't suspect
me, I can stay with him as long as I wish.

Exeunt. Enter Inés and Leonor.

---

that Moscatel or his master may have designs on the female members of Don Pedro's
household (including Inés).

810+   The stage is momentarily empty here, but the scene does not change. We have

INÉS   Confusa de mirar quedo
                            lo que ha sucedido aquí.
                            Informarse tan severo,
                            cobrarse tan recatado,
                            hablar con él tan pesado,   815
                            y seguirle tan ligero
                            muchos efectos han sido.
                            No sé qué ha de suceder.

LEONOR [a Beatriz,   ¡Válgate Dios por mujer!
    dentro]   ¡Qué temeraria has nacido!   820

INÉS   Señora, ¿qué te ha pasado,
                            que tan colérica vienes?

LEONOR   Que no me escuchó Beatriz,
                            porque ha estado impertinente,
                            con más soberbia que nunca,   825
                            tan cansada como siempre.
                            Dice que dirá a mi padre
                            el suceso.

INÉS   Cuando vienen
                            los pesares, nunca, ¡ay triste!,
                            vienen solos, pues de suerte   830
                            se eslabonan unos de otros
                            que, enredándose crüeles,
                            es víspera del segundo
                            el primero que sucede.
                            Aquel hombre que dejaste   835
                            aquí, para que supiese
                            yo quién era, te buscaba
                            a ti, señora, con este
                            papel; que Don Juan no quiso,
                            por el riesgo, que viniese   840
                            crïado suyo. El papel
                            me dio apenas, cuando quiere
                            el cielo que entre tu padre
                            y que con el hombre encuentre.
                            Llegó al empeño Don Juan,   845
                            e hizo que el hombre le diese
                            no sé qué necias disculpas;
                            pero aunque quiso prudente

---

let the stage direction stand as it is, but Leonor's entry is probably delayed until
819–20.

INÉS

I'm really baffled by the things I've seen here. Such pressing questions, such sly pretence, such solemn talk, and then such hot pursuit! So many quick changes! I don't know how this is going to end.

LEONOR (*to Beatriz, offstage*)   Confound you, woman, but you really have some nerve!

INÉS

But, madam, what has made you so angry?

LEONOR

Beatriz wouldn't listen to me. She was her usual unhelpful and tiresome self, more haughty than ever. She says she's going to tell Father what happened.

INÉS

Sorrows come not one by one, but linked together in a cruel chain where one misfortune brings on the next.

You asked me to find out who that man was that you left here. He was looking for *you*, madam, to give you this letter, because Don Juan thought it would be too risky to send one of his own servants. No sooner had he handed me the letter than it was Heaven's will your father should walk right in and catch him.

Don Juan joined the fray, and got the man to give him some crazy excuse or other. But, though my master shrewdly tried to

---

828-34 In Spanish as in English, proverbs have it that 'misfortunes seldom come alone'; e.g. in *Don Quixote*, I, 28, Dorotea tells us that 'un mal llama a otro' ('one misfortune summons another'). Cf. note 851-4, and *Casa con dos puertas mala es de guardar* (*A house with two doors is a hard one to guard*), where we find 'un mal a otro mal llama' (Aguilar II, 293b).

	disimular mi señor,
	no pudo, y tras él se vuelve. 850
LEONOR	¡Qué bien dicen que los males
	son, si hay uno, como el fénix,
	pues es cuna en que uno nace
	la tumba donde otro muere!
	Dame el papel, porque quiero 855
	al instante responderle
	a Don Juan en el peligro
	que estoy.
INÉS	No le guardes, léele,
	que quizá advertirá algo
	que en tu cuidado aproveche. 860
LEONOR	Dices bien; abrirle quiero,
	que nada en esto se pierde.

Lee

'¡Qué mal podré, hermoso dueño,
decirte ni encarecerte...!'

INÉS	Tu hermana viene.
LEONOR	¡Ay de mí! 865

Sale Beatriz

BEATRIZ	¿Qué misivo idioma es éste
	que ajado ocultas?
LEONOR	¿Yo?
BEATRIZ	Sí.
LEONOR	No entiendo lo que me quieres
	decir.
BEATRIZ	Con vulgar disculpa
	me has obstinado dos veces. 870
	Ese manchado papel
	en quien cifró líneas breves
	cálamo ansarino, dando
	cornerino vaso débil
	el etíope licor, 875
	ver tengo.
LEONOR	En vano pretendes

851–4 Here Leonor seems to paraphrase the remark of the unhappy Dorotea in *Don Quixote*: 'el fin de una desgracia suele ser principio de otro mayor' ('the end of one misfortune is usually the beginning of a greater one': see previous note).

The phoenix was a mythological bird of Arabia. It was enormously long-lived, but since there was only one, it reproduced itself by building a nest of aromatic wood

	hide his feelings, he couldn't, and now he has set off after him.
LEONOR	Troubles really are just like the phoenix; the tomb where one dies is the cradle where the next is born!
	Give me that letter. I must reply to Don Juan at once informing him of the danger I'm in.
INÉS	Don't just clutch it! Read it! Maybe it says something that will help you out of your difficulty.
LEONOR	You're right. I shall open it. What can I lose by doing so? *Reads* 'My lovely mistress, how can I adequately express...'
INÉS	Your sister is coming!
LEONOR	Oh, dear! *Enter Beatriz*
BEATRIZ	What verbal missive is this, which you crumple and secrete?
LEONOR	I?
BEATRIZ	Yes, you!
LEONOR	I don't know what you're talking about.
BEATRIZ	Twice you have obstinately parried my inquiries with vulgar excuses. I must see that maculate paper on which ansarine quill has scribed brief lines with niger liquid drawn from delicate cornuous jar.
LEONOR	You shan't see it. You would be doubly

which it fanned to flames with its wings, destroying itself. From the ashes a new phoenix was born.

869–76 One of Beatriz's most outrageous pieces of circumlocution. Pens were made from cut goose ('ansarine') quills, inkwells from horn ('cornuous jar'); 'niger liquid' is ink, though Calderón's adjective, Ethiopian, derives from the other side of Africa.

	ver el papel, porque fuera	
	también ser necia dos veces	
	no querer saber de mí	
	cuando de oírme te ofendes	880
	lo que yo quiero decir,	
	y querer saber aleve	
	lo que pretendo callarte.	

BEATRIZ   Mi fraternidad no atiende
a tu lengua, sí a tu acción,   885
porque aquélla mentir puede
y ésta ha de decir verdad;
y así, en la ocasión urgente,
si oír lo que quieres no quiero,
saber sí lo que no quieres.   890

LEONOR   ¿De qué suerte, si no quiero,
lo has de saber?

BEATRIZ   De esta suerte.

       Ásela el papel y porfían las dos
       Suelta la epístola.

INÉS [*ap.*]   No es
sino evangelio.

LEONOR   Aunque intentes
por fuerza verle, tirana,   895
poco podré o no has de verle.

BEATRIZ   Deja el papel.

       Sale ᴅon Pedro, y ellas lo rompen y se quedan
          cada una con su pedazo

DON PEDRO   ¿Qué papel
es? ¿Por qué reñís, aleves?

INÉS [*ap.*]   Cayóse la casa, como
dice el fullero que pierde.   900

DON PEDRO   Suelta este pedazo tú,
y tú suelta este otro.

LEONOR [*ap.*]   Déme
ingenio amor.

BEATRIZ   El que abstraes

893–4   The New Testament contains twenty-one epistles, but only four gospels. A letter from one's beloved is clearly in the gospel category.

899   **the roof has fallen in**: in Spanish one says 'house', not just roof. Covarrubias (s.v. *caer*) quotes 'caese la casa' ('the roof is falling in'), but not the rest, about the cardsharp. Arellano (p. 238) notes both expressions together in *¿Cuál es mayor*

foolish to take offence if you refuse to listen
to what I wish to say, while at the same
time slyly trying to discover what I wish to
keep concealed.

BEATRIZ   My sororial solicitude marks not your words
but your deeds. The tongue can lie, but
actions can speak only truth. Therefore, in
such a strait as this, I do *not* wish to know
what you are trying to tell me, but I *do* wish
to know what you are trying to conceal.

LEONOR   How can you, if I don't want you to?

BEATRIZ   Like this!
            She grabs hold of the letter, and they both pull at it
Release the epistle!

INÉS (*aside*)   It's not an epistle! It's a gospel!

LEONOR   Though you may try to force it from me,
you shan't succeed if I can help it.

BEATRIZ   Let go of that letter!
            *Enter Don Pedro. The letter tears and each is
            left with a portion.*

DON PEDRO   What letter is that? What unseemly quar-
rel is this?

INÉS (*aside*)   The roof has fallen in, as the cardsharp said
when he lost his shirt.

DON PEDRO   You, let go of this piece. And let go of this
other piece, you.

LEONOR (*aside*)   Love, inspire me!

BEATRIZ   The fragment you from my weak hand

---

perfección? (*Which is greater perfection?*). They also occur in *Los tres afectos de
amor* (*Love's three emotions*), Aguilar I, 1206a.

903–4 **The fragment you . . . abstract**: the hyperbaton of the Spanish will not stand
in English (literally, 'The, which you abstract, fragment'); it is, however, typical of
Góngora, e.g. the opening of his *Polifemo* is 'Estas que me dictó rimas sonoras...'
('These, which to me dictated, sonorous rhymes...').

	fragmento a mi mano débil	
	te referirá baldones	905
	que tu pundonor padece.	
LEONOR	El papel, señor, que miras,	
	yo no sé lo que contiene;	
	y pues que Beatriz lo sabe,	
	¿quién duda que suyo fuese?	910
	Leyéndole estaba cuando	
	llegué...	
BEATRIZ	¿Yo?	
DON PEDRO	¡Calla!	
LEONOR	Y sin verme,	
	llegando con tal cuidado	
	(que me le puso de verle),	
	quise quitársele, y ella	915
	me le defendió. No pienses	
	que fue atrevimiento en mí,	
	que después que sé que tiene	
	Beatriz quien la escriba, y quien	
	la hable de noche por ese	920
	balcón, mi virtud me ha dado	
	disculpas para atreverme,	
	aunque soy menor hermana,	
	a tratarla de esta suerte.	
INÉS [ap.]	De mano gana Leonor	925
	cuando un mismo punto tienen...	
DON PEDRO	¡Por cierto, Beatriz...!	
BEATRIZ	Ignoro,	
	atónita, responderte,	
	que me construyó su acento	
	estatua de fuego y nieve,	930
	porque cuanto me acumula	
	delito es suyo in especie.	
LEONOR	Pues ¿aquí no estaba Inés,	
	que decir la verdad puede?	
BEATRIZ	Pues ¿Inés no estaba aquí,	935
	que dirá lo que sucede?	
INÉS	Yo soy en fin la presencia	
	de todo el hecho presente.	
DON PEDRO	([Ap.] ¡Ay de mí!, que combatido	

932 **precisely:** *OED* lists the Latin expression *in specie* (*especie* is how Calderón would

abstract will things umbrageous to your name disclose.

LEONOR

Sir, I know nothing of the contents of this letter. Since Beatriz knows what's in it, surely it must be hers? She was reading it when I walked in...

BEATRIZ

I?

DON PEDRO

Silence!

LEONOR

The sight of her made me suspicious, so I stole up on her and tried to snatch the letter, but she fought me for it.

Please do not think I was being disrespectful. I found out that someone was writing to Beatriz and speaking to her at night on that balcony there, and my virtue gave me the courage to treat her in this way, even though she *is* my older sister.

INÉS (*aside*)

Leonor wins hands down when they're evenly matched...

DON PEDRO

Really, Beatriz...!

BEATRIZ

I am too dumbstruck to respond. Her words transmute me into a statue of fire and snow. Each offence that she ascribes to me is her own precisely.

LEONOR

But, wasn't Inés here? She can tell the truth.

BEATRIZ

But, was Inés not here? She will say what happened.

INÉS

I suppose I *was* present at this present business.

DON PEDRO

(*Aside.* Alas! I am beset by twin evils,

---

have pronounced it, i.e. as a three-syllable word) with this meaning, but Calderón's audience would have been much more at home with Latin than any modern one.

de uno y otro mal tan fuerte,   940
ambos me están mal, pues ambos
armados contra mí vienen;
que al averiguar (¡ay triste!)
cúya es la culpa evidente,
no es excusarme la pena,   945
pues cuando a saberla llegue,
tan sitiado mi dolor,
tan acosado mi suerte,
tan cercado mi desdicha
en este lance me tienen,   950
que habiendo (¡cielo!) que habiendo
de morir precisamente,
quién me da muerte sabré,
mas no excusaré la muerte.)
Vete tú, Beatriz, de aquí;   955
y tú, Leonor, de aquí vete.

BEATRIZ   Señor, yo...

DON PEDRO   Nada digáis.

LEONOR [ap.]   Quiera amor que no confiese
el papel lo que yo niego.   [Vase]

BEATRIZ [ap. a ella] Tú, mentil hermana, tienes   960
la culpa de todo.   [Vase]

DON PEDRO   Inés.

INÉS [ap.]   Aquí entro agora.

DON PEDRO   Deténte.

INÉS [ap.]   Honor, con quien vengo vengo.

DON PEDRO   Pues sola el testigo eres,
¿quién leía en el papel?

INÉS [ap.]   Yo   965
ni quito ni pongo leyes,
pero hago lo que debo.

DON PEDRO   ¿Qué es lo que dudas? ¿Qué temes?

---

960 **mendacious:** *mentil* appears to be a coining on Calderón's part, but it is so close
to *mentir* ('to lie') that it would give a Spanish audience no trouble.

963 **Here's where a friend in need is a friend indeed:** the Spanish *con quien vengo
vengo* is proverbial (Sbarbi, II, 435); Calderón uses it as a play title. Given Calderón's
fondness for advertising his own plays (see notes 1232 and 1245), we can probably
assume that *Con quien vengo vengo* was written before *No hay burlas con el amor*,
although the existence of the proverbial expression prevents complete certainty. It
was certainly published much earlier, in 1638.

both armed against me, both bearing my destruction.

Discovering which of my daughters is to blame will not cure my pain; for even if I do find out, I shall be so besieged by sorrow, so hemmed in by fate, so ringed round by misery, that (Heavens!) being doomed to die, I shall recognise my killer but be helpless to escape my death!)

	Please leave, Beatriz. And you, too, Leonor.	
BEATRIZ	Sir, I...	
DON PEDRO	Not another word!	
LEONOR (*aside*)	Love grant that the letter will not confess what I deny!	*Exit*
BEATRIZ (*aside to her*) You, mendacious sister, are to blame for all of this.		*Exit*
DON PEDRO	Inés!	
INÉS (*aside*)	This is where I come in!	
DON PEDRO	Wait!	
INÉS (*aside*)	Here's where a friend in need is a friend indeed!	
DON PEDRO	You were the only witness; tell me who was reading the letter.	
INÉS (*aside*)	I neither make nor unmake laws. I only do my duty.	
DON PEDRO	Why don't you answer? What are you afraid of?	

966–7 Inés here paraphrases a famous historical remark. When Peter I of Castile (the Cruel, 1350–69) was stabbed to death by his illegitimate half-brother Henry at Montiel, Henry was assisted by a third party (his page, or his ally Bertrand du Guesclin) who uttered the words 'Ni quito ni pongo rey, pero ayudo a mi señor' ('I neither make nor unmake a king, but I help my master') or (less commonly quoted), 'ni quito ni pongo reyes, pero hago lo que debo', almost exactly as here. Correas (p. 234) quotes the former version.

INÉS	([*Ap.*] El oficio de crïada	
	es ayudar a quien miente.)	970
	Señor, poco antes que tú	
	llegué yo, sin que pudiese	
	de la acción, ni de las voces,	
	saber cúyo el papel fuese.	
	Ésta es la verdad, so cargo	975
	del juramento que tiene	
	hecho cualquiera crïada	
	en el pleito que refieres.	
DON PEDRO	([*Ap.*] ¿Aun este pequeño alivio	
	del desengaño, no quiere	980
	darme el dolor?) Vete, Inés.	
INÉS [*ap.*]	¡Viva a toda ley quien vence! *Vase*	
DON PEDRO	Que el papel confesará	
	cuanto tú y ellas me nieguen.	
	Juntar quiero los pedazos	985
	de esta víbora, esta sierpe,	
	que dividido el veneno	
	en dos mitades contiene.	

Lee

	'¡Qué mal podré, hermoso dueño,	
	decirte ni encarecerte	990
	el cuidado con que estoy	
	de que anoche nos oyese	
	tu hermana! Avísame al punto	
	que a tu padre se lo cuente,	
	para que te ponga en salvo.'	995
	A entrambas a dos conviene	
	el papel, para que sea	
	hoy mi desdicha más fuerte,	
	pues si supiera de una	
	que con liviandad procede,	1000
	supiera también de otra	
	la virtud, y de esta suerte	
	templado estuviera el daño;	
	mas para que no se temple,	
	quiere el cielo que a ninguna	1005
	crea, y que en las dos sospeche.	

975–8 If anyone tells lies in this play, it is Inés: here she makes her fibbing funnier by burlesquing the antiquated jargon of legal documents. We translate freely to retain some of the original tone.

INÉS

(*Aside.* For a maidservant, helping liars is part of the job.) Sir, I arrived just before you did, but I couldn't tell from what they were doing or saying which of them owned the letter. That is the truth, the whole truth, and nothing but the truth. I swear it on my oath as a maidservant.

DON PEDRO

(*Aside.* Am I to be denied even the trivial relief of knowing the cause of my suffering?) Leave, Inés!

INÉS (*aside*)   Long live the winner!   *Exit*

DON PEDRO

The letter will confess what you and they deny. Now I shall join the two parts of this viper, this serpent, whose venom is contained in separate halves.

Reads

'My lovely mistress, how can I adequately express the anguish I have endured since your sister overheard us last night. Notify me the instant she informs your father, so that I may secure your safety.'

As this letter could refer to either of my daughters, it serves only to deepen my affliction. If I found that one of them had behaved licentiously, I should know the other was virtuous, and thus the blow would be tempered; but, to prevent this, Heaven has decreed I should believe neither, but suspect both.

---

982   Another proverbial expression (see Sbarbi, II, 466); also used by Don Quixote, who places it in Sancho's mouth (*Don Quixote*, II, 20). Calderón uses it again in *Las armas de la hermosura* (*Beauty's weapons*), Aguilar I, 981a/b.

Hallar un crïado aquí,
turbarse (¡ay de mí!) de verme,
llegar Don Juan, y dejarle,
salir tras él, y perderle,   1010
volver a casa y hallar
la confusión que me vence,
cosas son que han menester
atenciones más prudentes.
Y así, pues sé que el crïado   1015
es, si su temor no miente,
de Don Alonso de Luna,
saber quién es me conviene,
y atender a sus acciones;
y hasta que a mis manos llegue   1020
o desengaño o venganza,
¡valedme, cielos, valedme!

[*Vase*]

First I discover a servant who gets upset on seeing me; Don Juan arrives, I let the man go, I follow him, I lose him; I return home and am confronted by this mystery which quite perplexes me.   These things merit more careful consideration.

Since I know that the servant, unless his fear made him a liar, belongs to Don Alonso de Luna, I had better find out who *he* is and keep an eye on his movements.

Until I know the truth or am avenged, may Heaven help me!

Exit

JORNADA SEGUNDA

Salen Don Juan, Don Alonso y Moscatel

DON ALONSO	De buena salimos.
MOSCATEL	Yo soy el que salí de buena y entré en mala, pues me vi 1025 ya de la muerte tan cerca.
DON JUAN	Determinarme yo a entrar, viendo la ocasión tan cierta, tras Don Pedro, fue tu dicha.
MOSCATEL	Y aun la tuya, pues si dejas 1030 de entrar, confieso de plano.
DON ALONSO	¿Eso dices?
MOSCATEL	Y aun lo hiciera mejor que lo digo.
DON ALONSO	Mira, Don Juan, si amando hay quien tema.
DON JUAN	Pues ¿un amante es cobarde? 1035
MOSCATEL	Mucho más, por ver que arriesga una vida que no es suya, sino de su hermosa prenda; y si es deuda de un amante en su servicio perderla, 1040 ya es de amor estelionato hipotecarla a otra deuda.
DON ALONSO	Ya que por Don Juan te sufro esta locura, esta tema, y hemos todo el día tratado 1045 de tus disgustos y penas, este rato que el pesar firma, si no paces, treguas, hablemos de tus amores otro poco; ya que es fuerza 1050 sufrirlos, hagamos de ellos entretenimiento. Cuenta,

---

1022+ **Enter Don Juan**: once again we have no immediate indication of where this scene is set, but the free access of such characters as Don Luis and Don Diego (1149+) indicates that we are in the street. Evidently some time has passed, as Inés has been 'searching the whole of Madrid' for Don Juan (1107–8).

1041 **fraud**: *estelionato* refers to a particular kind of fraud perpetrated by suppressing

ACT II

Enter Don Juan, Don Alonso and Moscatel

DON JUAN	We were lucky to get out of that!
MOSCATEL	Certainly *I* was. But then I was unlucky ever to get in. I was at death's door!

DON JUAN	It's just as well for you that I decided to seize the chance and follow Don Pedro into the house.
MOSCATEL	It's just as well for you, too. If you hadn't arrived, I'd have confessed everything.
DON ALONSO	You would?
MOSCATEL	I would, and faster than it takes to say so.

DON ALONSO	Now, Don Juan, you can see whether lovers live in fear.
DON JUAN	Are you saying lovers are cowards?
MOSCATEL	They're worse, because the lives they risk don't belong to them but to their ladies.
	Since a lover is obliged to lay down his life in the service of his beloved, he'd be committing fraud if he mortgaged it against any other obligation.
DON ALONSO	For Don Juan's sake I've put up with your silly harping, and all day we've been hearing about your sorrows and your woes. Now that there's a temporary lull in Don Juan's troubles, let us talk a bit more about your love. As we have no choice but to put up with it, we might as well derive some amusement from it. Tell us who your lady

---

or concealing documents relating to previous contractual obligations. Covarrubias derives the word from *estelión*, a small lizard which eats its skin after shedding it. Whatever the derivation, the word has obvious metaphorical possibilities in the field of amorous relationships, e.g. Lope de Vega, Soneto 103 of his *Rimas*, ed. J.M. Blecua (Barcelona, 1983), p. 84. Calderón himself uses the word in a sacred love metaphor in his *auto*, *A María el corazón* (*To Mary the heart*), Aguilar III, 1147b.
1044 *tema*: see note 315.

           Moscatel, quién es tu dama,
           y en qué estado estás con ella.

MOSCATEL   En qué estado estoy diré;   1055
           quién es, no.

DON ALONSO   Pues ¿qué recelas?

MOSCATEL   Tu condición.

DON JUAN   ¿No soy yo
           seguro?

MOSCATEL   No hay cosa cierta.

DON ALONSO   Verdad es que yo he tenido
           por opinión siempre cuerda   1060
           que, para una vez, no hay
           mujer mala, ni comedia,
           como ni para dos veces
           comedia ni mujer buena.
           Verdad es que, en mi concepto,   1065
           todas, hay por qué quererlas,
           y todas, por qué dejarlas;
           y esto bien claro lo prueba
           el refrán: 'no vivirás
           ni con ellas ni sin ellas'.   1070
           Verdad es que la casada,
           por fruta vedada, alegra
           bien, como también por fruta
           agridulce la doncella.
           Y pues que de frutas va,   1075
           la viuda a mí me contenta,
           por fruta sin hueso, como
           me refrena la soltera,
           porque, a dos favores, es
           la soltera fruta enjerta;   1080
           la fregona, porque es fruta
           más barata, aunque más puerca;
           y a las demás del rebusco,
           ¡lavarlas para comerlas!
           Pero aunque esta condición   1085
           tras su variedad me lleva,

1059–84 Don Alonso can find justification in proverbs for his view of women, e.g. 'Viu-
das, casadas y doncellas, ¡buenas son todas ellas!' ('widows, wives or maids, all of
them are good'): Martínez Kleiser, 42.801.

1069–70 This proverb is recorded by Correas (1627) simply as 'Ni kon ellas, ni sin
ellas' ('neither with them nor without them'): p. 234.

	is, Moscatel, and what stage you've reached with her.
MOSCATEL	I'll tell you what stage I've reached, but not who she is.
DON ALONSO	What are you afraid of?
MOSCATEL	Of your character.
DON JUAN	Don't you trust *me*?
MOSCATEL	I trust nobody!
DON ALONSO	I admit I've always believed that, first time round, there's no such thing as a bad woman or a bad play, just as, second time round, there's no such thing as a good play or a good woman.

In my opinion, there are grounds for loving every woman and for leaving every woman, as is clearly illustrated by the proverb that says: 'We cannot live with them, and we cannot live without them.'

Certainly a married woman, being forbidden fruit, offers great satisfaction, as also does the bittersweet virgin.

Still on the subject of fruits, I am very fond of widows because they have no pips, but I can't stand spinsters, because, if you're nice to them twice, they graft themselves on to you.

Scullerymaids are cheaper but coarser. As for the remaining windfalls, you'd need to be sure to wash them first!

But, though I may have a certain taste for

1077 **no pips**: literally, 'no stone' (as in a peach). What Don Alonso means is that widows have no husbands who might impair one's enjoyment of them.

1083 **windfalls**: Don Alonso employs the unusual word *rebusco*, more commonly found in the feminine *rebusca*, 'the fruit which is left behind in the fields after the harvest, especially in vineyards' (*DLE*).

| | no por eso a los amigos | |
| | falta la correspondencia. | |

MOSCATEL   Aunque más digas ni hagas
                   de esta fruta culebresca,   1090
                   el querubín es mi amor,
                   que de ti me la defienda.

DON ALONSO   Pues vaya, ¿en qué estado estás?

MOSCATEL   Que venturoso merezca
                   alguna esperanza, quiso   1095
                   mi amor.

DON ALONSO   ¡Agora te diera
                   más de dos mil bofetadas
                   de buena gana! ¡Que quieras,
                   Don Juan, que yo sufra un loco
                   decir cosas como éstas!   1100
                   ¿Qué esperanza ni qué amor
                   entre quien almohaza y friega?

DON JUAN   Así se conserva el mundo.

DON ALONSO   Sí, mas con malas conservas.

                   Sale Inés, tapada, con un papel

INÉS   ¿Señor Don Juan?

DON JUAN   ¿Quién me llama?   1105

INÉS   Yo soy.

DON JUAN   Vengas norabuena,
                   Inés.

INÉS   Para haberte hallado
                   he dado en Madrid mil vueltas.

DON JUAN   ¿Qué ha sucedido, que así
                   vienes?

MOSCATEL [*ap.*]   Inesilla es ésta;   1110
                   quiera el cielo que mi amo
                   no la atisbe ni la vea.

INÉS   A darte aqueste papel
                   he venido. Adiós.

1090 **serpentine**: Moscatel appears to have invented the word *culebresca* from *culebra*,
a serpent. He is clearly thinking of the forbidden fruit which Eve, urged on by the
serpent, persuaded Adam to eat.

1103 **that's what makes the world go round**: the Spanish expression does not quite
have the currency of the English, but cf. Lope de Vega, *Fuenteovejuna* (*Sheepwell*):
'sin amor, no se pudiera / ni aun el mundo conservar' ('the world couldn't even
survive without love'): lines 369–70.

	variety, that doesn't mean I'm disloyal to my friends.
MOSCATEL	You can say and do what you like where those serpentine fruits are concerned, but my beloved is a cherub, and I pray that Love may save her from you.
DON ALONSO	Well then, how are things coming along?
MOSCATEL	Love has ordained I should have some happy expectations.
DON ALONSO	For two pins I'd beat you round the head! Don Juan, can you really expect me to put up with a fool who prattles like that? Expectations and cherubs, indeed! Between a groom and a scrubber!
DON JUAN	That's what makes the world go round.
DON ALONSO	Yes, round the bend!

Enter Inés, veiled, carrying a letter

INÉS	Don Juan?
DON JUAN	Who's calling me?
INÉS	I am.
DON JUAN	I'm glad to see you, Inés.
INÉS	I've had to search the whole of Madrid looking for you.
DON JUAN	What has happened? Why have you come?
MOSCATEL (*aside*)	This is my little Inés. Heaven grant that my master doesn't look at her too closely.
INÉS	I've come to give you this letter. Goodbye.

1104+, 1106 **veiled**: it was common for ladies, and even for ladies' maids, to wear veils in public places. By dramatic convention a lady wearing a veil was totally unrecognisable, even to her intimates. The plots of many plays depend on this convention, e.g. Tirso's *La celosa de sí misma* (*Jealous of herself*). Inés presumably removes her veil at 1106.

1108 **the whole of Madrid**: plans of Madrid dating from this period, e.g. Texeira's (1656), indicate that one could walk across Madrid in half an hour. The population in 1635 was still well short of 100,000.

DON JUAN   Espera;
    le leeré.

Lee Don Juan, y entretanto se pone Moscatel
en medio de Don Alonso e Inés

DON ALONSO [*ap.*]   No tiene, a fe,   1115
    mala cara la mozuela.

MOSCATEL [*ap.*]   ¡Vióla! No daré un ochavo
    por mi honra toda entera.

DON ALONSO   Oye, Moscatel.

MOSCATEL   ¿Señor?

DON ALONSO   Si como esta moza fuera   1120
    la tuya, te disculpara,
    si hay disculpa que amor tenga.

MOSCATEL   ([*Ap.*] Celos, vamos poco a poco;
    no matéis con tanta priesa.)
    ¿Ésta te parece bien?   1125

DON ALONSO   Pues ¿no es bien hermosa ésta
    para fregona?

MOSCATEL   No es,
    sino muy mala y muy fea.
    Si vieras, señor, la mía,
    pondría el alma que dijeras   1130
    que era el pecado nefando,
    si entraba en su competencia.

DON ALONSO   ¡Viven los cielos, que mientes!

DON JUAN   Ya he leído.

DON ALONSO   Y ¿qué hay?

DON JUAN   Mil quejas
    de Leonor, y en fin me avisa   1135
    que bien puedo ir a verla,
    que no hay sospecha de mí

1117 **He has seen her!**: if Moscatel is punning on *¡Vióla!* (i.e. *la vio*, 'he has seen her') and *¡Viola!* ('rape!', a verb, not a noun), the pun is untranslatable.

cent: strictly speaking, an *ochavo* ('an eighth') was a small copper coin worth two *maravedís*. It originally weighed an eighth of an ounce.

1117–18 In theory, if a man's beloved receives the attention of another, his honour suffers (cf. 127-8). Later in the play Don Luis invents a reason for not marrying Beatriz when Don Pedro invites him to do so (2689–2731), but the real cause of his reluctance is the knowledge that he has a rival (3083-6). In *El médico de su honra* (*The surgeon of his honour*), even the suspicion that he has a rival for the hand of Leonor is enough to make Gutierre consider his honour endangered and break off his courtship. Moscatel follows convention here, but the extent to which dramatic

DON JUAN	Wait. I'll read it.

*Don Juan reads, and meanwhile Moscatel places
himself between Don Alonso and Inés*

DON ALONSO (*aside*)	My word, but that's not a bad-looking wench!
MOSCATEL (*aside*)	He has seen her! I wouldn't give a cent for my honour now!
DON ALONSO	Listen, Moscatel.
MOSCATEL	Sir?
DON ALONSO	If ever there could be an excuse for falling in love, I'd forgive you if your girl looked like this one here.
MOSCATEL	(*Aside.* Oh! My jealous heart! Let's take this step by step. Don't kill me off so fast.) You think she's nice, do you?
DON ALONSO	Why, she's quite good-looking for a scullery-maid, isn't she?
MOSCATEL	Not at all! She's just plain ugly! If you saw mine, sir, I bet my soul this one would only remind you of unnatural vice.
DON ALONSO	By Heavens, but you're a liar!
DON JUAN	I've read it.
DON ALONSO	And what's in it?
DON JUAN	A thousand complaints from Leonor, but she says I may freely visit her. Thanks to some ruse which she does not explain, nobody has any suspicions about me.

convention followed real life is a matter for speculation.

1124 The older spelling *priesa* (for modern *prisa*) is required by the assonance in e–a.
1130 **my soul**: this reading survived to reach the first Vera Tassis edition of 1682; by the time the second edition appeared (1694) Vera was an official play-censor, and 'my soul' became the innocuous 'my arm'.
1131–2 A textual crux makes Moscatel's meaning doubtful. Perhaps he means only that if this girl tried to compete with his, it would be 'a dreadful sin'; perhaps he means to imply that making love to this one would be sodomy in comparison; perhaps he means both. Our translation tries to retain these possibilities.
1133 **liar**: another example of Don Alonso's insensitivity. To call another gentleman a liar would be an offence which could lead to sword-play; but servants cannot retaliate.

por una industria; cuál sea
no dice. Después, de todo
yo volveré a daros cuenta.   1140
Vamos, Inés.   *Vase*

DON ALONSO   Moscatel,
no la dejes ir, deténla.

MOSCATEL [*ap.*]   ¿Esto más, celos?
DON ALONSO   ¡Ah, hermosa!
INÉS   ¿Qué queréis?
DON ALONSO   Veros quisiera
yo esa buena cara.

MOSCATEL [*ap.*]   ¡Ay, cielos!   1145
INÉS   Hay mucho que ver en ella,
y no vengo tan despacio.

DON ALONSO   Yo la sabré ver apriesa.
MOSCATEL [*ap.*]   Y aun dejar de verla y todo.
                     Salen Don Luis y Don Diego

DON DIEGO   La crïada suya es ésta.   1150
DON LUIS   Desde su casa la he visto
salir, y vengo tras ella
por ver si para Beatriz
darla un recado pudiera.

INÉS [*ap.*]   No sé lo que Moscatel   1155
me quiere decir por señas.

DON DIEGO   Con Don Alonso de Luna
habla.

DON LUIS   Cierta es mi sospecha;
que venir una crïada
de Beatriz de esta manera   1160
a buscarle, estar él siempre
en su calle y a sus rejas
con el otro amigo suyo,
mirar que cuando se aleja
se quedan los dos hablando,   1165
no es posible que no sean
lances de amor.

DON DIEGO   ¿Qué queréis
hacer?

1158–67 Calderón introduces a complication: Don Luis, seeing Don Alonso talking to

I'll come back later and tell you everything.

| | Let's go, Inés.   *Exit* |
| DON ALONSO | Don't let her go, Moscatel. Stop her. |

MOSCATEL (*aside*)	Oh, jealous heart! This too!
DON ALONSO	I say, my lovely!
INÉS	What do you want?
DON ALONSO	I want to see your pretty face.

MOSCATEL (*aside*)	Oh, Heavens!
INÉS	There's plenty to be seen there, but I can't wait around that long.
DON ALONSO	I won't take long to see it!
MOSCATEL (*aside*)	Nor to stop seeing it, either!

Enter Don Luis and Don Diego

| DON DIEGO | There's her maid. |
| DON LUIS | I saw her come out of the house, and I've been following her to see if I could slip her a message for Beatriz. |

| INÉS (*aside*) | I can't make out what Moscatel is trying to tell me with this sign-language. |
| DON DIEGO | She's talking to Don Alonso de Luna. |

| DON LUIS | My suspicions are confirmed. If Beatriz's maid has gone in search of him like this, and if he is forever in Beatriz's street and at her window with that friend of his, and if he now continues talking to the maid after his friend's departure, this must certainly be an affair of the heart. |

| DON DIEGO | What do you propose to do? |

Beatriz's maid, assumes that Don Alonso is his rival (which he will be, but not until much later).

DON LUIS	Que aquí no me vean,	
	que no tengo yo favores	
	para que empeñarme pueda,	1170
	y reñir un desvalido	
	es valentía muy necia.	
DON DIEGO	Decís bien, y quizá mienten	
	los viles celos que os cercan.	
DON LUIS	Nunca son viles los celos,	1175
	Don Diego.	

DON DIEGO   Opinión es nueva.

DON LUIS   ¿Hay más nobleza que hablar
verdad? Pues esta nobleza
sólo los celos la tienen,
porque no hay celos que mientan. *Va[n]se* 1180

INÉS   Bien está. Adiós, que es muy tarde.

DON ALONSO   Dejad que vaya siquiera
con vos aquese crïado.
No vais sola.

INÉS   Norabuena;
venga el crïado conmigo.   1185

MOSCATEL [*ap.*]   ¡Que esto escuche! ¡Que esto vea!

DON ALONSO   Moscatel.

MOSCATEL   ¿Señor?

DON ALONSO   Escucha:
Inés me ha dado licencia
para que en mi nombre vayas
hasta su casa con ella;   1190
ve, y dirásla en el camino
que como tal vez se venga
a casa, no faltará
algún regalo que hacerla.

MOSCATEL   ¿Es posible que tal dices?   1195

DON ALONSO   Sí, que si en su amor ya es fuerza
acompañar a Don Juan,
no es muy mala conveniencia
tener quien aquel instante
también a mí me entretenga.   1200

MOSCATEL   Yo se lo diré.

DON ALONSO   En los trucos

1184 **Don't go**: the Spanish *vais* was a legitimate form of the subjunctive (i.e. **negative**

DON LUIS	I do not want them to see me here. I have been shown no favours to encourage me, and to fight over someone who spurns you is a silly kind of bravery.
DON DIEGO	You're right. But, maybe there's no ground for the base jealousy that assails you.
DON LUIS	Jealousy is never base, Don Diego.
DON DIEGO	That's a novel idea!
DON LUIS	Is there anything more noble than to speak the truth? Well, nowhere but in jealousy is such nobility found, for jealousy never lies.

Exeunt

INÉS	Very well. Goodbye, it's very late.
DON ALONSO	At least let my servant here accompany you. Don't go alone.
INÉS	All right, let him come with me.
MOSCATEL (*aside*)	What am I hearing? What am I seeing?
DON ALONSO	Moscatel.
MOSCATEL	Sir?
DON ALONSO	Listen, Inés has agreed to let you escort her home on my behalf. Go with her, and on the way explain that, if by any chance she were to call on me at home, she would not go unrewarded.
MOSCATEL	Do you really mean that?
DON ALONSO	Of course I do. If I have to help Don Juan in his love affair, then I might as well have someone to keep *me* amused at the same time.
MOSCATEL	I'll tell her so.
DON ALONSO	I'll be in the billiard-hall awaiting her

---

imperative) in the seventeenth century.
1201 **billiard-hall**: the game of *truco*, as described by Covarrubias (who says in 1611

	te aguardo con la respuesta.	*Vase*
MOSCATEL [*ap.*]	¡Quedamos buenos, honor!	
INÉS	Vamos, Moscatel, ¿qué esperas?	
MOSCATEL	Vamos, Inés.	
INÉS	Pues, ¿tan triste	1205
	conmigo vas, que aun apenas	
	alzas a verme la cara?	
	¿Qué es aquesto?	
MOSCATEL	¡Ay, Inés bella!	
	¡Ay, dulce hechizo del alma,	
	qué de cuidados me cuestas!	1210
INÉS	¿Qué tienes?	
MOSCATEL	Amor y honor.	
	Quiero y sirvo, y hoy es fuerza	
	entre mi dama y mi amo,	
	que no sirva o que no quiera.	
INÉS	No entiendo tus disparates.	1215
MOSCATEL	Pues yo haré que los entiendas.	
	Don Alonso, mi señor,	
	te vio, Inés, y a Dios pluguiera	
	que antes cegase, aunque yo	
	el mozo de ciego fuera.	1220
	Vióte, Inés, ¡ay Dios!, y al verte	
	fue precisa consecuencia	
	quererte; no tanto, Inés,	
	por tu infinita belleza,	
	como por su amor finito,	1225
	que eres, al fin, cara nueva.	
	Conmigo a decirte envía...	
	(Aquí se turba mi lengua,	
	aquí la voz se suspende,	
	y aquí los sentidos tiemblan.)	1230
	Con más afectos, que cuando	
	Prado hizo al rey de Suecia,	

---

that it was recently introduced from Italy) is not now played in the way he writes of, but the table was similar, with pockets. 'Billiards' was being played in England by this time (e.g. Shakespeare, *Antony and Cleopatra*, II, v, 'Let it alone, let's to billiards'). Florio (*A world of words, or most copious and exact dictionarie of Italian and English*, 1598), gives Italian *trucco* as 'billiards'. For further examples in Spanish texts, see Arellano, pp. 257–8.

1220 **blind man's boy**: Moscatel is probably thinking of the eponymous hero of *La vida de Lazarillo de Tormes*, which was published anonymously in 1554 and first

	reply. *Exit*

MOSCATEL (*aside*) Oh, honour, what a fine mess we're in!

INÉS Come along, Moscatel. What are you waiting for?

MOSCATEL Let's go, Inés.

INÉS Are you so upset at having to accompany me that you can't even raise your head to look me in the face? What's wrong?

MOSCATEL Oh, my beautiful Inés! Oh, sweet enchantress of my soul, what sorrows you bring on me!

INÉS What's the matter?

MOSCATEL Love and honour are the matter. I serve and I love, and today I must choose between loving my lady and serving my lord.

INÉS I can't understand your nonsense.

MOSCATEL Then I shall explain. My master Don Alonso spotted you, Inés, and I wish to God he had been blinded first, even though that would make me a blind man's boy.

He spotted you, Inés, and no sooner had he done so than he naturally took a fancy to you; not so much for your infinite beauty as for his own very finite appreciation of it. In short, Inés, you are a new face.

He has sent me along to tell you... (Words fail me, I am struck dumb, my senses reel.) With more passion than Prado playing the King of Sweden, he says, Inés, that if

---

translated into English in 1586 (*The pleasaunt historie of Lazarillo de Tormes*). Lazarillo's first master was a blind man who treated him rather unkindly.

1232 **Prado playing the king of Sweden**: Shergold and Varey note that Antonio de Prado played *El rey de Suecia* (*The king of Sweden*) at the Pardo palace on 1 February 1633 ('Some palace performances of seventeenth-century plays', *BHS*, 40 [1963], 236). Their source does not say who wrote the play, but it almost certainly dealt with Gustavus Adolphus II, who fell at the battle of Lützen on 16 November 1632. On 4 March 1634 the Florentine ambassador in Madrid wrote that 'Two great

	dice que si vas, Inés,	
	a verle, tendrás (¡qué pena!),	
	si es por la mañana, almuerzo,	1235
	si es por la tarde, merienda.	
	Bien veo que es la mayor	
	infamia y mayor bajeza	
	de un amante ser tercero	
	(¡un volcán soy, soy un Etna!)	1240
	de su dama; mas también	
	veo que es mayor afrenta	
	ser desleal a su dueño.	
	Y así, entre una y otra deuda,	
	amigo, amante y leal,	1245
	cumplo con que de mí sepas	
	que él te quiere, y yo lo lloro,	
	porque al fin, de esta manera,	
	tu amor digan y mis celos	
	tu alegría y mi tristeza.	1250
INÉS	¡Grosero, descortés, loco!	
	Detén esa aleve lengua,	
	que no sé, no sé qué has visto	
	en mí para que te atrevas	
	a hablar con tal libertad	1255
	a una mujer de mis prendas.	
	Dile a tu amo, villano,	
	que soy quien soy, y no tenga	
	pretensiones para mí;	
	que de cualquiera manera	1260
	iré a servirle a su casa,	
	porque yo no soy de aquellas	
	mujercillas que se pagan	
	en almuerzos y meriendas,	
	que soy moza de capricho,	1265
	y eso le doy por respuesta.	
MOSCATEL	¿Eso dices?	

---

poets, Calderón and Coello, have together written a play on the deeds of the Duke of Friedland [i.e. Wallenstein]... It has given great pleasure because of its fine manner of portraying the warring factions, especially the defeat of the king of Sweden, celebrating his bravery'. There is a good chance that all three references (1 February 1633, 4 March 1634, and this) are to the same play. It will be remembered that Prado premiered *No hay burlas con el amor* in spring 1635 (see p. xxvii).

1245 **a loyal friend and a loyal lover**: the 'friend' is somewhat out of place, largely because Calderón is squeezing in another piece of self-advertisement, for his play

you go and see him (oh, grief!) you shall
have, if it's morning, breakfast, and if it's
evening, supper.

I realise there's nothing a lover could do
more vile or more disreputable (oh, I could
erupt like Mount Etna!) than to play pimp
to his own beloved, but it would be even
worse of him to be disloyal to his master.

And so, torn between being a loyal friend
and a loyal lover, I fulfil my duty by telling
you that he wants you and that this brings
tears to my eyes. Let your delight and my
dejection express your love and my jealousy.

INÉS   Oh, you uncouth, bad-mannered fool! Hold
your wicked tongue! I don't know what
you've seen in me that makes you think you
can take such liberties!

Tell your master, wretch, that I am who
I am; that he needn't entertain any fancy
notions about me; that I've no intention of
going to his house to be of 'service' to him;
that I'm not one of those creatures who
can be bought with breakfasts and suppers;
that I am a woman with a mind of her own.
That's the answer I give him!

MOSCATEL   That's your reply?

Amigo, amante y leal (*A friend, a lover and loyal*). It was not published until 1653,
although one critic has suggested on the basis of the verse-forms that it was composed
in the early 1630s. This reference seems to confirm the suggestion.

1258 **I am who I am**: the standard response of the honour-conscious noble when faced
with a dishonourable course of action. See p. xxv, and cf. Leo Spitzer, 'Soy quien
soy', *Nueva Revista de Filología Española*, 1 (1947), 113–27.

1262–4 **bought with breakfasts and suppers**: here it is Inés who echoes the *Vida
de Lazarillo de Tormes* (cf. note 1220), Part 3, where Lazarillo describes seeing his
master the squire talking to two young women, who 'were not ashamed to ask him
for breakfast, with the usual payment'. The edition of J. Cejador y Frauca (Madrid,
1959), p. 166, n. 4, explains that the payment was a sexual one.

INÉS   Eso digo;
                              y presto de aquí te ausenta,
                              no te vean en mi casa,
                              mira que ya estamos cerca.   1270
MOSCATEL   En fin, ¿te vas enojada?
INÉS   No me sigas, no me veas.
MOSCATEL   Obedecerte es forzoso.
                              Pues tan triste, Inés, me dejas,
                              'bien podéis, ojos, llorar,   1275
                              no lo dejéis de vergüenza.'

                                   Vase Moscatel

INÉS   Aquésta es mi casa; el manto
                              me he de quitar a la puerta,
                              que para esto solamente
                              creo que en las faldas nuestras   1280
                              usamos los guardainfantes.
                              Ahora, aunque mi ama la necia
                              me haya echado un rato menos,
                              no sabrá que he estado fuera.
                              Nadie de ustedes lo diga,   1285
                              que los cargo la conciencia.

                         [*Vase y*] *salen Don Juan y Leonor.*
                         [*Luego vuelve a salir Inés.*]

LEONOR   Esta mentira ha sido
                              la que nuestro cuidado ha divertido.
DON JUAN   Fue del ingenio tuyo,
                              que con eso que fue sutil arguyo.   1290
LEONOR   Ya del todo perdida
                              la vida, restauré en parte la vida,
                              pues lo que era evidencia
                              puse con el engaño en contingencia;
                              que no es pequeño aviso   1295
                              saber hacer dudoso lo preciso.
DON JUAN   Tu padre, en fin, ¿de entrambas sospechoso

1275–6 **'Eyes, well may you weep...'**: as Arellano points out (p. 261), Moscatel here
   quotes the opening lines of a ballad, and thus mimics Don Gutierre, the very honour-
   conscious protagonist of *El médico de su honra* (*The surgeon of his honour*), lines
   1599–1600: Aguilar I, 334a.
1281 **farthingales**: a framework of cane or whalebone hoops used to support a skirt.
   These reached extravagant proportions, as can be seen from Velázquez's portraits
   of members of the royal family, for example. They were much satirised, but Inés
   shows, as she hides her shawl under her skirt, that they had their uses; another was

INÉS	Yes, it is. Now clear off at once! I don't want anyone from my house to see you. We're almost there.
MOSCATEL	Are you leaving me in anger?
INÉS	Don't follow me. And don't come looking for me.
MOSCATEL	I'll do anything you say. Since you leave me in such sadness, Inés, I can only say: 'Eyes, well may you weep! Of tears be not ashamed!'

Exit Moscatel

INÉS	This is my house. I'll remove my shawl before going in: here's the real reason why we wear skirts with these big farthingales!

Now, even if that silly Beatriz has noticed my absence, she'll never know I've been out. None of you tell her! Promise! |

Exit, and enter Don Juan and Leonor.
Inés returns later.

LEONOR	That was the lie that got us out of trouble.
DON JUAN	It was you who thought of it; so, naturally, I think it was very clever.
LEONOR	With my life completely in ruins, I managed to salvage something by contriving to cast doubt on what was beyond question. It's no easy matter to make what is clear look cloudy.
DON JUAN	And your father has ended up suspecting

to conceal pregnancy, as the Spanish *guardainfante* ('child-keeper') suggests.
1285 **None of you tell her!**: addressed to the audience, who are thus invited to become collaborators in the deception of Beatriz, and to 'participate' in the play.
1286+ There is no indication in D that Inés leaves the stage, but the scene changes from the street to the interior of Don Pedro's house. Logic, and the convention of clearing the stage to indicate a change of scene, demands that she go off briefly.
1289–90 It is perhaps worth noting that Don Juan, the male character with whom the audience is invited to identify most, finds Leonor's cleverness worth flattering. Unlike Don Diego or Don Alonso, he seems to appreciate a woman for her mind.

quedó?

LEONOR   Tanto, que anda cuidadoso,
                 yendo a casa y viniendo,
                 escuchando a la una, a la otra oyendo.   1300
                 Hasta aquí no ha sabido
                 cúyo el papel, ni para quién ha sido,
                 porque Inés, que tenía
                 sola noticia de la culpa mía,
                 sin que a decirlo acuda,   1305
                 dejó en su fuerza la primera duda.

INÉS   Yo no dije que era
                 el papel de Beatriz, porque pudiera
                 el papel desmentirme,
                 y así en lo que dijiste estuve firme.   1310

DON JUAN   Dicha fue que viniera
                 el papel de manera
                 que a entrambas convenía,
                 que bien se acuerda la memoria mía
                 de que no te nombraba   1315
                 y de que escrito de otra letra estaba.
                 Pero dime, ¿qué ha hecho
                 Beatriz al testimonio?

LEONOR   Yo sospecho
                 que, sujeta al indicio,
                 si juicio tiene, ha de perder el juicio,   1320
                 pues sobre su melindre y su locura,
                 tan vana de su ingenio y hermosura,
                 verse indiciada tanto
                 de una sospecha, la convierte en llanto.
                 Y estoy, Don Juan, gustosa de manera   1325
                 de verla así, que diera
                 porque fuera verdad y no fingido
                 el amor que en su culpa he introducido,
                 la vida.

INÉS   Piensa tú, señor, qué haremos
                 por llevar adelante sus extremos.   1330

LEONOR   De nuestro amor industria lisonjera
                 el divertirla y el culparla fuera,
                 pues con eso dejara
                 de perseguirme a mí, y ella callara.

DON JUAN   Ahora bien: pues yo quiero   1335

	both of you?
LEONOR	So much so, he's forever prowling anxiously around the house trying to eavesdrop on one or other of us.
	So far he has been unable to discover who sent the letter, nor whom it was addressed to, because Inés, who is the only one who knows I'm the culprit, managed to leave his mind full of doubt.
INÉS	I didn't say the letter belonged to Beatriz, just in case what's in it might prove me a liar; but I said nothing that would contradict what *you* said.
DON JUAN	Luckily the letter was written in such a way that it could apply to either of you. It didn't mention your name, and, besides, it was written in another hand.
	But, tell me, how has Beatriz reacted to being held to blame?
LEONOR	I suspect the accusation will make her lose her wits, if she has any. Apart from her affectation and her silliness, she is so conceited about her brains and her beauty that these suspicions have driven her to tears.
	I'm so delighted to see her in this state, Don Juan, that I'd give anything to make a reality of the bogus love I concocted just to put her in the wrong.
INÉS	Sir, you try and think up some way to get her into an even worse state.
LEONOR	It would be splendid if we could distract her attention from our love and make her seem the guilty one. That should stop her persecuting me and keep her quiet.
DON JUAN	Very well, then! I'm only too happy to be

	de esta venganza tuya ser tercero,	
	y trayendo conmigo	
	para que la entretenga un cierto amigo,	
	haré... pero ella viene;	
	después lo oirás, que aquí callar conviene.	1340
LEONOR	Pues vete, no te vea;	
	que aunque aquesta sospecha en ti no sea	
	a toda ley, bien creo	
	que es mejor desvelar nuestro deseo.	
DON JUAN	Pues adiós, Leonor bella.	1345
INÉS	¡Santiago y cierra, España! ¡A ella, a ella!	

Vanse [Inés y Don Juan y] sale Beatriz

BEATRIZ	Aquí, que fénix estoy	
	(porque en fin la fantasía	
	hace y no hace compañía).	
	soliloquiar quiero hoy	1350
	en qué infelice soy,	
	y en qué horóscopo nací;	
	pues siendo mi honor en mí	
	sol que el día iluminó,	
	el eclipse padeció,	1355
	y yo el efecto sentí.	
	Entre mi nombre y mi ardor,	
	con epiciclo confuso,	
	el cuerpo opaco me puso	
	la mentira de Leonor.	1360
LEONOR	¿Qué me quieres?	
BEATRIZ	Es error,	
	aunque a solas te he nombrado,	
	fantasear que te he llamado;	
	que si el nombrar es llamar,	

1346 **For Spain and St James!**: St James (the greater) is the patron saint of Spain, and was supposed to have appeared in battle, leading Christian Spaniards against Moors; hence this battle-cry, usually translated as 'Saint James, and close with the enemy, Spain!'. Among those to whom its meaning was not clear is Sancho Panza, who questions Don Quixote about its meaning (*Don Quixote*, II, 58).

1347 **phoenix**: as stated earlier (851–4), there was only one phoenix at a time; Beatriz uses this as a metaphor for being alone.

1351 The spelling *infelice* (for normal *infeliz*) was a permitted way of adding an extra syllable to suit the metre.

1352 **horoscope**: although the seventeenth century had its sceptics, it was widely believed that individuals were influenced by the position of the heavenly bodies at the moment of their birth. Beatriz is beginning to think that her horoscope must

the instrument of your vengeance. I'll bring
along a certain friend of mine to make up to
her. I'll... But here she comes. I'll explain
later. For the moment, not a word!

LEONOR   Go quickly. Don't let her see you. Though
                nobody has the slightest suspicion about
                you, I think we should be very careful about
                this affair.

DON JUAN   Farewell, then, lovely Leonor.

INÉS   For Spain and Saint James! Up and at her!

          Exeunt Inés and Don Juan, and enter Beatriz

BEATRIZ   Now, like the solitary phoenix, with naught
                for company but my own imagination, I
                shall deliver a soliloquy about my unhappi-
                ness and about the horoscope under which
                I was born.

                My honour, which for me is the sun that
                illumines the day, suffered an eclipse which
                has gravely affected me.

                An opaque body, describing an erratic
                epicycle, was placed twixt that light and
                my good name by the lies of Leonor.

LEONOR   Did you call me?

BEATRIZ   Though I uttered your name in solitude,
                you are wrong to imagine I summoned
                you. If naming were summoning, my sorrow

---

have been particularly unfavourable.

1353–60 The mechanism of eclipses was well understood in Calderón's time, even
though the Catholic Church had not accepted the Copernican (heliocentric) system.
There were two main sorts of heavenly body, luminous and opaque (*cuerpo opaco*).
The former, like the sun, produced light; the latter, like the moon and the earth,
did not (though they might reflect it). An eclipse of the moon is produced when
the 'opaque body' of the earth intervenes between it and the 'luminous body' of the
sun. An epicycle is a circle which has its centre on the circumference of another;
the concept was used by Ptolemy (2nd century A.D.) to explain the movement of
the planets in terms of circles, when observation indicated that their orbits were *not*
circular. Copernicus abandoned the geocentric system, but not epicycles, and even
Galileo (died 1642) insisted on them, though Kepler had proved that the orbits were
ellipses. Calderón's metaphor is a little confused (a textual crux does not help),
but Leonor's lie is the 'opaque body' which has been interposed between the sun of
Beatriz's honour and her good name.

                                    hoy desvía con nombrar   1365
                                    al contrario mi cuidado.

LEONOR   Pues ¿por qué crüel conmigo
                                    tu voz a solas se emplea?

BEATRIZ   ¿Por qué? ¿Me interrogas? Sea
                                    tu mendacio tu castigo.   1370
                                    ¿Tú no fuiste, amor testigo,
                                    la escrita?

LEONOR   Sí.

BEATRIZ   ¿Tú no fuiste
                                    la que al paterno dijiste,
                                    al fin, que era para mí
                                    el lineado papel?

LEONOR   Sí.   1375

BEATRIZ   ¿Tú no fuiste quien hiciste
                                    tan valida la mentira
                                    que embeleció a la verdad,
                                    acuada su puridad?

LEONOR   Sí, Beatriz.

BEATRIZ   Pues, ¿qué te admira   1380
                                    lamentar tu fraude?

LEONOR   Mira
                                    lo que tu enfado causó;
                                    que no lo inventara, no,
                                    si tú ayudaras mi engaño;
                                    mas ya sucedido el daño,   1385
                                    Beatriz, primero era yo.
                                    Negarte a solas no quiero
                                    que mía la culpa fue,
                                    pero tampoco querré
                                    confesársela a un tercero.   1390
                                    Yo amo, yo adoro, yo muero
                                    de amor... ([Ap.] ¡Mi padre, ay de mí!)

1365 **vanish:** *desviar* was used intransitively in classical Spanish to mean 'go away' (e.g. *The trickster of Seville*, III, 228).

1370 **mendacity:** another Latinism on Beatriz's part. *Mendacidad* is normal Spanish for 'mendacity'. *DLE* lists *mendacio* as obsolete, meaning 'lie'.

1377 **plausible:** modern Spanish has the adjective *válido*, stressed (like English 'valid') on the first syllable. Classical Spanish had only *valido*, the past participle of the verb *valer*, meaning 'accepted', 'believed', 'generally esteemed', or as we translate. Cf. line 2270.

1379 **diluted:** the correct spelling of the Spanish verb is *aguar* ('to water down,

would vanish if I merely named its opposite.

LEONOR	But why do you speak so cruelly about me when you are alone?
BEATRIZ	Why? You need to inquire! Let your mendacity be its own punishment. Were not you (as Love is your witness) the addressee of that letter?
LEONOR	Yes.
BEATRIZ	Was it not you who told our progenitor that the lineated paper was for me?
LEONOR	Yes.
BEATRIZ	Was it not you who made the lie so plausible that truth was diluted and confounded?
LEONOR	Yes, Beatriz.
BEATRIZ	Then why should you be surprised when I lament your deceitfulness?

LEONOR	Just look what your spitefulness has done!
	
	    I wouldn't have invented the lie if you had helped me keep my secret.
	    But, once the damage was done, it was every man for himself.
	    Now that we're alone, I shall not deny the fault was mine, but I shall on no account confess this to a third party.
	    I love, I adore, I die of love... (*Aside.* Good gracious! There's my father!)

dilute'), not *acuar*. However, some related words are still written with *c*, e.g. *ácueo*, 'aqueous'; we suspect that this is another of Beatriz's Latinisms. *DLE* lists *puridad* as being in current use, but the normal Spanish word for 'purity' is *pureza*.

1386   **every man for himself**: *primero soy yo* is a proverbial expression (Cejador, *Refranero castellano*) roughly equivalent to 'charity begins at home'. *Primero soy yo* is also the title of a Calderón play. We cannot assume that this is another advertisement, given that the play was published only posthumously (1683) and that the proverb already existed. The proverbial nature of the phrase evidently discourages Leonor from using the feminine form *primera*; the same happens in *Casa con dos puertas mala es de guardar* (*A house with two doors is a hard one to guard*), Aguilar II, 306a.

Sale al paño Don Pedro por las espaldas de Beatriz, y cara
a cara de Leonor; ella le ve, y él se encubre

DON PEDRO [*ap.*]   'Yo muero de amor', oí
                       a Leonor.

LEONOR   ([*Ap.*] Cure mi error
                       mi voz.) ¡'Yo muero de amor'   1395
                       dices delante de mí!
                       ¡'Yo quiero'!

DON PEDRO [*ap.*]   ¿Esto llego a ver?
LEONOR   ¡'Yo amo'!
BEATRIZ   ¿Aquesto llego a oír?
LEONOR   ¿'De amor muero' ha de decir
                       una principal mujer?   1400
                       Mi padre lo ha de saber;
                       que aunque tú me has dicho aquí
                       que a él no, pero a mí sí
                       lo confiesas, brevemente
                       lo sabrá.

BEATRIZ   ¿Qué dices?
LEONOR   Tente;   1405
                       no te apropincues a mí.

BEATRIZ   El concepto dificulto
                       de tus extremos, Leonor.

LEONOR   No me empañes el candor
                       de mi castísimo bulto.   1410

BEATRIZ   ¡Qué mudanza!
LEONOR   ¿Tal insulto
                       pronunciar tu lengua osa?

DON PEDRO [*ap.*]   Leonor es la virtüosa.
BEATRIZ   Oye, hermana.
LEONOR   Aqueso no,
                       que tener no puedo yo   1415
                       hermana libidinosa.

                       Vase Leonor

BEATRIZ   ¿Quién tales extremos vio?
                       ¿Quién vio tales sentimientos?
                       ¿Quién vio tales fingimientos

1392+ Still 'prowling around the house trying to eavesdrop' (1299–1300), Don Pedro
    manages to catch Leonor in the middle of a potentially incriminating confession;
    but, since he does not realise she has seen him, she is able to turn matters to her

Don Pedro appears at the backcloth behind Beatriz and
facing Leonor. Leonor sees him. He hides.

DON PEDRO (*aside*) 'I die of love' I heard Leonor say.

LEONOR   (*Aside.* I'll change my tone of voice to cover
                         my mistake.) 'I die of love' you say, to my
                         face! 'I am in love'!

DON PEDRO (*aside*) What's this I'm seeing?
LEONOR   'I love'!
BEATRIZ   What's this I'm hearing?
LEONOR   'I die of love' on the lips of a wellbred lady!
                         Father shall learn of this!   And, though
                         you've just told me you'd confess this thing
                         to me but not to him, he shall hear of it at
                         once.

BEATRIZ   What are you saying?
LEONOR   Desist! Seek not such propinquity with me!

BEATRIZ   I cannot comprehend your sudden changes,
                         Leonor.
LEONOR   Do not sully the purity of my most chaste
                         bosom!
BEATRIZ   What a transformation!
LEONOR   Does your tongue dare utter such insolence?

DON PEDRO (*aside*) Leonor is the virtuous one.
BEATRIZ   Listen to me, sister.
LEONOR   I am no such thing! I cannot have a libidi-
                         nous sister!

                         Exit Leonor
BEATRIZ   Who ever saw such sudden changes, such
                         contradictory feelings, such pretences, from

---

advantage.
1405–6; 1409–10; 1411–12; 1414–16 Leonor turns the tables on Beatriz by echoing,
  slightly altered, her sister's earlier remarks and accusations (603–6; 618–20; 640).

de un instante a otro?

Don Pedro	Yo,	1420

yo los vi, Beatriz, y no
en vano el cuidado ha sido
que con las dos he tenido.

Beatriz   Señor, ¿tú estabas aquí?

Don Pedro   Sí, sí, Beatriz, aquí estaba.   1425

Beatriz   ¿Oíste a Leonor lo que hablaba?

Don Pedro   Lo que hablaba a Leonor oí.

Beatriz   Luego ¿ya estarás de mí
desengañado?

Don Pedro   Sí estoy,
pues he llegado a ver hoy   1430
que una hermana menor pueda
reñirte.

Beatriz   ¡Que tal suceda!
Infausta y crinita soy.

Don Pedro   ¿Qué crinita, ni qué infausta?

Beatriz   Señor...

Don Pedro   Beatriz, bueno está;   1435
basta lo afectado ya,
lo enfadoso, Beatriz, basta,
que es lo que más te contrasta
para que vencida quede
tu opinión: bien verse puede,   1440
si a hablar así te acomodas,
que quien no habla como todas,
como todas no procede.
Yo sé que el cuidado ha sido
y el papel de un caballero   1445
bachiller y chocarrero,
leve y mal entretenido,
y que le quieres he oído,
cuando Leonor te reñía.
Culpa ha sido tuya y mía,   1450
mas remediarélo yo:
aquí el estudio acabó,
aquí dio fin la poesía.

1433–4 Beatriz returns to the notion of her bad horoscope. The Spanish *crinito* literally meant 'hairy', and so was associated with comets (a word of Greek origin, meaning 'hairy stars'). The influence of comets was generally thought to be bad.

	one minute to the next?
DON PEDRO	I did, Beatriz. My vigilance over both of you has not been in vain.

BEATRIZ	Sir, were you there all the time?
DON PEDRO	Yes, Beatriz. I was.
BEATRIZ	And did you hear Leonor's words?
DON PEDRO	I heard Leonor's words.
BEATRIZ	Then you know the truth about me?

| DON PEDRO | I do indeed.   Today I have seen how your younger sister has earned the right to remonstrate with you. |

BEATRIZ	Oh, that such a thing should befall me! Ill-starred and planet-stricken am I!
DON PEDRO	Ill-starred and planet-stricken indeed!
BEATRIZ	Sir...
DON PEDRO	Enough, Beatriz. Enough of your tiresome affectation. It is this, more than anything else, that has earned you a bad name. It's all too plain that, if you can bring yourself to talk like that, instead of talking like everybody else, you will also behave differently from everybody else.

I now know that the 'anguish' and the letter belong to a glib young gentleman who is nothing but a scurrilous waster, and I know from Leonor's rebuke that you are in love with him.

The blame for all of this is mine as well as yours, but the remedy shall be mine alone.

There shall be no more study, and no more poetry.

---

infausta should rhyme with *basta* and *contrasta* (1437, 1438), and Calderón may well be making a joke by permitting Don Pedro, unfamiliar with Beatriz's vocabulary, to echo it incorrectly by using the non-existent *infasta*, which *would* rhyme. Góngora uses *infausto* (e.g. *Soledad* I, 800).

	Libro en casa no ha de haber	
	de latín, que yo no alcance;	1455
	unas *Horas* de romance	
	le bastan a una mujer.	
	Bordar, labrar y coser	
	sepa sólo; deje al hombre	
	el estudio, y no te asombre	1460
	esto; que te he de matar	
	si algo te escucho nombrar	
	que no sea por su nombre.	
BEATRIZ	Subordinada al respeto,	
	girasol de tu semblante,	1465
	en estilo relevante	
	no frasificar prometo.	
	Deja, empero, a tu conceto	
	desvanecer la apariencia	
	que el engaño hizo evidencia,	1470
	que hizo caso la malicia,	
	queriendo con su injusticia	
	captar tu benevolencia.	
DON PEDRO	¡Perdiendo, Beatriz, el vicio,	
	bien enmendada te veo!	1475
BEATRIZ	Por tu anticipata...	
DON PEDRO	Creo	
	que hoy me has de quitar el juicio.	

Vanse. Salen Don Alonso y Moscatel.

DON ALONSO	¿Eso la pícara dijo?	
MOSCATEL	De tu amor tan ofendida,	
	como si fuera hija Inés	1480
	del Preste Juan de las Indias,	
	'Decid', dijo, 'a vuestro dueño	
	que de mi valor no vista,	
	que soy grande para dama,	

1456 **Book of Hours**: a book of prayers to be said at various hours of the day, usually to the Virgin Mary. Intended for pious laywomen, such works were not as popular in 1635 as they had once been, for writers were producing a greater variety of 'edifying' works.

1464–77 It is worth noting that Beatriz's lack of immediate reformation does not prompt Don Pedro to take his threat to her (1461–3) literally (cf. note 359–60). His remark carries as much weight as a harassed modern parent's 'I'll murder you if...'.

1473 **prevail upon your benevolence**: the Spanish phrase *captar tu benevolencia* echoes the Latin expression 'captatio benevolentiae' (literally, 'securing of goodwill'). The securing of goodwill in the listener or reader was an important part of the study of

I will not permit so much as a single Latin
book in the house. A Book of Hours in the
vernacular is quite sufficient for a woman.

Let her stitch and sew and embroider, and
leave studying to men. And there's no need
to look surprised! I shall kill you if I ever
again catch you referring to anything except
by its proper name.

BEATRIZ   Respectfully subordinate, like the sunflower
                           following your countenance, I promise not
                           to verbalise in lofty style.

                           However, please permit your reason to
                           penetrate the appearances which deceit has
                           presented as evidence, and which malice
                           has adduced, attempting thus unjustly to
                           prevail upon your benevolence.

DON PEDRO   So much for mending your ways, Beatriz!

BEATRIZ   In the name of your ancestrix...
DON PEDRO   I do believe you'll drive me mad!
              Exeunt. Enter Don Alonso and Moscatel.
DON ALONSO   The little hussy said that?
MOSCATEL   She was so upset by your suggestion, you'd
                           think she was the daughter of Prester John
                           of the Indies. 'Tell your master,' she said,
                           'that he needn't think he can sport *my*
                           virtue; say I'm too good to be his plaything,

---

rhetoric. Calderón's use of the phrase is more likely to be a subconscious reflection
of his own education than a conscious attempt to suggest that Beatriz had studied
rhetoric.
1477+ *Exeunt...* : once again the scene changes. As we are some distance from Don
   Pedro's house (1680–1), we are probably in Don Alonso's.
1481 **Prester John of the Indies**: a mythical priest-king (*prester* = presbyter = priest)
   of the Orient, supposedly Christian and also fabulously wealthy. Martin Behaim's
   map of the world (1491) puts his kingdom roughly in modern Tibet, as Marco Polo
   had done; by the time of Covarrubias (1611) he was identified with the emperor of
   Ethiopia.
1484–9 A little self-parody on Calderón's part. When the noblewoman Mencía tells

	y para esposa soy chica'.	1485
DON ALONSO	Eso a reyes de comedia	
	no hay condesa que no diga	
	de Amalfi, Mantua o Milán,	
	mas no las de Picardía.	
	Si a mí se me diera algo,	1490
	fuera la historia muy linda,	
	porque no hay cosa que tanto	
	me canse y me dé mohina	
	como ver una fregona	
	que a lo dama se resista.	1495
	¡Válgate el diablo, picaña!	
	¿Cómo no tienes a dicha	
	que te hable un hombre que al fin	
	trae una camisa limpia?	
MOSCATEL	Señor, cada ropa blanca	1500
	su semejante codicia.	
DON ALONSO	Y ¿qué te pasó con Celia?	
MOSCATEL	Estaba a su celosía	
	asomada, y aun borracha,	
	pues dijo por qué no ibas	1505
	a verla, y esto, señor,	
	en juicio no lo diría,	
	porque ¿cómo has de ir a verla,	
	si ya la viste ha tres días?	
DON ALONSO	Mi firmeza me destruye,	1510
	porque todas imaginan,	
	siendo galán al quitar,	
	que lo he de ser de por vida.	
	Pues mejor es lo que a mí	

---

prince Enrique in *El médico de su honra* (*The surgeon of his honour*) that their
love-affair could have no future, she says 'soy para dama más, / lo que para esposa
menos' ('I am by the same degree too good to be your plaything as I am not good
enough to be your wife', i.e. I have insufficient status to marry someone of your rank,
but enough concern for my status not to wish to be your mistress), Aguilar I, 320b.
Don Alonso's reply suggests that the motif is commoner than it is. Arellano (p. 275)
quotes another example from Juan Ruiz de Alarcón. The story of the Duchess
(i.e. not Countess) of Amalfi did give rise to some plays, notably Lope de Vega's *El
mayordomo de la duquesa de Amalfi* (probably written 1604–1606, published 1618)
and John Webster's *The duchess of Malfy* (published 1623). Mantua and Milan are
also duchies, not counties.

1489 **Roguesborough**: in the original, 'Picardy', an untranslatable pun. The Spanish
word *pícaro-a*, a rogue, is taken to mean a native of *Picardía* (Picardy), which
consequently comes to mean 'knavery' or 'sexual naughtiness'.

	and not good enough to be his wife.'
DON ALONSO	That's the kind of answer kings in plays are forever receiving from Countesses of Amalfi or Mantua or Milan, but never from a Countess of Roguesborough!

If I were to take the notion, this could turn out to be a pretty little episode, because there's nothing that gets my back up so much as seeing a scullerymaid playing hard to get like a lady.

The devil take the little slut! She should be only too delighted to be addressed by a man with a clean shirt!

MOSCATEL   Sir, birds of like linen flock together.

DON ALONSO   And what news have you about Celia?

MOSCATEL   She was sitting at her window, and she must have been tipsy, or maybe even drunk, because she wanted to know why you hadn't been to see her, and she wouldn't have said that, sir, if she were in her right mind; for, why would you go and see her when it's only three days since you were there last?

DON ALONSO   My constancy is my undoing. Because I treat them well on my departure, they think I have to go on doing so for ever.

But let me tell you about something more

1500–1 Moscatel garbles a proverb, which exists in various forms, e.g. 'Todo semejante apetece y codicia a su semejante' (Sbarbi, II, 352), 'cada cual quiere a su igual', or 'cada par con su igual' (Correas, p. 378). All mean more or less that every creature seeks its like.

1502–4 The word-play here is untranslatable. Celia was looking out (*asomada*) of her lattice-window (*celosía*, the type called *jalousie* in French); but *celosía* also means 'jealousy', an emotion poor Celia probably had reason to feel, as even her name suggests; and *asomada* also means 'tipsy', which leads Moscatel to *borracha*, 'drunk'.

1502–41 This discussion about women, two of whom are named and spoken of rather disparagingly, reminds us uncomfortably of the similar discussion between Don Juan Tenorio and his friend Mota, early in Act II of *The trickster of Seville*.

1512 Don Alonso puns on the expression *al quitar*: in the legal sense, it means 'temporary', and his relationships with women are certainly that; but he also means that he behaves gallantly 'on his departure'.

me ha pasado: como iba   1515
en un coche Doña Clara,
llamóme, lleguéme a oírla,
y díjome que a la tarde
(¡ahí es una niñería!)
le enviase veinte varas   1520
de lama, porque quería
hacer en mi nombre una
pollera, y a media risa
pregunté de qué color.
Respondió que de la mía,   1525
y así al propósito hice
de repente esta quintilla:
'De mi color, bien mi amor
dar la pollera quisiera;
mas es tanto mi temor   1530
que no me dejas color
de qué hacerte la pollera'.
Con esto me descarté
de la lama.

MOSCATEL   Linda finca
es un desenfado.

DON ALONSO   ¿Cómo?   1535

MOSCATEL   Como paga a chanza vista.

DON ALONSO   ¿No sabes lo que en aquesto
más me mata, más me admira?
Que usándose hombres que nieguen,
se usen mujeres que pidan.   1540

MOSCATEL   Piden por su devoción.
([*Ap.*] ¡Qué presto de Inés se olvida!
Celos, adiós.)

DON ALONSO   Moscatel.

MOSCATEL   ¿Señor?

DON ALONSO   ¿Quieres que te diga
una verdad?

1515–34 There were of course predatory females who were a match for predatory males
like Don Alonso. They would unashamedly ask for presents, and their men-friends,
either hoping for favours in return, or fearing to lose face by refusing, would have to
pay. Don Alonso has no such compunction.

1525 **leave the colour to me**: Clara actually said that the skirt should be 'of Don
Alonso's colour'. She meant that the colour should be of his choosing, but he responded to the literal meaning of the phrase by pretending to blanch at the thought
of paying for so much material. Now masculine, *color* could be feminine (thus *mía*) in

interesting that happened to me. Doña Clara, passing in her carriage, called to me and I approached, and she asked me (such childishness!) to send her that evening twenty yards of lamé, as she wanted to make up a skirt in my honour. Half-laughingly I inquired what colour she wanted.

She replied that she would leave the colour to me, so I dashed off these lines:

'My love is such I'd soon donate
A skirt that was my colour's mate;
But such is the fear by which I'm reft,
I simply have no colour left.'

And so I got out of providing the lamé.

MOSCATEL	A good quittance is a great relief!
DON ALONSO	What do you mean?
MOSCATEL	Never pay cash till the goods are delivered!
DON ALONSO	Do you know what really amazes me about this sort of thing? It's that, when men refuse women, the women implore them even more.
MOSCATEL	They show devotion by imploring. (*Aside*. How quickly he has forgotten Inés! Jealousy, farewell!)
DON ALONSO	Moscatel!
MOSCATEL	Sir?
DON ALONSO	Do you want me to tell you the truth?

---

the seventeenth century.

1534–6 Moscatel puns using financial terminology: *pagar a letra vista* means 'to pay on sight'; by analogy, he makes up *pagar a chanza vista*, which could mean 'to pay when the joke's been seen': as Clara doesn't see the joke, she doesn't get paid. However, we also think that Moscatel may be using the jargon of commercial dealing to imply that Don Alonso did well to avoid giving Clara an expensive present in return for a possible (but by no means guaranteed) sexual favour.

1541 Moscatel seems to imply that, because women are more devout than men (in the religious and 'romantic' sense), they 'implore' more (i.e. make more requests).

MOSCATEL	Si contigo	1545
	lo puedes acabar, dila.	
DON ALONSO	La Inesilla me ha picado.	
MOSCATEL	¿Tan aguda es la Inesilla?	
DON ALONSO	Y por hacer burla de ella	
	solamente, he de rendirla.	1550
	Allá has de volver.	
MOSCATEL	¿Yo?	
DON ALONSO	Sí.	
MOSCATEL [ap.]	Celos, no adiós tan aprisa.	

Sale Don Juan

DON ALONSO   Y dirás...

DON JUAN
      ¡Gracias al cielo
que os traigo nuevas un día
de contento, porque amor   1555
no siempre ha de ser desdichas!
Ya cesaron sus disgustos,
sus pesares, sus rencillas,
que, como es niño, el semblante
que ayer fue llanto, hoy es risa.   1560
Ayer de vuestro valor
me valí, cuando tenía
empeños de honor, y agora
que han mejorado de dicha,
me he de valer, Don Alonso,   1565
de vuestra cortesanía,
buen gusto y sutil ingenio,
porque en dos iguales líneas
los dos extremos toquéis
del pesar y la alegría.   1570

DON ALONSO   Pues bien, ¿qué os ha sucedido?

DON JUAN
De cuanta culpa tenía,
Leonor hizo a Beatriz dueño,
cautelosa y prevenida;
dudó el padre entre las dos   1575
cúya fuese la malicia,
y quedó por fe dudosa
la que era culpa precisa.
Para ayudar este engaño

1559 **but a child**: Don Juan's image is of the child Cupid, son of Venus.
1566 **social graces**: the usual Spanish word is *cortesía*; this is an Italianism, found

MOSCATEL   If you think you can manage it, go ahead.

DON ALONSO   Little Inés has stung me.
MOSCATEL   Is little Inés barbed, then?
DON ALONSO   Now, if only to teach her a lesson, I will
                   have her. You must go to her again.

MOSCATEL   What? Me?
DON ALONSO   Yes, you.
MOSCATEL (*aside*) Jealousy! I said farewell too soon!
                       Enter Don Juan
DON ALONSO   Tell her...
DON JUAN   Thank Heaven I bring you good news on
                   one day at least, and that love need not be
                   all misfortune.

                   All sorrows, woes and quarrelling have
                   ceased, and Love (who, after all, is but a
                   child) today shows a smiling countenance
                   where yesterday there were only tears.
                       Yesterday I had recourse to your valour
                   when questions of honour were involved.
                   Now that my position has improved, Don
                   Alonso, I wish to avail myself of your social
                   graces, your good judgment and your wit,
                   so that you may in equal measure know the
                   extremes of my sorrow and my joy.

DON ALONSO   What's happened, then?
DON JUAN   Shrewdly and cleverly, Leonor shifted the
                   blame on to Beatriz.

                   Their father could not decide which of
                   them was the schemer, and blatant guilt
                   became indistinguishable from doubtful
                   innocence. To promote this deception, and

---

first in Boscán (died 1542). Calderón also uses it in *De una causa dos efectos* (*Two
effects from a single cause*), Aguilar II, 475a, when one of the characters (Fadrique)
complains that he has never bothered to learn the social graces.

con Beatriz, y divertirla,   1580
que si hay envidia entre hermanos,
es la más crüel envidia,
me ha pedido que con ella
algún nuevo amante finja,
porque la importa en extremo   1585
o culparla o divertirla.
Y aquéste habéis de ser vos,
ayudándoos ella misma
a la entrada de su casa.
Y así, desde aqueste día   1590
la habéis de asistir, pasear,
adorar su celosía,
solicitar sus crïadas,
donde saliere, seguirla,
escribirla...

DON ALONSO   Deteneos,   1595
que ni hablarla, ni servirla,
ni pasearla, ni mirarla
sabré yo hacer en mi vida.
¿Yo mirar a una ventana
embobado todo el día,   1600
haciendo el amor ardiente
a un cántaro de agua fría?
¿Yo sobornar a una moza
porque mis penas la diga?
¿Yo abrazar un escudero   1605
con la barba hasta la cinta?
¿Yo seguir a una mujer,
ni saber dónde va a misa,
ni si la oye?, que al fin, yo,
Don Juan, en toda mi vida   1610
la he averiguado a mi dama
si tiene o no tiene crisma;
y ellas se huelgan, pues todas

1601-2 Muir and Mackenzie suggest (p. 204) that the pitcher of cold water refers to
the occupational hazard of suitors, the slops which were flung from windows into
the street, there being no other method of waste disposal. This was not normally
a daytime occurrence, however. It was (and still is) the custom in Spain to place
unglazed pitchers of water on a shaded windowsill to catch the breeze; evaporation
through the unglazed clay cools the water. A poem attributed to Calderón supports
this interpretation: the *Romance a un galán que enamoró un cántaro pensando que
era su dama* (*Ballad to a young gallant who paid court to a pitcher thinking it was
his lady-love*), MS 2100, Biblioteca Nacional, Madrid. The reference in our text, on

to confuse her sister further (envy between brothers or sisters is the cruellest kind), Leonor has asked me to find someone who will pretend to be in love with her sister, because Beatriz must either be incriminated or thrown off the scent.

You are to be the feigned lover. Leonor herself will get you into the house.

So, from this day forth, you must wait on Beatriz, frequent her street, worship at her window, bribe her servants, follow her wherever she goes, write to her...

DON ALONSO   Just a minute! Not on my life am I going to talk to her, wait on her, follow her, gaze at her!

Me, staring all day at a window like an idiot, and making passionate declarations of love to a pitcher of cold water!

Me, bribing a maidservant to tell her mistress about my woes!
Me, embracing a footman with a beard down to his waist!
Me, following a woman about, or trying to discover where she goes to Mass, or if she goes to Mass at all! Me, who have never cared whether a lady friend of mine had *ever* been baptised. (And they prefer it that way, because they're never too keen to

---

the other hand, increases the chances that this poem, which survives only in MS 2100 (of the eighteenth century) really is by Calderón.

1610–14 What Don Alonso is referring to, obliquely, is the kind of investigations that would be carried out if marriage were in the offing between two people of apparently good family. Each family would check that the other was 'old Christian' (i.e. with no Moorish or Jewish ancestry). One way to do this was to look into parish baptismal records. Such investigations would reveal information regarding date of birth, and Don Alonso's lady friends are allegedly glad that his lack of curiosity enables them to keep their age secret.

niegan dónde se bautizan.
¿Yo escribir papel tan cuerdo   1615
que mil locuras no diga,
donde el retozar no ande
entre el afecto y la dicha?
¿Yo parlar a una ventana,
después de una noche fría,   1620
para pedir una mano?
¿Yo sufrir que muy esquiva
me responda 'es de mi esposo',
y con aquesta porfía
me ande con su doncellez   1625
dando en cara cada día?
¡Vive Dios, que antes me deje
morir, que a una mujer siga,
ni solicite, ni ronde,
ni mire, ni hable, ni escriba!   1630
Porque en no teniendo yo
libre entrada a mis visitas,
donde tome mi despejo
a la primera vez silla,
la segunda taburete   1635
y la tercera tarima,
siendo mi lecho el estrado
y mi almohada una rodilla,
y haciéndola que me rasque
la cabeza si me pica,   1640
no daré por cuanto amor
hay en el mundo dos higas.
Y mirad, pues, qué mujer
tan chistosa y entendida
me traéis: una mujer   1645
que habla siempre algarabía,
y sin Calepino no
puede un hombre entrar a oírla.
Y así, mirad si tenéis

1619–23 Cf. note 333–7, and also Brenan, *South from Granada*, ed. cit., p. 285.

blethering: the Spanish *parlar* is a Gallicism; cf. *La cisma de Ingalaterra* (*The schism of England*), Aguilar I, 153a.

1634–40 Etiquette in upper-class Madrid society was at this time extremely strict, and no translation can convey Don Alonso's appalling familiarity and total disregard of the proprieties. Ladies sat on cushions on a dais (see note 321), and gentlemen who were not close friends would be expected to stand. Don Alonso sits down at his first visit, and very quickly reaches a lower and lower level (that is to say, a greater and

reveal where they were christened.)

Me, writing sensible letters where there's no room for a bit of titillation amid all the 'affection' and the 'bliss'.

Me, spending the whole of a cold night blethering at a window, just in the hope of holding hands.

Me, accepting her disdainful reply that 'it shall be my husband's alone', and letting her obstinately flaunt her maidenhood daily in my face!

By God, I'd die before I'd chase a woman, or plead, or haunt her street, or gaze, or make small-talk, or write love-letters!

Unless I can come and go as I please, taking a chair on my first visit, an arm-chair on my second and an ottoman on my third, using the divan for a bed and a lap for a pillow, and getting the lady to scratch my head if it's itchy, I wouldn't give two figs for all the love in the world.

And just look what a clever blue-stocking you've got for me; a woman who talks constant gibberish and whom nobody can make sense of without the aid of a Latin dictionary. So, if you have any quarrels in

---

greater degree of familiarity), ending up sprawled on the dais with his head on the lady's lap.

1642 **two figs**: not the fruit, which would be *dos higos*, but the obscene gesture, made with the thumb between the index and middle finger, with the fist closed. To the English mind, this seems to have been a particularly Spanish gesture, e.g. '...figo for thy friendship! ...The fig of Spain!' (Shakespeare, *Henry V*, III, vi).

1647 **Latin dictionary**: the surname of Ambrosio Calepino, whose Latin/Italian dictionary was published in 1502, came to be used for any Latin dictionary. Quevedo drops the name in his *Culta latiniparla* (see above, p. xxi). In the form Calepin, it even entered French and English (the latter as early as 1568).

	algún disgusto en que os sirva,	1650
	que voto a Dios que primero	
	con diez hombres legos riña	
	que con una mujer culta,	
	que ha de ser la dama mía,	
	como fianza, abonada,	1655
	sobre lega, llana y lisa.	
Don Juan	En la corte, Don Alonso,	
	¿cada día no se mira,	
	por hacer tercio a un amigo,	
	enamorar a una amiga?	1660
Don Alonso	También se mira, Don Juan,	
	en la corte cada día	
	perder uno su dinero	
	por hacer tercio a una rifa.	
Don Juan	Yo no quiero que tu amor	1665
	sea, sino que lo finjas,	
	que esto todo ha de ser burla.	
Don Alonso	Mucho el ser fingido obliga,	
	y hacer burla de una loca	
	tan vana y tan presumida...	1670
Moscatel [ap.]	¡Qué presto hizo la razón	
	a la ocasión que le brinda!	
	Tan loco nos venga el año.	
Don Alonso	Cuanto sea engaño y mentira,	
	vaya; mas pensar que tengo	1675
	de obligarla ni sufrirla,	
	es pensar un imposible.	
Don Juan	Ni nadie a aqueso os obliga.	
Don Alonso	Pues desde aquí empiezo a amarla.	
Don Juan	Vamos a su casa misma,	1680
	y en el camino os diré	
	de ella cosas conocidas	
	que importan, y haré que entréis	
	a hablarla.	
Don Alonso	Vamos aprisa,	
	que ya, de pensar, Don Juan,	1685

1655–6 Don Alonso uses an expression from the legal language relating to contracts. The phrase *llano y liso* ('plain and simple') is still in current use; *lego*, as we have seen (597) means illiterate, so Alonso is punning on the mental rather than physical qualities of his ideal woman.

which I may be of service to you, I swear
to God I'd rather fight ten illiterate men
than one educated woman. Any lady friend
of mine must come with a guarantee, signed
and sealed, that she's not only illiterate, but
down-to-earth and plain-spoken as well.

DON JUAN

Here in Madrid, Don Alonso, is it not
common practice for one gentleman to
help another by paying suit to a lady's
best friend?

DON ALONSO

Yes, and it's also common practice for
gentlemen to lose all their money by helping
to support a lottery.

DON JUAN

I'm not asking you to be in love with her,
only to pretend you are. The whole thing
is just a joke.

DON ALONSO

I like the idea of pretending, and also of
playing a joke on such a conceited and
pretentious woman.

MOSCATEL (*aside*)

How quickly he rises to the bait! Let's hope
it's not us that get caught.

DON ALONSO

Deceit and lies are fine by me, but wooing
her in earnest and putting up with her
nonsense is quite out of the question.

DON JUAN

But nobody is asking you to do that!

DON ALONSO

Very well, then. I fall for her here and now.

DON JUAN

Let us go to her house, and on the way I'll
tell you what you need to know, and then
I'll get you in to talk to her.

DON ALONSO

Let's go at once, Don Juan. I'm already

1665–6 Don Juan suddenly adopts the familiar form of address (*tú*, as opposed to
vosotros). Possibly the assonance (í-a) made it easier to use this form (*finjas*). He
goes back to *vosotros* in 1678.

1673 **Let's hope...**: literally, 'Let's hope the year is as good', a proverbial expression,
recorded by Correas, p. 492. Correas explains that *año loco* means a fertile, abundant
year. Cf. *La hija del aire* I (*The daughter of the air*), Aguilar I, 739b. We know of
no English equivalent.

lo que hoy a las burlas mías
han de responder sus veras,
me estoy muriendo de risa.

MOSCATEL   Quiera amor no pare en llanto.

DON ALONSO   ¿Qué llanto, necio, si miras   1690
que todo es burla?, pues sólo
mi libertad solicita
hacer buen tercio a Don Juan,
vengar a Leonor divina,
burlar a Beatriz hermosa   1695
y retozar a Inesilla.

MOSCATEL [ap.]   No será, no, sino echarse
con la carga de mis dichas.

Vanse. Salen Beatriz e Inés.

INÉS   Grande es, señora, tu melancolía.

BEATRIZ   ¿Cómo no ha de ser grande, y más si es mía? 1700
¿Y harta razón no tengo,
pues por Leonor con mi ascendiente vengo
a padecer calumnias de que amo,
cuando la misma ingratitud me llamo?
¿Yo, pensar que he escuchado a un hombre amores,
que admití un papel, que di favores,
que entró en mi cuarto abriendo una fenestra,
que fue el tacto la nube de mi diestra?
Cosas son que el escrúpulo más leve
dentro de mí, ni aun a pensar se atreve.   1710
Y así, aqueste retiro,
donde la luz del sol apenas miro,
lúgubre será esfera
en que, engañando lo que vivo, muera;
estancia será esquiva   1715
en que, burlando lo que muero, viva.
El sol, Narciso de carmín y grana,
desde el primer fulgor de la mañana
al paroxismo de la noche fría
adonde espera el parangón del día,   1720
no me ha de ver la cara,
si ya con luz no se penetra avara

1698+ **Exeunt... :** the scene changes to a room in Don Pedro's house.
1707 **casement:** the English hardly conveys the extravagance of the word *fenestra*,
which is a pure Latinism.
1717 **Narcissus:** the narcissus is illustrated in herbals of the sixteenth and seventeenth

dying of laughter at the thought that false love on
my part may be met by true love on hers.

MOSCATEL   Let's hope Love won't make it end in tears.

DON ALONSO   What tears, you jackass! Don't you see it's all a
joke? I'm only going to give Don Juan a hand,
avenge the divine Leonor, play a joke on the
beautiful Beatriz, and have a little frolic with Inés.

MOSCATEL (*aside*) No, that's *not* all you're going to do. You're also
going to run away with my happiness.

Exeunt. Enter Beatriz and Inés.

INÉS   Your melancholy is very great, madam.

BEATRIZ   How could it be otherwise, being mine?
    Do I not have good reason? Thanks to Leonor,
I am calumniated before my progenitor. I stand
accused of being in love, when I am in this respect
indifference incarnate.
    The very idea that I would allow a man to speak
to me of love, or that I would accept a letter, or
grant favours, or permit a man to enter my room
through an open casement, or besmirch my dexter
with his touch!
    The least proclivity in me towards such be-
haviour is quite unthinkable. Therefore this refuge,
where I scarcely glimpse the light of day, shall
be the lugubrious domain, the minuscule retreat
where, feigning life, I die, and where, cheating
death, I live. The sun, like a crimson-red Narcissus, from its first resplendence in the morn until
its paroxysm in the cold night, where its counterpart awaits, shall not look upon my face, unless
some meagre ray of light should penetrate this

---

centuries (see also Covarrubias); it was the flower into which the mythological
Narcissus changed when he pined away for love of his own reflection in a pool of
water. There is no special resemblance between the sun and the flower, but when
the sun is at its reddest, i.e. as it rises from the sea or sets in it, it will be reflected
in the water like Narcissus.

1720 **its counterpart** (i.e. of the day): Beatriz must be alluding to the moon, which
was a victim of one of her circumlocutions earlier.

a esta mansión adonde
mi profanado pundonor me esconde.
Lloren aquí mis ojos   1725
sinónimos neutrales, digo, enojos
de torpes desvaríos,
que son ajenos, y parecen míos.
Inés, ¿no me he quejado
en bien humilde estilo, en bien templado?   1730
Si mi padre me oyera,
¡oh, cuánta enmienda en mis discursos viera!

INÉS   Mucha, aunque del tema reformado
algunas palabrillas te han sobrado.

BEATRIZ   Dime cuáles han sido.   1735

INÉS   'Lúgubres' y 'crepúsculos' he oído,
'equívocos', 'sinónimos neutrales',
'fenestras', 'paroxismos', y otros tales
de que yo no me acuerdo.

BEATRIZ   ¡Con la estulticia que hay, el juicio pierdo!   1740
Pues ¿ésas no son voces de cartilla,
que un portero las sabe de la villa?
Mas desde aquí prometo
que calce mi conceto,
a pesar de Saturno,   1745
vil zueco, en vez de trágico coturno.

INÉS [ap.] Enmendándose va.

BEATRIZ   Y tú, si me oyeres
frase negada a bárbaras mujeres,
por ver si en esto topa,
tírame de la manga de la ropa.   1750

INÉS   La concesión aceto,

1726 **equivocal imputations**: Beatriz, as she goes on to explain, is referring to her sister's behaviour (1392ff), which has misled Don Pedro into thinking Leonor innocent and Beatriz guilty.

1733 See note 315.

1736–8 **prolixity**: this list echoes our translation of Beatriz's speech (1700–28) rather than translates the words Inés uses in the Spanish. Inés in fact lists two words that Beatriz did not use: *crepúsculos* ('twilights') and *equívocos* ('equivocal'). The former may be her malapropism for *escrúpulos* ('scruples', a commoner word in English); hence our 'prolixity', and 'equivalent disputations'. Both *crepúsculo* and *equívoco* were favoured by Góngora, who had a special fondness for proparoxytones (words stressed on the third-last syllable). Perhaps Inés knows more about 'learned' vocabulary than she has been letting on.

1740 **stultitude**: another pure Latinism from Beatriz.

dwelling where the profanation of my name
has made me hide myself away.

Now let my eyes lament those equivocal
imputations, I mean those sorrows caused
by the sins of others, blamed on me.

Inés, have I not grieved in humble,
temperate style?   If my father were to
hear me now, how improved he would find
my speech!

INÉS	He surely would! But one or two little words escaped reforming.
BEATRIZ	Tell me which ones they were.
INÉS	I heard 'lugubrious' and 'prolixity', 'casements' and 'paroxysms', 'minuscule', 'equivalent disputations', and a few more I can't remember.
BEATRIZ	Oh, such stultitude will make me lose my reason! Surely these are common-or-garden terms known to every doorman in the city? But I promise that, Saturn notwithstanding, my thoughts henceforth shall be shod in rough clogs instead of tragic buskins.
INÉS (*aside*)	Some improvement!
BEATRIZ	And, should you hear me lapse into any expression alien to untutored women, try plucking at my sleeve to see if that helps.
INÉS	I accept the commission, and agree to play

1745 **Saturn notwithstanding**: Beatriz is thinking of her horoscope again. The planet
   Saturn's influence is supposedly baleful, and prompts a state of melancholy in those
   affected by it. Cf. English 'saturnine'.

1746 **tragic buskins**: the buskin was a kind of high-heeled shoe, worn by actors in
   Greek tragedy to look taller (and more imposing). *Calzar el coturno* ('to put on the
   buskin') came to mean to write or speak in the high style considered appropriate for
   tragedy. Ordinary clogs were worn by comic actors (and, metaphorically, by those
   who used the low comic style). Beatriz means that despite the melancholy influence
   of Saturn on her life, and the resulting appropriateness of the tragic style, she is going
   to try to use the plainer (and more cheerful) language of comedy. López Pinciano
   discusses the significance of the different types of footwear in his *Filosofía antigua
   poética* (*The poetic philosophy of the ancients*), Epístola IX: see vol. III, pp. 29–30
   of the Madrid, 1953 edition.

y ser fiscala de tu voz prometo.

Salen Leonor, Don Alonso y Moscatel

LEONOR [*a Don Alonso*]   Ésta es Beatriz, y puesto que has venido
a divertirla, su galán fingido,
hablarla aquí podrás seguramente;   1755
yo, atenta a que no haya inconveniente,
con Don Juan allí hablando,
hoy las espaldas te estaré guardando.

Vase Leonor

DON ALONSO [*ap.*]   ¿Quién creerá que he tenido
mudo el amor, aun siendo amor fingido?   1760

INÉS   Moscatel, ¿qué es aquesto?

MOSCATEL   La droga introducir que se ha dispuesto.

INÉS   ¿Para qué entras tú acá?

MOSCATEL   ¿Para qué? Amo,
y no has de estar a tiro de mi amo
sin escucha.

BEATRIZ   Inés, ¿qué es esto?   1765

INÉS   Un hombre, señora, es
que hasta aquí se ha entrado.

BEATRIZ   ¡Un hombre en mi cubículo! [*A Inés*] ¿Qué haces?

INÉS   Tirarte de la manga.

BEATRIZ   ¡Necio intento!
Detén, que sólo digo en mi aposento.   1770

DON ALONSO   Hermosa Beatriz, la voz
no des al aire, no des
al cielo quejas, huïdas
de la prisión del clavel.
Oye piadosa mis ansias   1775
sin enojarte, porque
no siempre fue de lo hermoso
patrimonio lo crüel.

BEATRIZ   ¿Andáis por antonomasias?

INÉS   Dos veces tiro.

BEATRIZ   ¡Está bien!   1780

1760 **at a loss for words**: this is the first time Don Alonso, faced with a woman, has ever been at a loss for words. Since his attraction to Beatriz appears to be largely physical, perhaps we are to assume that it begins right here, when his first sight of her takes him by surprise.

1774 **ruby**: in the original, 'carnation', which is a red flower in Spain, but which rarely

censor to your speech.

Enter Leonor, Don Alonso and Moscatel

LEONOR (*to Don Alonso*) There's Beatriz. If you're ready to try turning her head in your role of mock suitor, you can safely address her now. To make sure you're not interrupted, I'll go and talk to Don Juan over there and keep a lookout.

Exit Leonor

DON ALONSO (*aside*)Who would have believed I'd be at a loss for words to speak my love, even though it's only pretended love?

INÉS Moscatel, what's going on?

MOSCATEL The drug is about to be administered.

INÉS But why have *you* come here?

MOSCATEL Why? Because I'm in love. My master won't get within range of you except with me standing guard.

BEATRIZ Inés, what is this?

INÉS This is a man, madam, that has just walked in.

BEATRIZ A man in my boudoir! (*To Inés*) What are you doing?

INÉS I'm plucking at your sleeve!

BEATRIZ How silly! Stop it! In my room, I mean.

DON ALONSO Lovely Beatriz! Cast not your voice upon the air, send not your sighs to heaven, fleeing their ruby prison.

Compassionately hear my plaints and be not angered, for cruelty was not always beauty's legacy.

BEATRIZ You like antonomasia, do you?

INÉS That's *two* plucks!

BEATRIZ Enough! Enough!

---

carries that association in English.

1779 **antonomasia**: a figure of speech in which a descriptive phrase is used for a proper name, or a proper name for the quality associated with it. Thus the first edition of Góngora's poems called him the 'Spanish Homer'. Calling Beatriz's lips a carnation is just a metaphor, and Don Alonso has not actually used antonomasia.

—Atrevido caballero
(que te has osado a romper
la clausura donde el sol,
que fénix y hoguera es,
si tal vez entra atrevido,   1785
sale cobarde tal vez;
y a no traer por disculpa
que me viene el día a traer,
no osara donde estoy yo
a entrar en átomos él),   1790
¿qué atrevimiento, qué audacia
rige tu alevoso pie?
¿Qué osadía, qué ardimiento
te ha conducido, bajel
derrotado, a investigar   1795
enjutos piélagos, que
surcó tarde, mal o nunca
racional piloto? Pues
en Sirtes de mi recato,
Escilas de mi desdén,   1800
en Caribdis de mi honor,
sólo has de hallar, has de ver
o para que a fondo vayas,
o para dar al través
cuatro o seis desnudos troncos   1805
de dos escollos o tres.

INÉS [ap.]   Aquí empiezan sus engaños.

MOSCATEL [ap.]   Él mismo vaya con él.

DON ALONSO   Peritísima Beatriz,
                  Beatriz, dulce enigma en quien   1810
                  vive de más el hablar
                  o de más el parecer,
                  pues a una deidad le sobra
                  que hermosa en extremo es

1784 **fire and phoenix**: as already pointed out (851–4), the phoenix destroyed itself by fire, in order to be reborn. The sun is a fire which is reborn every morning.

1797–8 Beatriz here echoes lines 63–4 of Góngora's *Polifemo*: 'su pecho inunda, o tarde, o mal, o en vano / surcada aun de los dedos de la mano' ('floods his breast, furrowed late, badly or in vain by the fingers of his hand'): a reference to the flowing beard of Polyphemus.

1799–1806 The exact meaning of this passage is obscured by textual problems in the original. Scylla was a maiden who loved Glaucus, a fisherman; the envious Circe changed her into a monster. In despair, Scylla cast herself into the sea and became a rock. In some versions (e.g. Homer, *Odyssey*) the monstrous Scylla inhabits a

Bold sir, you have dared to breach the cloister where the sun (which is both fire and phoenix), if perchance it boldly enters, meekly takes its leave again.

If the very atoms of the sun dare not enter where I am, except on the pretext of bringing me the day, what brashness or audacity governs *your* perfidious step?

What boldness, what passion has borne your bark off course to explore these waterless deeps where rational pilot badly or tardily or never ploughed the waves?

On the shoals of my modesty, on the Scylla of my scorn, on the Charybdis of my honour, you will founder or run yourself aground on four or six bare trunks of two or three reefs.

INÉS (*aside*)	Now his hoaxing will begin!
MOSCATEL (*aside*)	Let's hope the Devil looks after his own!
DON ALONSO	Most learned Beatriz! Sweet enigma in whom either eloquence or beauty could be deemed redundant; for a goddess of such surpassing beauty has no need of such

---

cave in the rock, and with each of her six heads snatches a sailor from every passing ship. To avoid Scylla, ships had to go close to Charybdis, a whirlpool which sucked down and then spewed up the sea three times every day. (Charybdis had been changed into the whirlpool by Jupiter for stealing Hercules's oxen.) Beatriz tells Don Alonso he will founder on the Charybdis of her honour, or be dashed against the Scylla of her disdain; this sense persuaded us to adopt *sirtes* ('shoals, sandbanks') instead of *fletes* ('cargoes') in 1799. The two words would be very alike in seventeenth-century handwriting. Juan Pérez de Moya (*Filosofía secreta*) deals with Scylla, Charybdis and the Syrtes together (pp. 98–102 of the 1611 edition); the Syrtes were feared by the sailors taking St Paul to Rome (Acts XXVII, 17: 'the shallows of Syrtis' in the New English Bible, 'quicksands' in the Authorised Version). In lines 1805–6 Beatriz quotes a version of the opening lines of Góngora's ballad, 'Cuatro o seis desnudos hombros' (Millé 70).

	ser en extremo entendida:	1815
	no admires de salto que	
	golfo navegue, ignorando	
	(naufragio mi aliento, pues)	
	tu discreción, tu belleza;	
	entre el mirar y el saber	1820
	hurtar pude sitio al mar,	
	y mucho agradable en él.	
Inés [ap.]	También ha menester éste	
	que le tire Moscatel.	
Don Alonso	Yo soy aquel que dos años	1825
	viviente girasol fue	
	de la luz de tu beldad:	
	fragante al llegarte a ver	
	cuanto mustio al ausentarse,	
	que entre el morir y el nacer	1830
	no hubo más distancia que entre	
	si se ve o si no se ve.	
Inés [ap.]	Atención, señoras mías:	
	entre mentir o querer,	
	¿cuál será lo verdadero,	1835
	si esto lo fingido es?	
Don Alonso	La causa hoy de este alboroto	
	es haber hallado ayer	
	tu padre el crïado mío	
	que te traía un papel;	1840
	y viendo la obligación	
	que tengo a quien soy, osé,	
	temeroso de tu riesgo,	
	ahora que ocasión hallé,	
	entrar hasta aquí.	
Beatriz	Detente,	1845
	que ya me incumbe saber,	
	aunque mi riesgo derogue	

1816–22 The presence of *golfe* in the original strongly suggests that this passage is
corrupt, for there is no such word (although Don Alonso might possibly be capa-
ble of inventing words, as Beatriz does, when trying to impress). We have made
three modest changes, all compatible with the other identifiable errors in D. Don
Alonso claims to have admired Beatriz from afar for two whole years (line 1825);
but now that he has crossed the high seas, as it were, and seen her beauty and wit
close to, he has become aware of his previous ignorance of them, and as a result has
been metaphorically shipwrecked. Previously he had been content between seeing
and knowing (i.e. having seen her but not known what she was like). Apparently

	surpassing knowledge! Be not alarmed that, of your loveliness and discernment unaware, I should have sailed, all hopes dashed, into these deep waters.
	Here have I found balmy sea-room that delights the eye and the mind alike.
INÉS (*aside*)	This fellow should have his sleeve plucked by Moscatel.
DON ALONSO	I am he who for two long years has turned like a human sunflower towards the light of your beauty, fragrant when it beheld you and wilting when you were gone, for whom the difference between life and death was the difference between beholding you and not beholding you.
INÉS (*aside*)	Observe, ladies. If this is make-believe, how can we tell lying from loving?
DON ALONSO	The reason for today's commotion is that yesterday your father caught my servant bringing you a letter.
	In view of the obligations which correspond to my position, I dared, being fearful of the risk to you, to seize the first available opportunity to come here.
BEATRIZ	Stay! Although the risk to me invalidates the most inviolable of laws, it behoves me

recognising Beatriz's literary allusion, Don Alonso completes his speech with a paraphrase of the next two lines of the Góngora ballad quoted by her (see lines 1805–6, and note).

1826 The sunflower supposedly keeps its face towards the sun, moving to follow its revolution throughout the day; a very common metaphor for the lover, forever turned towards the beloved.

1837–45 Don Alonso cleverly leads Beatriz to believe that Don Juan's letter really was meant for her, and that Don Alonso wrote it. The 'risk' refers to what her father may do to her when he discovers that she has an unauthorised suitor (see note 359–60).

la más inviolable ley,
qué papel o qué crïado
aquése que dices fue.   1850

DON ALONSO   El crïado, este crïado;
el papel, aquel papel
que abrió Leonor, siendo tuyo,
porque a ella se le dio Inés.

INÉS   Yo no se le di, que ella   1855
me le quitó sin querer.

BEATRIZ   ¿Tuyo era el crïado?
DON ALONSO   Sí.
BEATRIZ   ¿Y tuyo el papel?
DON ALONSO   También.
BEATRIZ   ¿Y para mí?
DON ALONSO   Pues ¿qué dudas?
BEATRIZ   Antes no dudo, pues sé   1860
que mi muerte y mi homicida
fuiste de mi paz, crüel
tirano, que introdujiste
escrúpulos en mi fe.
Vuelve, vuelve las espaldas   1865
de piadoso, o de cortés,
que solicitas mi muerte
si aquí mi hermana te ve,
porque hará verdades hoy
los fingimientos de ayer.   1870

INÉS [ap.]   ¡Qué fácilmente creyó
lo que él contó y yo afirmé!

MOSCATEL [ap.] En fin, no hay cosa más fácil
que engañar una mujer.

BEATRIZ   Y no quieras más victoria   1875
de mi vanidad, que ver
que por ti lloran mis ojos,
que puede, en efecto, hacer
costar lágrimas un hombre
sin quererle una mujer,   1880
que no las lágrimas siempre
señas son de querer bien.
Vete.

DON ALONSO [ap.]   Más lo deseo yo,

to ascertain what letter and what servant you refer to.

DON ALONSO   The servant was this servant here. The letter was that letter which, being yours, was opened by Leonor, because it was to her that Inés gave it.

INÉS   I didn't give it to her. She took it from me.

BEATRIZ   That servant was yours?

DON ALONSO   Yes.

BEATRIZ   And the letter yours?

DON ALONSO   Also.

BEATRIZ   And for me?

DON ALONSO   Do you doubt it?

BEATRIZ   I do not doubt it. I know, and know full well, that it was you who slew my peace of mind, oh! cruel tyrant!, when you cast doubt upon my honesty.

Depart, depart, in compassion or in courtesy, for you will provoke my death if my sister sees you here, and she will turn yesterday's lies into today's truths.

INÉS (*aside*)   How easily she believes what he says when I confirm it!

MOSCATEL (*aside*)   In short, there's nothing as easy as fooling a woman.

BEATRIZ   Seek no further triumph over my vanity than to behold my eyes shed tears because of you; for a man can make a woman weep though she does not love him, and tears are not always a sign of love.
Now leave.

DON ALONSO (*aside*)There's nothing I'd like better!   I'm at my

que estoy ya para perder
el juicio, pensando modos   1885
para responderte.

BEATRIZ   No des
más escándalo en mi casa,
que basta el primero ser
que concupiscible oí.

Tírale de la manga Inés

No tires más, déjame,   1890
que tienes traza, por Dios,
de dejarme muda.

DON ALONSO   En fe,
dïámetro al menos serte
no rehusa aquesta vez
mi opuesto planeta: quiero   1895
obedeceros cortés,
pero en sabiendo mi amor.

BEATRIZ   Pues adiós, que ya lo sé.

DON ALONSO [a   No se ha empezado muy mal.
Moscatel]

MOSCATEL [a Don   Ni se ha acabado muy bien: 1900
Alonso]   que viene gente.

INÉS   ¡Ay, señora,
ir no le dejes!

BEATRIZ   ¿Por qué?

INÉS   Porque al paso están hablando
Leonor, Don Juan, y también
tu padre.

MOSCATEL   El padre es el diablo   1905
de estos enemigos tres.

BEATRIZ   Mi climatérico día
es hoy, ¡ay de mí!, si os ven,
porque contra mí los cielos
han sabido disponer   1910

1892–7 Don Alonso's original remark was so impenetrable that the compositors or
scribes gave up: D's version is defective both in assonance and in number of syllables.
However, his meaning is clear: he will leave, politely and obediently, if Beatriz admits
to understanding his protestations of love. Other modern editions alter 1893 and
1895, as well as inventing a line; we invent 1894, but leave the other lines unmodified.

1905–6 **three enemies**: the three enemies of man are the world, the flesh and the
devil, the devil being the worst. That is to say, the arrival of Don Juan, Leonor and
Don Pedro will interrupt Don Alonso's feigned courtship of Beatriz, but it is only

wits' end trying to think of a reply.

BEATRIZ   Create no further turmoil in my house.
                  Suffice it that you have been the first man
                  to address me concupiscently.

                  Inés plucks at her sleeve
                  Stop plucking! Let me be! At this rate, by
                  God, you'll make a dummy of me!

DON ALONSO   My planet cannot now refuse to move to
                  that point where it shall furthest lie from
                  yours; I'll do your bidding like a gentleman,
                  but I must first acquaint you with my love.

BEATRIZ   Then goodbye. I am acquainted.
DON ALONSO (*to Moscatel*)   This isn't starting too badly.

MOSCATEL (*to Don Alonso*)   No, but it isn't finishing too well;
                  someone's coming!
INÉS   Oh, madam, don't let him go!

BEATRIZ   Why not?
INÉS   Because Leonor and Don Juan are outside
                  talking to your father!

MOSCATEL   Three enemies hath man, and the Devil
                  here is the father!
BEATRIZ   Alas! This will be my climacteric day if
                  they find you here, for the heavens have

Don Pedro's arrival that matters. In Calderón's *auto, A tu prójimo como a ti* (*Thy neighbour as thyself*), Man is set upon by the World, the Flesh and the Devil, in the guise of bandits, and left for dead; he is rescued by Christ, in the guise of the Samaritan.

1907 **climacteric day**: as a noun, 'climacteric' has an increasing tendency to mean 'menopause'; as an adjective, it simply meant 'crucial', 'critical' or 'fatal', used of any stage of human life. Climacteric years are seven and nine, or multiples of them by the odd numbers 3, 5, 7, 9. Saturn, with his malevolent influence (see note 1745), presided over these.

<table>
<tr><td></td><td>evidencias que acreditan
culpas que no imaginé.
Para el cuarto de mi padre
el paso esta cuadra es:
no podéis salir de aquí,
ni allá dentro entrar podéis;
y así, antes que aquí entren,
fuerza el esconderos es.</td><td>1915</td></tr>
</table>

Don Alonso	¿Es comedia de Don Pedro Calderón, donde ha de haber por fuerza amante escondido o rebozada mujer?	1920
Beatriz	Esto conviene a mi honor.	
Don Alonso	¿Yo me tengo de esconder?	
Moscatel	Inés, mala burla es ésta.	1925
Inés	Y muy mala, Moscatel.	
Beatriz	Esto he de deberos.	
Don Alonso [*ap.*]	Cielos, considerad que no es bien darme tan fino el pesar, siendo tan falso el placer.	1930
Beatriz	¿Qué esperáis?	
Don Alonso	¿Qué he de esperar? Saber adónde ha de ser donde tengo de esconderme.	
Inés	Donde estar mejor podréis es en aquella alacena de vidrios.	1935
Beatriz	Has dicho bien.	
Don Alonso	¡Lindo búcaro del Duque o de la Maya seré! ¿Yo en alacena de vidrios? ¡Voto a Dios!	
Beatriz	Preciso es.	1940

1919–22 This *could* be a reference to Calderón's play *El escondido y la tapada* (*The hidden lover and the veiled lady*), were it not that there is evidence that Calderón wrote it about a year later than this: there was a performance by Antonio de Prado on 3 April 1636 (Shergold and Varey, 'Some early Calderón dates', *BHS*, 38 [1961], 278). Quite a number of Calderón comedies have hidden lovers and veiled ladies—as do several by other contemporary dramatists.

1935 We are not certain whether, in seventeenth-century Spanish houses, these 'china

ranged against me evidence of crimes I have never even dreamed of.

My father must pass through here on the way to his room.

You cannot get out of here, and you cannot go in there. So, before they enter, you must hide.

DON ALONSO   Is this a play by Don Pedro Calderón, where there's bound to be a hidden lover or a veiled lady?

BEATRIZ   My honour demands it.

DON ALONSO   So I have to hide, do I?

MOSCATEL   This is a bad joke, Inés!

INÉS   A *very* bad joke, Moscatel!

BEATRIZ   You would oblige me by doing so.

DON ALONSO (*aside*) Heavens above! It's not fair I should receive such real punishment for such false pleasure!

BEATRIZ   What are you waiting for?

DON ALONSO   What do you think I'm waiting for? I'm waiting to be told where to hide.

INÉS   The best place for you is in that china-cupboard over there.

BEATRIZ   You are right.

DON ALONSO   A fine piece of china I'll make! Me, in a cupboard! My God!

BEATRIZ   It is imperative!

---

cupboards' were permanent fixtures or articles of furniture. Given the nature of public theatres at the time, we must assume that a readily transportable piece of furniture was used in the play.

1937–8 The Spanish original refers to what are apparently two types of earthenware. Arellano (p. 303) presents evidence that La Maya ware came from Lisbon. We do not know exactly what *el Duque* refers to. Strictly speaking, a *búcaro* was an earthenware vase, made of an aromatic clay, which gave off a pleasant smell when filled with water.

INÉS	Entrad.
DON ALONSO	Sin un calzador no es posible.
INÉS	Entra también.
MOSCATEL	¿Es alacena de dos, como mula de alquiler?

Éntranse en una alacena, quiébranse vidrios y salen
Don Pedro, Leonor y Don Juan

INÉS	Mirad que quebráis los vidrios.	1945
DON PEDRO	Hola, unas luces traed a esta sala.	
DON JUAN [ap.]	¡Vive Dios, que no sé lo que he de hacer si halla a Don Alonso aquí Don Pedro! Que yo bien sé que no tiene el cuarto puerta por donde salir, y en fe de haberle empeñado yo, y ser mi amigo también, no sé, como llegue a verle, qué remedio puede haber.	1950 ... 1955
LEONOR [ap.]	¡Oh, nunca hubiera inventado la venganza que busqué, pues empezando de burlas, tan de veras viene a ser!	1960
DON PEDRO	Aquestas noches, Don Juan, ¿a qué hora os recogéis?	
DON JUAN	Temprano. ([Ap.] Aquesto es decirme que me vaya, y fuerza es. En grande peligro dejo a Don Alonso, por ser mi amigo; el estarme aquí no es posible; lo que haré será estar siempre a la mira de lo que ha de suceder.) Quedá adiós.	1965 ... 1970
DON PEDRO	Adiós. —Alumbra al señor Don Juan, Inés.
DON JUAN [a Don Pedro]	No habéis de salir de aquí.

1944 **a hired mule**: mules (and horses, etc.) were readily available for hire to travellers

INÉS	Get in!
DON ALONSO	It's not possible without a shoehorn!
INÉS	You, too!
MOSCATEL	Is this cupboard a two-seater, like a hired mule?

They get into the cupboard, breaking some china. Enter Don Pedro, Leonor and Don Juan.

INÉS	Careful! You're smashing the china!
DON PEDRO	Hello! Bring some lights for this room.
DON JUAN (*aside*)	My God, I don't know what I'll do if Don Pedro finds Don Alonso here! I'm only too well aware that there's no other way out of this room. It was I who got him into this fix, and he is my friend, but I don't know what I'll do if Don Pedro catches sight of him.
LEONOR (*aside*)	Oh, how I wish I'd never dreamed up that idea of getting revenge. What began as a joke is turning out to be deadly serious!
DON PEDRO	At what time do you retire these nights, Don Juan?
DON JUAN	Early. (*Aside.* This is his way of asking me to go, so I really have no choice. I'm leaving Don Alonso in great danger, and all because he was trying to help me. But it's impossible for me to stay here. All I can do is remain constantly on the alert to see what happens.) Goodbye.
DON PEDRO	Goodbye. Light Don Juan to the door, Inés.
DON JUAN (*to Don Pedro*)	You needn't accompany me.

in Spain at this time. Stingy or impoverished travellers would burden one poor mule
with two people, rather than hire a second.

Va Inés alumbrando, y vase Don Juan

DON PEDRO   Yo sé bien lo que he de hacer.

[Vase con Don Juan]

LEONOR [ap.]   ¿Adónde Beatriz habrá,   1975
                 pues yo no lo puedo ver,
                 a Don Alonso escondido?

BEATRIZ [ap.]   ¡Que tantos sustos me dé
                 un hombre que no conozco!

Vuelve Don Pedro e Inés con la luz; a tiempo que
se quiebra un vidrio, déjase Inés caer la luz

DON PEDRO   Entra aquesa luz, Inés,   1980
                 en mi cuarto.

LEONOR [ap.]   Ahora sin duda
                 da en su aposento con él.

DON PEDRO   Entrad conmigo las dos,
                 que os tengo que hablar... mas ¿qué
                 es aquello?

Déjase caer el candelero Inés

INÉS   El candelero   1985
                 se me cayó.

DON PEDRO   ¡Que no estés
                 nunca, Inés, en lo que haces!

INÉS   Sí estoy, señor.

Vanse Don Pedro y Leonor

BEATRIZ   Oye, Inés;
                 pues mi padre se recoge
                 tan presto, haz al punto que   1990
                 salgan de ahí aquestos hombres
                 sin que lo llegue a entender
                 Leonor.

INÉS   No lo entenderá.
                 Mas dime cómo ha de ser,
                 que mi señor no bajó   1995
                 con Don Juan por ser cortés
                 tanto como por cerrar
                 las puertas.

1974 A double-entendre understood by the audience, but not by the other characters.
Don Juan has politely told Don Pedro that there is no need to see him out. Don
Pedro appears to insist on the courtesy, but he really means to see to the locking of

Exit Don Juan, lighted by Inés

DON PEDRO	I know exactly what I need to do!

Exit with Don Juan

LEONOR (*aside*)	Where can Beatriz have hidden Don Alonso? I can't see him anywhere.

BEATRIZ (*aside*)	To think I should receive such frights from a man I do not even know!

Don Pedro returns, accompanied by Inés with the light.
Just as some china breaks, Inés drops the light.

DON PEDRO	Put that light in my room, Inés.

LEONOR (*aside*)	Now I suppose he's going to walk right in on top of Don Alonso.

DON PEDRO	Come with me, you two. I wish to speak to you... But, what's that?

Inés drops the candlestick

INÉS	I dropped the candlestick.

DON PEDRO	You never keep your mind on what you're doing, Inés!
INÉS	Oh, but I *do*, sir!

Exit Don Pedro and Leonor

BEATRIZ	Listen, Inés. Since my father is retiring early, get those two men out of here at once, and be sure Leonor does not learn about this.

INÉS	She won't learn about it. But tell me, how are they to be got out? My master didn't go down with Don Juan out of politeness, but because he wanted to lock the doors.

---

the front door, in order to prevent any further intrusions like Moscatel's. Inés soon realises that this was his real reason (1995–8).

1985 **candlestick**: this specific reference to a candlestick clarifies the earlier vague references to 'light' (1971–80).

BEATRIZ	Procura hacer
	que salgan como pudieren.

Vase Beatriz

INÉS	Ya por donde salgan sé.	2000
	—Mis aprensados señores,	
	bien desdoblaros podéis.	
DON ALONSO	¡Vive Dios, que si no fuera,	
	pícaro, por no sé qué,	
	que te matara!	
MOSCATEL	No pude	2005
	más, si los vidrios quebré,	
	que eran vidrios, en efecto.	
INÉS	Venid conmigo.	
DON ALONSO	¡Ay, Inés!	
	Si fuera por ti el secreto,	
	fuera empleado más bien.	2010
MOSCATEL	No fuera sino es más mal.	
DON ALONSO	¿Que ahora de temor estés?	
	No puedo conmigo más;	
	Vamos. [*A Inés*] Mas, por no perder	
	ocasión, toma un abrazo.	2015
MOSCATEL [*ap.*]	Cordero en brazos de Inés,	
	el hombre le vio mil veces,	
	pero sola aquesta vez	
	es el abrazado el hombre	
	y el cordero el que lo ve.	2020
INÉS	Salgamos presto de aquí.	
DON ALONSO	¿Quién dice que no?	
INÉS	Que aunque	
	mi señor cerró las puertas,	
	bien salir los dos podréis;	
	arrojaos sin que os sientan	2025
	por este balcón. Ea, pues.	
DON ALONSO	¿Eso tenemos agora,	
	Inés? ¿Balconear, después	
	de una alacena?	
INÉS	Esto es fuerza.	

2016–20 **St Agnes**: Santa Inés (died ca. 304) is traditionally portrayed holding a
lamb, and 'every man' has seen her so portrayed. This time, however, Agnes/Inés is

BEATRIZ

Just see that they leave here in any way they can.

Exit Beatriz

INÉS

I know how they can leave.
  Closeted sirs, you may now safely unfold yourselves.

DON ALONSO

By God, you rogue, for two pins I'd kill you!

MOSCATEL

I couldn't help breaking the china. It was made of china, after all.

INÉS

Come with me.

DON ALONSO

Oh, Inés! If only this intrigue were for you, it would be much more worth while.

MOSCATEL

It would not, sir, but much less.

DON ALONSO

Now you choose to be scared! I can stand no more! Come along! (*To Inés*) But don't let me lose this opportunity; here's another kiss.

MOSCATEL (*aside*)

Many a man has seen a lamb cuddled in Saint Agnes's arms, but this time it's the man that's being cuddled and it's this poor lamb that's looking on.

INÉS

Let's get out of here at once.

DON ALONSO

Who's objecting?

INÉS

My master has locked the doors, but you can still get out. Jump from this balcony here, and don't make any noise. Come on!

DON ALONSO

So this is what we're reduced to, Inés! Out of the cupboard and over the balcony!

INÉS

There's no alternative.

---

holding the man, while the lamb (i.e. Moscatel, afraid to object) sees it happen. Zurbarán (1598–1664) has three different versions of St Agnes holding her lamb.

MOSCATEL   Y digas, la tal Inés,   2030
                   ¿es muy alto?

INÉS   Del segundo
                   cuarto no más; no aguardéis.

DON ALONSO   ¿Mas que me quiebro una pierna?
                   Hombres que enamoráis, ved:
                   si estos lances en quien ama   2035
                   se dejan aborrecer,
                   en quien no ama, ¿qué será?
                   ¡Mal haya quien quiere bien!

                   [*Vanse*]

MOSCATEL	And tell me, my *dear* Inés: is there much of a drop?
INÉS	Only from the second floor. Hurry up!
DON ALONSO	But, what if I break a leg? You men who go courting, take note. If scrapes like this are hard on someone who's in love, just imagine what they're like for someone who isn't! The Devil take all true lovers!

Exeunt

JORNADA TERCERA
Salen Inés y Beatriz

Inés	Porque del balcón habiendo
	los dos Luzbeles caído... 2040
Beatriz	¡Ay Dios! ¿Cómo, Inés, ha sido?
Inés	...llegaron con mucho estruendo
	unos hombres, pretendiendo
	conocerlos, y después
	repararon (tanta es 2045
	de amo y mozo la destreza)
	el uno con la cabeza
	lo que el otro con los pies.
Beatriz	¿Qué dices?
Inés	Lo que ha pasado.
Beatriz	¿Quién, Inés, te lo contó? 2050
Inés	Cuanto he referido yo
	relación es de un crïado
	del galán de pie quebrado,
	como copla, que por ti
	saltó del balcón.
Beatriz	Y di: 2055
	¿quién le vulneró?... le ha herido,
	digo.
Inés	Eso no se ha sabido.
Beatriz	¿Doliente en fin yace?
Inés	Sí;
	pierna y cabeza llevó
	quebradas, aunque ya está 2060
	mucho mejor.
Beatriz	¿Quedará
	claudicante?

2040 **Lucifers**: Lucifer was the name given to Satan in his role as leader of the rebellion against God. When the rebellion failed, Lucifer and his adherents were thrown out of heaven and fell into hell: in Milton's *Paradise Lost* the fall lasted nine days (VI, 871); it was the basis of numerous metaphors involving a fall, as here. The name means 'light-bearer', and is applied to the morning star (the planet Venus); its transference to Satan is the result of a mistaken interpretation of Isaiah XIV, 12, where the expression 'morning star' is really a metaphor for the king of Babylon.

2045–9 The fact that we have had to intervene editorially here makes the interpretation of this passage doubtful, but we can be sure that Inés's use of the word 'cleverly' is ironic. Don Alonso has hurt both leg and head (2058–61), the former

ACT III

Enter Inés and Beatriz

INÉS	When those two Lucifers fell from the balcony...
BEATRIZ	Oh, my goodness! What happened, Inés?
INÉS	...some men burst on to the scene and tried to discover who they were, but master and servant cleverly managed to get away, one by using his head, the other by using his feet.
BEATRIZ	What are you saying?
INÉS	I'm saying what happened!
BEATRIZ	Who told you this, Inés?
INÉS	What I'm telling you was told to me by a servant of the limping lover who had to leap from the balcony because of you.
BEATRIZ	And tell me: who inflicted those lesions? I mean: who wounded him?
INÉS	Nobody knows.
BEATRIZ	Lies he, then, injured?
INÉS	He does. He cracked his leg and his head, but he is already much improved.
BEATRIZ	Will he be left halt?

---

presumably in the jump from the balcony. He managed to evade his attackers (Don Luis and Don Diego, as will later become clear) at the cost of an injury to the head ('by using his head'); Moscatel ran away ('by using his feet').

2051–5 Once again a textual crux renders the meaning doubtful. The Spanish *pie quebrado* ('broken foot') alludes to a type of verse, *coplas de pie quebrado*, with stanzas of twelve lines (8, 8, 4, 8, 8, 4, 8, 8, 4, 8, 8, 4 syllables). Though Inés is illiterate (593–6), we need not be surprised that the limping lover makes her think of limping verse: Jorge Manrique's *Coplas* (1476), the best known-poem in this metre, still survived in oral tradition.

2062–3 **halt**: the Spanish *claudicante* is a Latinism; although now unexceptional, it was 'learned' at this time. Góngora uses it in a wickedly funny sonnet directed at

INÉS   ¿Qué sé yo
que es claudicante? ¡Que no
has de perder vicio tal!

BEATRIZ   ¿Hay demencia? ¿Hay tosca igual?   2065
Di, ¿el claudicante no es
hombre de alternados pies
que se ambula desigual?

INÉS   No sé lo que es ni que no;
sólo sé, de temor llena,   2070
que ha estado herido.

BEATRIZ [ap.]   Su pena,
¡ay de mí!, padezco yo.
¿Qué pócima que bebió
(¡Qué delirio! ¡Qué ardimiento!
¡Qué ultraje! ¡Qué tormento!)   2075
el alma por el oído,
que la concibe un sentido,
y la aborta un sentimiento?
¿Qué es lo que pasa por mí?
Pero si yo de mí sé,   2080
yo misma me lo diré:
conjurado contra mí
al dios de los necios vi,
por ver cuánto baldonaba
su deidad; y cuando estaba   2085
más fiera en la ofensa mía,
ya los efectos sentía
de las causas que ignoraba.
Un hombre en mi cuarto entró
de mis ansias informado,   2090
resuelto y determinado;
acción fue que me obligó
al compás que me ofendió,
pues si ofensa el amor piensa,
la acción ser en mi defensa   2095
la construye obligación:
luego compatibles son
la obligación y la ofensa.

Quevedo, whom he likens to the patron-saint of plague victims, St Roch, who had a
limp (as did Quevedo): Millé LXXV, line 10.

2071–2118 *aside*: D contains no indication that Inés goes off stage here; however,
she is clearly not meant to hear the speech, since it would prompt her to draw the
conclusions which she draws rather later, in line 2148. Presumably she busies herself

INÉS	How am I supposed to know what 'halt' means? Are you never going to give up that dreadful habit?
BEATRIZ	What imbecility! How can anyone be so ignorant? Tell me: do we not say that an alternate-footing man who ambulates unevenly is 'halt'?
INÉS	I don't know whether we do or not. All I know, I'm sorry to say, is that Don Alonso is hurt.
BEATRIZ (*aside*)	Oh, how I feel his every pain! What potion did my soul imbibe through the medium of my ears, begetting a passion which through sorrow will miscarry? What madness! What boldness! What effrontery! Oh! What torment!

What is this that is happening because of me? Did I myself but know, I could myself explain it!

The god of fools conspired against me, because he saw how I slighted his divinity; and, when I was harshest in my scorn, I was already experiencing the effects of causes still concealed from me.

A man entered my room, resolute and determined, believing me to be in some peril.

This action simultaneously indebted and offended me; for, though his talk of love insulted me, he earned my gratitude by coming to protect me.

Thus, being indebted and being offended are compatible.

---

sweeping or dusting while Beatriz speaks to the audience, and realises only from her mistress's tears at the end of the speech that something is amiss.

2073–8 A difficult passage from which we have extracted some sense by changing part of one line and the faulty original punctuation.

2083 **the god of fools**: she must mean Cupid, god of love.

Vino mi padre, y aquí
trágica mi historia fuera,   2100
si cortés no obedeciera
los preceptos que le di.
Por mí escondido, y por mí
precipitado y caído,
quedó de otra mano herido: 2105
pues si iguales llego a ver
que sentir y agradecer,
¿cuál será lo preferido?
Es decir que su mal siento
ilícito a mi valor,   2110
y lícito no a mi amor
faltarme agradecimiento;
sentir por mi parte intento
que a mí se pueda atrever;
por la suya, que a tener   2115
llegue por mí tal pesar;
y temo acabar de amar
donde empiezo a agradecer.

INÉS   ¿Qué pena es ésta, señora?
            ¿Qué tienes, que triste estás?   2120

BEATRIZ   ¿Qué quieres que tenga más?

INÉS   No le gastes a la aurora
            las blancas perlas agora
            que has de echar menos después.

BEATRIZ   ¡Ay, Inés mía! ¡Ay, Inés!   2125
            Si tú guardarme quisieras
            un secreto, tú supieras
            mi tormento.

INÉS   Dile pues;
            que aunque siempre en mi lugar
            San Secreto esclarecido   2130
            día de trabajo ha sido,
            le quiero canonizar
            y hacer fiesta de guardar.

2119 The line requires an ending in -*ora* for the rhyme with 2122 and 2123. D's odd
reading, *ya*, can be explained by the common practice of writing *señora* as *S^a* with
a long looped 'ʃ' which is very like the letter 'y'.
2122–3 **the dawn's white pearls**: perhaps catching some of Beatriz's disease just as
that young lady is recovering from it, Inés refers poetically to Beatriz's tears (and
hints darkly that she may have more reason to weep in due course).
2129 **my home town**: Madrid was expanding rapidly in the early seventeenth century.

My father arrived, and tragic would have
been my tale indeed had not Don Alonso
gallantly obeyed my precepts.

On my account obliged to hide, and then
on my account precipitated, he fell, and was
wounded by an unknown hand. If, then, I
have equal grounds for gratitude and grief,
how am I to choose between them?

To say I feel his pain would be improper,
but not to show due gratitude would be
improper, too.

For my part, I try to be displeased with
him for being so bold. For his part, I regret
he has suffered so because of me.

And I am afraid that, if I start with
gratitude, I may end with love.

INÉS	Why are you so sad, madam? What has upset you so?
BEATRIZ	How else should I be?
INÉS	Waste not the dawn's white pearls, for you may need them by and by.
BEATRIZ	Oh, Inés! My dear Inés! If you would agree to keep a secret for me, you would learn what is tormenting me.
INÉS	Then tell me. Though the Feast of Saint Secret was always a working day in my home town, I'm willing to canonise him and make it a holiday of obligation.

Many servants in particular were first generation citizens of the capital, having left
the land in search of a better living. Inés refers again, if more vaguely, to this in
lines 2500–1.

2133 **a holiday** (or 'holy day') **of obligation** is a day on which the Catholic Church
expects the faithful to attend mass. To facilitate this, the day would usually be a
holiday in the normal modern sense. Although Inés admits that she was never one
to keep the Feast of St Secret (i.e. a secret), she claims she will do so now.

BEATRIZ   Pues si eso ha de ser así,
                  yo he de fïarme de ti.   2135
                  A este galán caballero
                  agradecer, Inés, quiero
                  lo que ha pasado por mí.
                  Pero no quisiera que él
                  sepa que lo siento yo,   2140
                  porque ser piadosa, no
                  es dejar de ser crüel.
                  A mi obligación fïel,
                  y fiel a mi honor, que intente
                  saber de él mi fe consiente,   2145
                  no por él, sino por mí.

INÉS   Claro está que será así.
                  ([Ap.] ¡Ay, señores, que ya siente!)

BEATRIZ   Quisiera que te llegaras,
                  como que de ti salía,   2150
                  a visitarle, Inés mía,
                  y de su mal te informaras.

INÉS   ¿Y qué más?

BEATRIZ   Que le llevaras
                  una banda, y le dijeras
                  que tú la ladrona eras   2155
                  del favor.

INÉS   Está muy bien;
                  y haré este papel tan bien
                  como tú misma lo hicieras.
                  Dame la banda, y verás
                  cuál mi chinelita anda.   2160

BEATRIZ   Yo voy, Inés, por la banda;
                  pero mira que jamás
                  nada a Leonor le dirás.

INÉS   Nada le diré a Leonor.
                  Vase Beatriz y sale Leonor
                  ¡Victoria por el amor!   2165

LEONOR   ¿De qué es el contento, Inés?

INÉS   Yo te lo diré después,

2143-4 Calderón takes certain liberties to produce the correct number of syllables
here: *fiel* is worth two syllables in line 2143, one in 2144.
2156-7 It is rare but not unknown for Calderón to rhyme a word with itself, a habit
frowned upon by poetic theorists. D's reading *también* ('also') would solve the

BEATRIZ	Then I shall trust you. I wish, Inés, to express my gratitude to that gentleman for what he has endured because of me.
	But I do not wish him to know what I feel; after all, one can be compassionate while remaining aloof.
	I believe I can fulfil my obligations without damage to my honour, by attempting (for my own sake, not for his) to ascertain his condition.
INÉS	But of course! (*Aside.* Ladies and gentlemen, she is beginning to feel something!)
BEATRIZ	I want you to call on him, my dear Inés, as if it were your own idea, and inquire about his injuries.
INÉS	Anything else?
BEATRIZ	Yes, I want you to take him a ribbon, and say you stole it for him as a token.
INÉS	Very good. I'll perform this task as well as you would yourself. Give me the ribbon, and you'll see how fleet-footed I can be.
BEATRIZ	I shall go and fetch it at once, Inés. Be sure you do not say anything to Leonor!
INÉS	I won't tell Leonor a thing!

Exit Beatriz and enter Leonor

	Love has conquered!
LEONOR	What are you so happy about?
INÉS	I'll tell you later. But no, I'll tell you now,

---

problem of rhyme, but since Inés has performed no previous tasks for Beatriz, this word is out of place.

2167 **I'll tell you later**: the Spanish here is part of a saying, 'un poco te quiero, Inés; yo te lo diré después' ('I'm a bit fond of you, Inés; I'll tell you about it later') recorded

	aunque primero es mejor,	
	que reviento, te prometo,	
	porque en Dios y mi conciencia	2170
	que hizo vuestra diligencia	
	en Beatriz un grande efeto.	

Leonor   ¿Qué fue?

Inés   Encargóme un secreto,
y fue haberme encomendado
que le cuente de contado;   2175
claro es, pues cuando no fuera
por decirlo, lo dijera
por habérmelo encargado.
De Beatriz la fantasía
ya Don Alonso rindió;   2180
en tal lenguaje le habló
que, a pesar de su porfía,
conmigo una banda envía:
en fin, en fin, ha de ser
mujer cualquiera mujer.   2185
Por la banda quiero ir,
y, pues te lo he de decir
yo, tú no lo has de saber.   *Vase*

Leonor   Digo que no lo sabré.

Sale Don Juan

Don Juan   Pues ya yo lo tengo oído;   2190
ahora veo que en amor
número hay, pues en rigor,
por no dejarte infeliz,
crece un afecto en Beatriz
cuando ha faltado en Leonor.   2195

Leonor   Pues, ¿en mí ha faltado?

Don Juan   Sí,
en ti, Leonor, ha faltado;
que aunque he sufrido y callado
mis desdichas hasta aquí,
fue porque pensé hoy de ti   2200

---

by Correas (p. 177). It is also quoted in Lope's *El caballero de Olmedo* (*The knight from Olmedo*), lines 998 and 1010, where the heroine's name is Inés. Calderón himself quotes the first half in *No siempre lo peor es cierto* (*The worst isn't always true*), Aguilar II, 1460b.

2171–2 Although the last two lines of Inés's speech do not make sense in the D version, her meaning is clear: that the scheme devised by Leonor and Don Juan worked very

because I swear I'm just bursting to tell it.
As God is my judge, your little trick has
had an amazing effect on Beatriz.

LEONOR   What has she done?

INÉS   She has let me into a secret. Of course,
telling me was telling the world. Even if
it wasn't worth relating, I'd broadcast it
if only because I was asked not to. Don
Alonso has taken Beatriz's fancy.

He spoke such words to her that, in spite
of her obstinacy, she is sending me to him
with a ribbon. In short, every woman is a
woman in the end.

I'm off now to get the ribbon. I'll tell you
the whole story later; but remember, you're
supposed to know nothing about it!   *Exit*

LEONOR   I won't know a thing!
                Enter Don Juan

DON JUAN   I overheard everything. Now I realise there
is a quota for love. With Beatriz love waxes,
with Leonor it wanes.

LEONOR   Has mine waned, then?

DON JUAN   Yes, Leonor, it has. Until now I've borne
my grief in silence, because I hoped to learn

---

effectively on Beatriz. We have edited the lines accordingly. If Calderón did write
vuestra (meaning 'yours and Don Juan's' in this case) in line 2171, his habit of
spelling it *vr̃a* could have given rise to the reading *vna* (i.e. *una*), and this in turn
might have led copyists to tinker with 2172 in attempts to restore some sense.

2193 In isolation, line 2193 means 'so as not to leave you unhappy'; in the context, it
makes no sense. This is not surprising, as it occurs in a *décima* that lacks three of
its original ten lines (2189–95). We cannot tell exactly where the gaps are, let alone
reconstruct the missing lines, so we have 'solved' the problem by not translating the
line.

que averiguarlas pudiera
sin que a ti te lo dijera;
mas siendo fuerza sentirlas,
no muera yo sin decirlas,
ya que sin vengarlas muera.   2205
Don Alonso por tu gusto
a hablar a Beatriz entró:
ni arguyo ni pruebo yo
si fue justo o no fue justo.
Por excusar su disgusto,   2210
a costa de su opinión
se arrojó por un balcón;
y ya que en la calle estaba
a esperar en qué paraba
su empeño, fue en ocasión   2215
el bajar, que habían entrado
dos hombres en ella, y yo
me desvié, porque no
les diese el verme cuidado.
Estando, pues, apartado,   2220
las cuchilladas oí,
y a ellas al punto acudí;
y por presto que llegué,
ya los dos hombres no hallé
y herido a mi amigo vi.   2225
Mira si de mis recelos
puede haber causa mayor,
pues en su fingido amor
vi mis verdaderos celos.
Quien acuchilla (¡ay de mí,   2230
Leonor!) en tu calle así
a quien sale de tu casa,
bien dice que en ella pasa
mi agravio. Por ti y por mí
disimular he querido,   2235
como he dicho, hasta llegar
(¡ay, Leonor!) a averiguar
quién ese galán ha sido;
y viendo que no he podido
y que son intentos vanos,   2240
porque mis celos villanos
no murmuren en mi mengua,
quiero que diga la lengua

the truth from you today without the need
to ask.

But, though I am obliged to accept my
wretchedness, at least let me not die without expressing it, even if I do have to die
without avenging it.

To please you, Don Alonso came and
spoke to Beatriz. (Whether this was right
or wrong, I do not say.) To save her an
unpleasantness, he accepted the indignity
of leaping from the balcony.

I was waiting down there in the street to
see how his escapade would end, and I saw
two men arrive just as Don Alonso dropped
to the ground. I slipped into hiding, lest
the sight of me might alarm them.

From where I stood, at a little distance, I
heard the clash of swords. I rushed to the
scene at once, but, by the time I got there,
the men had disappeared and my friend lay
wounded.

Could I have greater reason to feel dis-
mayed, now that, as a result of Don Alonso's
false love, I have discovered grounds for real
jealousy?

When a man has a sword drawn on him
in your street, Leonor, just because he is
coming out of your house, it is pretty obvious that something injurious to *me* is going
on inside. For your sake and for my own,
I decided to turn a blind eye until I could
learn the identity of the assailant, but all
my attempts have been in vain.

Therefore, to save me from the shame of
what my worst suspicions fear, my tongue

lo que no han hecho las manos.
¡Quédate, ingrata, que no,   2245
pues que ya me he declarado,
me has de ver desengañado
en tu vida!

LEONOR   Pero yo,
¿no tengo una hermana?

DON JUAN   No;
que si tú hermana tuvieras   2250
de quien amores supieras,
no culparla procuraras
ni de burlas ni de veras;
y supuesto que has querido
fingirla un galán, infiero   2255
que a tenerle verdadero
no se le dieras fingido.

LEONOR   ¡Plegue al cielo...!

DON JUAN   No te pido
satisfacciones, Leonor.

LEONOR   Ni éstas lo son, que es error   2260
cuando nunca te he ofendido.

DON JUAN   Pues que tú la causa has sido,
deja que muera mi amor.

                Vanse. Salen Don Alonso y Moscatel.

MOSCATEL   Señor, ¿qué tienes? ¿Qué es eso?
¿En qué piensas? ¿En qué tratas?   2265
¿En qué discurres? ¿En qué
imaginas? ¿En qué andas?
¿Tú melancólico? ¿Tú
divertido? ¿Qué mudanza
es aquésta? ¿Tan valida   2270
ha sido una cuchillada?
¿Tanto poder ha tenido
tu herida, tanta privanza
un balcón, que han acabado
contigo no hablar de chanza?   2275

DON ALONSO   ¡Ay de mí!, que no sé, no,
qué es lo que siento en el alma,
que es bien y parece mal,
que es gusto y parece ansia,
que es gloria y parece pena;   2280

shall remedy what my hands could not. Farewell, inconstant creature! I have stated my position; you shall never change my mind.

LEONOR

But, have I not got a sister?

DON JUAN

No, you have not! If you had, and if you knew she had a lover, you would not have tried to incriminate her, either in jest or in earnest.

Since you've chosen to invent a suitor for her, I assume she doesn't have a real one.

LEONOR

I swear to Heaven...

DON JUAN

I'm not asking for apologies, Leonor.

LEONOR

And I'm not offering any! There's no call for apologies where there has been no offence.

DON JUAN

It is you who are to blame, so let my love expire.

Exeunt. Enter Don Alonso and Moscatel.

MOSCATEL

What's the matter, sir? What's this? What are you thinking of? What are you trying to do? What have you got in mind? What are you dreaming of? What are you *at*? You, melancholy? You, distracted? What transformation is this?

Are you so upset by a little skirmish, so affected by your wound, so altered by dropping from a balcony, that you have entirely lost your sense of humour?

DON ALONSO

Alas! I don't know what it is I feel within my soul. It is good, but it seems bad. It is pleasure, but it seems like pain.
It is glory, and it seems like misery. It is

2263+ *Exeunt...* : the scene changes back to Don Alonso's house.

dicha, y parece desgracia,
contento, y parece agravio;
lisonja, y parece rabia;
porque es un loco accidente
que a un tiempo da vida y mata,   2285
como veneno compuesto
de calidades contrarias.

MOSCATEL   ¡Hemos hecho buena hacienda!

DON ALONSO   ¿De qué te ríes?

MOSCATEL   No es nada.

DON ALONSO   ¡Ay de mí!

MOSCATEL   ¡Otra vez!

DON ALONSO   ¿De qué es,   2290
Moscatel, la carcajada?

MOSCATEL   Del suspiro, 'ay de mí'.

DON ALONSO   ¿Por qué?

MOSCATEL   Porque, señor mío, engañan
los señores: 'ay de mí' es,
amor te cogió en su trampa.   2295

DON ALONSO   Sin duda que estás borracho.
¿Yo amor?

MOSCATEL   Tú amor.

DON ALONSO   Pues ¿qué hallas
en mí, para imaginar
cosa de mí tan contraria?

MOSCATEL   Unas cosas que se dicen,   2300
y otras cosas que se callan.

DON ALONSO   ¿Yo enamorado? ¿De quién,
si yo no he visto a otra dama
sino a Beatriz?

MOSCATEL   De Beatriz.

DON ALONSO   ¿Yo, de un Ovidio con sayas?   2305
¿Yo, de un Virgilio con ropa,
y un Cicerón con enaguas?

MOSCATEL   ¡Tú, señor! ¿No me dijiste
que no era tan afectada
como Don Juan te había dicho?   2310

DON ALONSO   Es verdad.

2305–7 Three great Latin writers, two of poetry and one of prose. None is noted for

happiness like misfortune, contentment like
rage, flattery like insult.

What strange illness is it that kills and
at the same time cures, like a poison that
contains both venom and antidote?

MOSCATEL	This is a fine state of affairs!
DON ALONSO	What are you laughing at?
MOSCATEL	Nothing!
DON ALONSO	Oh, my!
MOSCATEL	Again!
DON ALONSO	What are you guffawing at, Moscatel?
MOSCATEL	At your sighing and 'oh-my-ing'.
DON ALONSO	Why so?
MOSCATEL	Because, my dear sir, you fine gentlemen deceive yourselves. 'Oh, my!' means Love has caught you in its trap.
DON ALONSO	You must be drunk! Me, love!
MOSCATEL	Yes. You, love!
DON ALONSO	But, what have you ever seen in me that could make you imagine something so outlandish?
MOSCATEL	Some things you've said, and some you haven't.
DON ALONSO	Me, in love? With whom, when the only woman I've seen is Beatriz?
MOSCATEL	With Beatriz.
DON ALONSO	Me? With that Ovid in a frock, that Virgil in skirts, that Cicero in petticoats!
MOSCATEL	You, sir! Didn't you tell me she was not as affected as Don Juan made out?
DON ALONSO	That's true.

---

obscurity, so Don Alonso must be thinking of Beatriz's Latinate vocabulary here.

MOSCATEL   ¿Tú no la alabas
                       de hermosa?

DON ALONSO   Sí.

MOSCATEL   Tú no sientes
                       que hombres en su calle haya
                       que acuchillen?

DON ALONSO   No lo niego,
                       pero tal tengo la causa.   2315

MOSCATEL   Luego son celos.

DON ALONSO   No son;
                       que no se me diera nada
                       que hubiera hombres, como dieran
                       celos y no cuchilladas;
                       fuera de que, si yo fui   2320
                       a verla, fue por burlarla,
                       de Don Juan apadrinado,
                       y fuera historia muy mala
                       haberme llevado a ser
                       el burlado yo.

MOSCATEL   En la plaza   2325
                       un toricantano un día
                       entró a dar una lanzada,
                       de un su amigo apadrinado;
                       y airoso terció la capa,
                       galán se quitó el sombrero,   2330
                       y osado tomó la lanza
                       veinte pasos del toril.
                       Salió un toro, y cara a cara
                       hacia el caballo se vino,
                       aunque pareció anca a anca,   2335
                       porque el caballo y el toro,
                       murmurando a las espaldas,
                       se echaron dos melecinas
                       con el cuerno y con el asta.
                       Cayó el caballero encima   2340
                       del toro, sacó la espada
                       el tal padrino, y por dar

2326 **novice bullfighter**: the English cannot fully convey Moscatel's witticism: he uses
toricantano by analogy with *misacantano*, a priest singing his first mass: 'novice'
retains a religious association. The word is still encountered, 'used jocosely in the
sense of a novice bullfighter', although only Martín Alonso, *Enciclopedia del idioma*
(Madrid, 1982), records it. In Moscatel's day, gentlemen fought bulls on horseback;

MOSCATEL	Don't you praise her beauty?
DON ALONSO	I do.
MOSCATEL	Doesn't it upset you to find men in her street ready to draw swords over her?
DON ALONSO	I don't deny *that*, for a very good reason!
MOSCATEL	Then you're jealous!
DON ALONSO	Of course I'm not jealous! I wouldn't care tuppence about men in her street, so long as there was only jealousy to worry about and not bloodshed. Besides, I called on her only as a joke, at Don Juan's behest. It would be a sad little tale if the joke turned out to be on me!
MOSCATEL	Once upon a time a novice bullfighter, accompanied by a friend who was sponsoring his first performance, rode into the bullring. Dashingly he flung back his cape and jauntily doffed his hat, then boldly poised his lance, some twenty paces from the bull-pen. A bull emerged and charged head on at the horse, though it might just as well have charged tail on, because, when lance hit bull and horns hit horse, both animals started rumbling at the rear and proceeded to knock the stuffing out of each other. The rider was thrown on top of the bull. The sponsor drew his sword and attempted

---

it was normal for novices to be accompanied by 'experts', as here.

2333–9 The joke is not easy to translate fully: *murmurar a las espaldas de alguien* means 'to gossip behind someone's back', but *murmurar* also means 'to murmur'. A good horseman would never let the bull touch his horse, since it was likely to come off worst; in this case the animals collided so forcefully that the shock acted like a purge, causing both to defecate copiously, making some noise as they did so.

al toro una cuchillada,
a su ahijado se la dio,
y siendo de buena marca;   2345
levantóse el caballero
preguntando en voces altas:
'¿Saben ustedes a quién
este hidalgo apadrinaba?
¿A mí, o al toro?' Y ninguno   2350
le supo decir palabra.
Aplícate: apadrinado
de Don Juan, fuiste a la casa
de Beatriz, la suerte erraste,
y nadie a saber alcanza   2355
si era Don Juan tu padrino,
o de Beatriz.

DON ALONSO   ¡Calla, calla!
¡Qué mal aplicado cuento!

MOSCATEL   Bien o mal, doy a Dios gracias
de que ya no reñirás   2360
mi amor, pues que ya en la danza
entras también.

DON ALONSO   Si es así,
dime ya de aquesa dama
qué es el nombre, enamorado.
¿De qué servicio es guardarla?   2365

MOSCATEL   Eso no, que no se pierde
tan presto una mala maña.

                    Llama Inés [dentro]

DON ALONSO   Mira quién llama a esa puerta.

MOSCATEL   ¿Quién es?

                    [Sale Inés]

INÉS   ¿Está tu amo en casa,
Moscatel?

MOSCATEL   ([*Ap.*] ¡Cielos! ¿Qué miro?   2370
Inés es ésta.) ¡Ay, ingrata!
¡Viven los cielos, que vienes

2354 **you made a mess**: Spanish *suerte* means 'luck', 'lot' or 'fate', but it also means
one of the phases of a bullfight. Moscatel means that Don Alonso made a mess of
his 'performance' (like the gentleman in his story), but also implies that he has been
unlucky.

2362–5 In D, lines 2363–4 make no sense. Perhaps part of the speech is missing,
but the context permits only one explanation of the exchange: Don Alonso must

to strike the bull, but he struck his friend a
first-class blow instead.

The rider picked himself up and cried:
'Does anyone know whom this noble gentleman is sponsoring, me or the bull?' But
they were stuck for an answer.

Similarly, you were sponsored by Don
Juan to go and call on Beatriz, and you
made a mess. And nobody can be sure
whether it was you Don Juan was sponsoring or Beatriz.

DON ALONSO   Be quiet! Your story is not at all apt.

MOSCATEL   Well, apt or not, thank God you'll have to
                  stop complaining about *me* being in love,
                  now that you've joined the dance as well.

DON ALONSO   In that case, you can tell me the name of
                  the woman you're in love with. What's the
                  point of hiding her?

MOSCATEL   Ah, no! Bad habits don't die *that* fast!
                  Inés knocks (offstage)

DON ALONSO   See who's at the door.
MOSCATEL   Who is it?
                          Enter Inés
INÉS   Is your master at home, Moscatel?

MOSCATEL   (*Aside.* Heavens! What's this I'm see-
                  ing?) Oh, but you're fickle! By Heaven,

---

say something along the lines of 'All right, if I'm in love, and you know who my
beloved is, why don't you, who are also in love, let me know who yours is?' We have
edited the lines accordingly. The accuracy of Moscatel's reply about Don Alonso's
philandering habits is confirmed by the next scene.
2366–7 A variation on a proverb, 'quien malas mañas ha, tarde o nunca las perderá'
('he who has bad habits will lose them late or never': Sbarbi, s.v. *maña*); cf. *El
segundo Scipión* (*The second Scipio*), Aguilar I, 1431b.

a verle!

INÉS	Pues, ¿qué pensabas?
	([*Ap.*] Quiero decir que es verdad,
	porque lo que más me agrada 2375
	es dar celos de poquito.)
	Porque le importa a mi fama
	que Don Alonso conozca
	que sé cumplir mi palabra.
MOSCATEL	¡Bien honrado pundonor! 2380
INÉS	Quita.
MOSCATEL	No has de entrar.
INÉS	Aparta.
DON ALONSO	¿Quién habla contigo?
MOSCATEL	Nadie.
INÉS	Miente, que alguien es quien habla.
DON ALONSO	Y muy alguien. Inés mía,
	una y mil veces me abraza. 2385
INÉS	Mil veces te abrazo y una,
	por pagarte en otras tantas.

Pellízquela Moscatel

	¡Ay!
DON ALONSO	¿Qué es eso?
INÉS	Diome un golpe
	la guarnición de tu daga.
DON ALONSO	No dudo que tu venida 2390
	sea a darme vida y alma,
	que aunque tú con Moscatel
	me respondiste enojada,
	en fin sabes que te quiero,
	y no has de ser siempre ingrata. 2395
INÉS	Nunca lo fui yo contigo,
	que a la primera palabra
	dije que a verte vendría.
DON ALONSO	¡Pícaro! Pues ¿tú me engañas?
MOSCATEL	¿Yo, señor?
DON ALONSO	¡Viven los cielos 2400
	que he de matarte a patadas!
MOSCATEL [*ap.*]	Cumplióse el refrán; mas no,

2402–3 Unfortunately Moscatel's proverb does not have an English equivalent. The

	you've come to visit him!
INÉS	What did you expect? (*Aside*. It suits me to let him misunderstand, because I simply adore making him just a little bit jealous.) For the sake of my good name, I must show Don Alonso I'm a woman of my word.
MOSCATEL	A fine way to protect your good name!
INÉS	Stand aside!
MOSCATEL	You're not getting in!
INÉS	Out of the way!
DON ALONSO	Who's talking to you?
MOSCATEL	Nobody.
INÉS	He's lying. Somebody *is* talking.
DON ALONSO	And a very special somebody! My dear Inés! Give me a thousand kisses, and then one more.
INÉS	I kiss you in return a thousand times, and then once more.
	Moscatel pinches her
	Ouch!
DON ALONSO	What's wrong?
INÉS	You poked me with the hilt of your dagger!
DON ALONSO	Your visit here will give me back my life and soul.
	Though you sent an angry answer through Moscatel, you know how much I love you, and your coldness cannot last forever.
INÉS	I was never cold towards you. At the first word, I said I would come and see you.
DON ALONSO (*to Moscatel*)	You scoundrel! Were you trying to cheat me?
MOSCATEL	Me, sir?
DON ALONSO	By Heavens, I'll kick the daylights out of you!
MOSCATEL (*aside*)	And so the proverb is fulfilled; except that

Spanish one he has in mind is 'Cornudo y apaleado, mandalde que baile' (or *mandarle*

	que hacerme bailar les falta.	
INÉS [ap.]	En sabiendo a lo que vengo,	
	Moscatel se desengaña.	2405
	Duren los celos un poco.	
MOSCATEL	¡Voto a Dios! De una picaña...	
INÉS	Pícaro, hablad con respeto;	
	mirad que soy vuestra ama.	
	[A D. Alonso] A solas quisiera hablarte.	2410
MOSCATEL	¿A solas?	
DON ALONSO	Salte allá, y guarda	
	esa puerta.	
MOSCATEL [ap.]	¿Yo la puerta?	
	¡Viven los cielos!	
DON ALONSO	¿Qué hablas?	
MOSCATEL	Que soy leal, y no tengo	
	de consentir tal infamia,	2415
	que por una picarona	
	exceso ninguno hagas	
	y se aventure la vida.	
DON ALONSO	¿De cuándo acá tanto guardas	
	mi salud? Salte allá fuera.	2420
MOSCATEL	No me saldré, si me matas,	
	que esto conviene a tu vida.	
DON ALONSO	Nunca te he visto con tanta	
	lealtad.	
MOSCATEL	Guardéla otras veces	
	para esta ocasión.	
DON ALONSO	Ya basta.	2425

Échale a empellones

	Ya estás sola; vuelve, Inés,	
	a abrazarme.	
INÉS	Aunque culpada	
	me has hecho en venir a verte,	
	por la opinión de mi ama	
	ha sido, no porque vengo,	2430

bailar): Correas, p. 421. The alleged explanation is that a husband, having been cuckolded (*cornudo*) and beaten (*apaleado*) by his wife's lover, is then made to dance (*mandarle bailar*): see Arellano, p. 334. Moscatel has been neither cuckolded nor beaten, but the sight of Inés apparently falling in with Don Alonso's plans makes him feel hard done by. Calderón refers obliquely to the same proverb in *El maestro*

	they haven't made me dance yet!
INÉS (*aside*)	When Moscatel learns what has really brought me here, he'll soon recover. But let his jealousy last a little longer!
MOSCATEL	I swear to God that such a hussy...
INÉS	Speak with respect, you scoundrel! Remember your place! (*To Don Alonso*) I wish to speak to you alone.
MOSCATEL	Alone!
DON ALONSO	You get out, and watch that door!
MOSCATEL (*aside*)	Me! Watch the door? By Heaven!
DON ALONSO	What are you saying?
MOSCATEL	That I am loyal, and that I can't permit such an outrage. I won't allow a brazen wench to make you do something foolish that might put your very life at risk.
DON ALONSO	Since when exactly have you started worrying about my health? Get outside!
MOSCATEL	I won't! Not even if you kill me! This is a matter of life and death!
DON ALONSO	I've never seen you show such loyalty before!
MOSCATEL	I was saving it for now.
DON ALONSO	Enough!
	He pushes Moscatel out
	Now that you're alone with me, give me another kiss.
INÉS	Though you made it look as if it were you I came to see, I've really come at the request of my mistress, and not, as I said, because

---

de danzar (*The dancing-master*), Aguilar II, 1559a.

2409 **remember your place**: Inés actually says 'remember I'm your mistress', using *ama*, the feminine form of *amo*, 'master'. The word has no sexual connotations; what she means is that, in her new (and feigned) role of lady-friend to Moscatel's master, she becomes Moscatel's 'mistress'. It is worth noting that in this speech Inés uses the formal mode of address (*vosotros*); this was not normally used to address servants, but by one person of rank to another.

como dije, por tu causa.

DON ALONSO   No sé qué quieras decirme.

INÉS   Dirélo en breves palabras.
Beatriz, habiendo sabido
cómo hubo unas cuchilladas   2435
de donde herido saliste
a las puertas de su casa,
de tu herida condolida,
de tu término obligada
y de tu salud dudosa,   2440
te envía toda esta banda.
Favor es suyo, aunque ella
me mandó que no llegaras
a saber que ella la envía.
Con esto, adiós.

DON ALONSO   Oye, aguarda.   2445
¿Beatriz se acuerda de mí?
¿Beatriz siente mis desgracias?
¿Beatriz me envía favores?
Novedad se me hace extraña.

INÉS   A mí no, porque en sabiendo   2450
que era tu voluntad falsa,
supe que sería dichosa;
que por no acertar en nada,
más con nosotras merece
quien finge, que no quien ama.   2455

Sale Moscatel

MOSCATEL [*ap.*]   ¡Qué mal descansa un celoso!
¡Qué mal un triste descansa!
Mis penas veré, que menos
es verlas que imaginarlas.

DON ALONSO   Inés bella, pues Beatriz   2460
hoy de extremo a extremo pasa,
paso yo de extremo a extremo;
que aunque fineza no haga
de enamorado, de noble
la he de hacer. Aquí aguarda   2465
a que le escriba un papel.

MOSCATEL   ([*Ap.*] Él se entra en esotra cuadra;
descanse mi corazón.)
Tigre fregatriz de Hircania,

of you.

DON ALONSO | I don't know what you mean.

INÉS | I'll tell you in a word. Beatriz learned that there had been a swordfight at her door, and she was upset to hear you had been wounded. As she feels responsible for your plight, she wishes to know how you are.

She sends you this ribbon as a token, though she told me not to let you know it was from her. And so, goodbye.

DON ALONSO | Hold on! Listen! Does Beatriz remember me? Does she worry about my misfortunes, send me tokens? What a novel turn of events!

INÉS | I don't find it the least bit novel. I knew your love was only faked, so I realised it would succeed. Since we women never get anything right, false lovers fare better with us than true ones.

Enter Moscatel

MOSCATEL (*aside*) | How jealousy and sorrow make a man fret! I must learn the worst. Knowing it can't be as bad as imagining it.

DON ALONSO | My lovely Inés, as Beatriz today has swung from one extreme to another, I too from one to another extreme will swing. Though I may not observe the niceties of a lover, I will observe those of a gentleman. Wait here while I go and write her a note.

MOSCATEL | (*Aside.* He has gone into the other room. Now my heart can stop pounding.) Oh, Hircanian tiger of a scullery-maid! Vile

---

2469–71 Hircania (in Asia, south of the Caspian Sea) was noted in Classical times

	vil cocodrilo de Egipto,	2470
	sierpe vil, león de Albania,	
	¿tendrá mi lengua razones,	
	tendrán mis labios palabras	
	para quejarse de ti?	

INÉS   No.

MOSCATEL   Pues si voces me faltan,   2475
tengan mis manos licencia
de darte de bofetadas
siquiera.

INÉS   No quiera hacer
tu mano tal, que ya bastan
las burlas, que todo ha sido   2480
por sólo tomar venganza
de que dudases de mí
que soy casta.

MOSCATEL   ¿Qué haces casta?
Creeré primero traidora.

INÉS   No vine a ver...

MOSCATEL   Tú me engañas.   2485

INÉS   ...a tu amo.

MOSCATEL   Pues ¿por qué?

INÉS   A traerle...

MOSCATEL   ¿Qué?

INÉS   ...una banda.

MOSCATEL   ¿Cúya?

INÉS   De Beatriz, que ya
un poco más claro habla.

MOSCATEL   Y ¿el abrazo?

INÉS   Fruta fue   2490
de palacio; eso no agravia,
que si él abrazó el cuerpo,
el alma tú.

MOSCATEL   Inés ingrata,
si le das el cuerpo al otro,
¡dale a Barrabás el alma!   2495

---

for the ferocity of its tigers, and there are numerous references to them in classical Spanish literature (although Moscatel's reference is an absurd one). As for crocodiles, their reputation for shedding tears is of similar antiquity. According to Covarrubias (s.v. *cocodrilo*), they imitated the sound of weeping in order to attract

crocodile of Egypt, base serpent, Albanian
lion! How can my tongue find phrases, or
my lips words, to condemn you?

INÉS	They can't.
MOSCATEL	Well, then, if I'm lost for words, let my hands be allowed to thump you.
INÉS	Let them do no such thing! The joke is over! I was only getting my own back on you for doubting I was true to you.
MOSCATEL	True, how are you! False, more like!
INÉS	I didn't come here to see...
MOSCATEL	You're fooling me!
INÉS	...your master.
MOSCATEL	Then, why?
INÉS	To bring him...
MOSCATEL	What?
INÉS	...a ribbon.
MOSCATEL	From whom?
INÉS	From Beatriz, who at last is beginning to make her meaning clear.
MOSCATEL	And what about those kisses?
INÉS	Just lip-service. Quite harmless. Though he held my body, you hold my soul.
MOSCATEL	Oh, false Inés! If you give the other fellow your body, you can let the Devil have your soul!

---

human victims. Albania (not the modern country, but in Asia) was famous for the
ferocity of its lions. (See Arellano, p. 339, for references to these three creatures.)
2495 **the Devil**: properly, *Barrabás* is Barabbas, the convicted criminal who was
pardoned instead of Christ; by extension, any wicked person, even the devil.

INÉS   Picón fue.

MOSCATEL   Pues los picones,
si juegan, muden baraja
o truequen la suerte. Dame
los brazos.

INÉS   De buena gana.

Sale Don Alonso

DON ALONSO   ¿Qué es esto?

INÉS   ¿Esto? Abrazar,   2500
en mi tierra.

MOSCATEL   Ha sido tanta
la alegría de haber visto
que ya esa fiera se ablanda
(la curiosidad perdona,
si he escuchado cuanto hablas),   2505
que le di a Inés este abrazo
en albricias de la banda.

DON ALONSO   Toma, Inés, este papel
que le has de dar a tu ama,
y para ti este diamante.   2510

INÉS   ¡Vivas edades más largas
que...! Claro está que es el fénix
suegra mentira de Arabia.

Vase Inés

MOSCATEL   ¿Diamante la diste?

DON ALONSO   Sí.

MOSCATEL   ¿Y de balde?

DON ALONSO   ¿Qué ignorancia!   2515

MOSCATEL   Mil me lleven diablos hoy
heréticos, si no amas
a Beatriz.

DON ALONSO   ¿En qué lo ves?

MOSCATEL   En que das sin esperanza.

2496–9 Covarrubias (s.v. *picatoste*) explains that *picón* means 'a joke that one plays
by pretending something'; but he also explains that *picarse* has a meaning associated
with gambling: 'to be annoyed when one loses, and to persist in playing'. That this
meaning is involved here is apparently confirmed by the gambling terminology used
by Moscatel in the next lines.

2511–13 The usual expression is 'may you live longer than the phoenix' (see 851–4).
The rest of the translation is very free, and the original means 'It's clear that the
phoenix is a mother-in-law Arabian lie'. Jokes about mothers-in-law abounded even

INÉS	I was only teasing! You can't bear to lose a trick, can you?
MOSCATEL	When I start losing tricks, I get a new deck to change my luck. Come to my arms!
INÉS	Gladly!

Enter Don Alonso

DON ALONSO	What's this?
INÉS	This? It's called kissing, where I come from.
MOSCATEL	I was so overjoyed to learn that your shrew had relented (forgive my curiosity, but I was listening to what you just said), that I gave Inés a kiss to celebrate the good news about the ribbon.
DON ALONSO	Inés, take this note and give it to your mistress. And, for yourself, here is a diamond.
INÉS	May you live longer than... I was going to say 'than the phoenix', but of course the phoenix is just a cock-and-bull story.

Exit Inés

MOSCATEL	You gave her a diamond?
DON ALONSO	Yes.
MOSCATEL	For nothing?
DON ALONSO	What a fool you are!
MOSCATEL	May I be carried off by a thousand heretical devils if you're not in love with Beatriz!
DON ALONSO	How can you tell?
MOSCATEL	Because you're giving something away

---

in the seventeenth century, and the clown in *La hija del aire* I (*The daughter of the air*) expresses the wish that his generous monarch may 'survive two mothers-in-law' (Aguilar I, 768a). Here, however, Inés merely means that the phoenix (which supposedly lived in Arabia) was the 'mother and father of all lies', i.e. a myth. Her compliment comes out somewhat left-handed, which may be no accident.

2515 **What a fool you are!:** Don Alonso tries to preserve his man-of-the-world image by implying that the diamond was a present for a favour conceded or promised by Inés; but Moscatel knows better.

No está en uso, ni está en rueca.   2520

DON ALONSO   Quien agradece no ama,
y yo estoy agradecido,
no enamorado.

MOSCATEL   Eso basta,
que en el infierno de amor,
dicen que tiene más almas   2525
la virtud, de agradecidas,
que no los vicios, de ingratas.
Y así, hagamos, señor, cuentas,
que no he de quedar en casa.

DON ALONSO   ¿Por qué, Moscatel?

MOSCATEL   Porque   2530
amo no quiero que ama,
y que no me acuda a mí
por acudir a su dama.

DON ALONSO   Bien el haberte sufrido
tantas locuras me pagas.   2535

MOSCATEL   Esto ha de ser.
                    Sale Don Juan

DON JUAN   ¿Qué ha de ser?

DON ALONSO   Irse quiere de mi casa.

DON JUAN   ¿Por qué, Moscatel?

MOSCATEL   Porque
ha hecho la mayor infamia,
la mayor ruindad, mayor   2540
bajeza, mayor...

DON JUAN   ¡Acaba!
¿Qué ha sido?

MOSCATEL   ¡Hase enamorado!
Mira si tengo harta causa.

DON ALONSO   En esta locura ha dado
por haber visto con cuánta   2545
fineza sirvo a Beatriz
por vuestro amor.

DON JUAN _____   A amor gracias...

2520 **that's not your normal, wily way**: the pun of the original is untranslatable. *no está en uso* means 'it isn't in fashion', while *no está en huso* (same pronunciation) translates as 'it isn't in bobbin', a meaningless phrase; this second meaning is then picked up by *ni está en rueca* ('it isn't in distaff'). Bobbins and distaffs are both

	without expecting anything in return. That's not your normal wily way.
DON ALONSO	Gratitude is not love. I am grateful, but I'm not in love.
MOSCATEL	That's bad enough! They say virtue has sent more grateful souls to love's hellfire than vice has ever sent ungrateful ones. Let us settle our accounts, sir; I cannot remain in this house.
DON ALONSO	Why not, Moscatel?
MOSCATEL	Because I do not want a lovestruck master who neglects me in order to serve his beloved.
DON ALONSO	This is how you thank me for putting up with all your nonsense!
MOSCATEL	That's how it has to be!

Enter Don Juan

DON JUAN	How what has to be?
DON ALONSO	He wants to leave my house.
DON JUAN	Why, Moscatel?
MOSCATEL	Because he has gone and committed the most disgraceful, the most ignoble, the most vile, the most...
DON JUAN	Enough! Enough! What has he *done*?
MOSCATEL	He has fallen in love! Tell me now if I'm not justified!
DON ALONSO	He has got hold of this crazy notion because he has seen how diligently I courted Beatriz for the sake of your love.
DON JUAN	Thanks be to Love...

used in spinning.

2521–3 Like Beatriz earlier (2131–2, 2141–6), Don Alonso insists feebly that what he feels for Beatriz is gratitude (for the concern she shows for his welfare), not love.

2528–41 Moscatel, determined to make Don Alonso suffer, echoes the words his master used in the opening scene of the play, especially lines 73–8 and 154–6.

Don Alonso   ¿Cómo?

Don Juan   ...que ya de ese empeño
libre estáis, como se acaba
hoy mi amor.

Don Alonso   Pues, ¿y Leonor?   2550

Don Juan   Leonor de mi pecho falta,
que como amor es fortuna,
sujeto vive a mudanzas.
¿Vuestra amada, Don Alonso?

Don Alonso   Yo no he ni de hablarla   2555
ni de verla en mi vida.
Pues, ¿volveré yo a su casa
y a su calle a hablarla y verla,
por la tarde y la mañana,
siendo yo el descalabrado,   2560
y vos, la cabeza sana,
no lo haréis?

Don Juan   No, porque herida
más penetrante y tirana
son mis celos, porque son
mortal herida del alma.   2565

Don Alonso   Pues troquemos las heridas,
que yo primero tomara,
sea mortal o venial,
tener hoy descalabrada
el alma que la cabeza,   2570
y esto bien claro se saca
del efecto, pues si curan
en falso una herida, mata,
y a los celosos da vida
cualquier cura, aunque sea falsa.   2575

Don Juan   En fin, Don Alonso, sea
con poca o con mucha causa,
no he de volver a poneros
en la confusión pasada.

Don Alonso   Ni por mí habéis de dejarlo,   2580
que a mí no se me da nada.

Don Juan   Por mí lo dejo, y por vos,
porque vuestra herida basta.

2568 **mortally or venially**: wounds may be mortal, but they cannot be venial. Don
  Alonso uses adjectives normally applied to sins; a venial sin is a minor one that is

DON ALONSO	What?
DON JUAN	...you are now relieved of that task. My love is finished.
DON ALONSO	But what about Leonor?
DON JUAN	Leonor no longer dwells in my heart. Like fortune, love is fickle. And how is *your* beloved, Don Alonso?
DON ALONSO	I shall never speak to her nor look on her again. Why should I, who have had my skull cracked, go back to her house or her street to talk to her and look on her, morning and night, when you, whose skull is in one piece, do not do likewise?
DON JUAN	I do not go, because my jealousy has inflicted even deeper and more cruel wounds on me, for it has mortally wounded my soul.
DON ALONSO	Then let's swop wounds. Mortally or venially, I'd prefer a cracked soul to a cracked skull, for the very simple reason that, if a wound is incorrectly treated, it can kill, whereas jealousy can be cured by any old piece of quackery.
DON JUAN	Don Alonso, rightly or wrongly, I shan't get you into the same scrape again.
DON ALONSO	Don't give up anything on my account; scrapes don't mean a thing to me.
DON JUAN	I'm giving up for my own sake *and* for yours; you've been wounded enough.

---

readily forgivable, whereas a mortal sin can lead to the 'death' of the soul, i.e. damnation. Don Alonso cannot resist rising to his friend's high-sounding metaphor.

DON ALONSO	De una herida no escarmientan caballos de buena casta.	2585
DON JUAN	¿Yo me volveré a llegar allá? ¡Süerte excusada!	
DON ALONSO	Pues cuando por vos no sea, por ver si a saber se alcanza quién me ha herido, he de volver.	2590
DON JUAN	Cuando importe a vuestra fama, desde acá fuera podremos hacer diligencias varias.	
DON ALONSO	Yo más pretendo, Don Juan, buena opinión con las damas que con los hombres, y no es bien que mujer tan vana como Beatriz, de mí piense...	2595
DON JUAN	Yo sabré desengañarla de todo.	
DON ALONSO	Don Juan, Don Juan, hablemos verdades claras: yo he de ir a ver a Beatriz.	2600
MOSCATEL	¡Hablara para mañana! ¡Y dirá que miento yo!	
DON JUAN	Si eso os importa, ¿qué os falta? Id vos muy en hora buena.	2605
DON ALONSO	¿Cómo, sin que las espaldas me guardéis vos y Leonor?	
DON JUAN	Yo no he de volver a hablarla.	
DON ALONSO	Esto habéis de hacer por mí; que no es cosa tan extraña, por hacer tercio a un amigo, volver a hablar a una dama.	2610
DON JUAN	Por vos, Don Alonso, haré lo que en mi vida pensaba.	2615
MOSCATEL	¿Qué os andáis haciendo puntas, nobles de capa y espada, si ambos deseáis ir a verlas?	

2603 **now the cat is out of the bag!**: the reason Don Alonso did not admit this before is, as Moscatel well knows, that he could not bring himself to say—either to himself or to the others—that he wants to see Beatriz again. Hence his various false reasons for wishing to go back.

2611–13 Don Alonso echoes Don Juan's words (1657–60), and the appeal to friendship

DON ALONSO	One wound doesn't scare a thoroughbred warhorse.
DON JUAN	You expect me to go back there! Spare me that!
DON ALONSO	Well, even if I needn't go there for your sake, I'll go to see if I can find out who wounded me.
DON JUAN	If it's something touching your good name, we can take appropriate steps from a distance.
DON ALONSO	Don Juan, I've always been more concerned with having a good name among women than among men. Besides, it's not right that a woman as conceited as Beatriz should think I'm...
DON JUAN	I shall explain everything to her.
DON ALONSO	Don Juan, Don Juan, let's call a spade a spade. I mean to go and see Beatriz.
MOSCATEL	Now the cat is out of the bag! And he says *I'm* a liar!
DON JUAN	If that's what you mean to do, what's stopping you? Go, and the best of luck to you!
DON ALONSO	How can I, unless you and Leonor keep watch for me?
DON JUAN	I will never speak to her again!
DON ALONSO	You must do so for *me*. After all, it's not so unusual to resume talking to a woman in order to help a friend.
DON JUAN	For your sake, Don Alonso, I shall do something I thought I'd never do again.
MOSCATEL	Why must you cloak-and-dagger noblemen beat about the bush, when both of you are simply dying to go and see the ladies?

---

works. But of course Don Juan, like Don Alonso, needs only a reasonable pretext (see Moscatel's next speech).

2616 **beat about the bush**: the Spanish *hacer puntas* is a falconry term (Covarrubias and *Autoridades*): it means 'to turn', 'to sheer away', instead of flying straight at the prey. We have chosen a slightly different metaphor.

	Y no hay cosa más usada	
	que ser amancebamientos	2620
	en los estrados y salas,	
	ad perpetuam rei memoriam	
	litigados, y se hallan	
	contra los celos fiscales	
	dos amigos y dos damas,	2625
	porque cuando el uno riñe,	
	el otro las paces trata.	

DON JUAN   Ahora bien, por vos iré;
           mas mirad, antes que vaya,
           que hay alacena.

DON ALONSO   ¿Qué importa?   2630
MOSCATEL   Que hay balconazo.
DON ALONSO   Que haya.
MOSCATEL   Que hay cuchillada.
DON ALONSO   Eso no;
           fuera de que si amor traza
           que por sola una mentira
           me sucedan cosas tantas,   2635
           vengan ya, por ser verdades,
           alacena y cuchilladas.

Vanse. Salen Don Diego y Don Luis.

DON DIEGO Ya sabréis la voluntad
           con que siempre os he servido.

DON LUIS   Conozco vuestra amistad,   2640
           y sé, Don Diego, que ha sido
           con fineza y con verdad.

DON DIEGO Pues no me tengáis a exceso
           una reprensión.

DON LUIS   No haré.
DON DIEGO Aquel pasado suceso...   2645
DON LUIS   Queréisme decir que fue
           locura, ya lo confieso;
           porque haber a un hombre herido
           que conmigo no ha tenido
           lances de competidor   2650
           no trae disculpa mejor,
           Diego, que no haberla habido.

2621 **drawing-rooms**: see 321.

Drawing-rooms are often the scene of lovers'
quarrels; and, when two gentlemen and two
ladies conduct the case against jealousy, one
of the men can play peacemaker whenever
the other has had a row.

DON JUAN	Very well. I shall do it for *you*. But, before you go, remember there's a cupboard.
DON ALONSO	So what?
MOSCATEL	And a drop from the balcony.
DON ALONSO	Who cares?
MOSCATEL	And swordplay.
DON ALONSO	Swordplay, no! And yet, since I've endured so much for what was mere pretence, I'm sure I'll cope with cupboards and swords now that it's the real thing!

Exeunt. Enter Don Diego and Don Luis.

DON DIEGO	You know I'm only too glad to help you always.
DON LUIS	I acknowledge your friendship, Don Diego, and I know that it has been firm and true.
DON DIEGO	Then you will not take it amiss if I offer a criticism?
DON LUIS	Of course not.
DON DIEGO	That recent business...
DON LUIS	You're going to tell me it was madness, and I agree. My only excuse for wounding a man who has not thrown down a challenge to me, is that there *is* no excuse for it!

2622–7 Moscatel uses legalistic vocabulary; *ad perpetuam rei memoriam* is a phrase
    normally used of a judicial enquiry made as a precautionary measure.
2637+ **Exeunt...** : the scene changes to the street outside or near Don Pedro's house.

Fuerza es remediarlo, pues
quien lleva ya en sus recelos
perdido el miedo a los celos,   2655
no se le tendrá después.

DON DIEGO   Y ahora, ¿qué habéis de hacer
de lo que ya se trató?
Pues es cierto que a saber
vuestros intentos llegó   2660
Don Pedro.

DON LUIS   ¿Qué hay que temer?
Deshácese un casamiento,
siendo santo sacramento,
después que se efectüó,
¿y no lo desharé yo   2665
sin efectüarle?

                    Sale Don Pedro

DON PEDRO [*ap.*]   Atento
a este hielo que me abrasa,
a este, que me hiela, ardor,
a lo que en mi agravio pasa,
y al respeto de mi honor,   2670
salgo tan tarde de casa.
A Don Luis pretendo hablar,
que mejor es acabar
de una vez con mi recelo,
que no esperar que un mozuelo   2675
que es fábula del lugar
se me atreva. Él viene aquí.
¡Cuánto de verle me alegro
galán y noble! Éste sí.

DON DIEGO   Vuestro suegro viene allí.   2680

DON LUIS   Pues huyamos de mi suegro.

DON PEDRO   ¡Señor Don Luis! Informado
de deudos vuestros he estado
de que honrar habéis querido
mi casa, y agradecido,   2685
como es justo, os he buscado

2653–6 A view expressed by various honour-sensitive noblemen, e.g. Gutierre in *El
médico de su honra* (*The surgeon of his honour*): to feel jealousy implies the existence
of a rival, and having a rival implies potential dishonour; so any man who cares about
his honour must necessarily be afraid of feeling jealous. The stanza has lost a line,
and the original probably expressed the idea more clearly.

	I must undo the damage, for a man who is so preoccupied that he loses his fear of being made jealous will soon cease to care about his very honour!
DON DIEGO	Then, what are you going to do about the plans you've already made?
	Don Pedro must surely have come to know of your intentions.
DON LUIS	What is there to worry about? Wedlock is a holy sacrament, but marriages can be unmade even after they have been solemnised; so why shouldn't I unmake one that hasn't?

Enter Don Pedro

DON PEDRO (*aside*)	I am out and about so late because I am scalded by this ice, chilled by this fire, which discredits and dishonours me.
	I must talk to Don Luis, for it's better I should put an end to my worries once and for all, rather than wait for advances to be made by a certain young pup who is the talk of the town. Here comes Don Luis.
	How glad I am to see him looking so fine and noble! He's the one!
DON DIEGO	Here comes your father-in-law.
DON LUIS	Then let us hide from my father-in-law.
DON PEDRO	Don Luis! I have been informed by relatives of yours that you wish to honour my house, and I have sought you out to say that,

---

2662–6 Then as now, the Catholic Church, while not permitting divorce, could annul a marriage for a variety of reasons. Don Luis is asking the question, 'If a marriage can be broken off after it has taken place, why should I worry about breaking one off before it has happened?'

2680–1 **father-in-law**: not literally, of course; he would have been if Don Luis had decided to go ahead with his plan to marry Beatriz. Don Luis wants to hide in order to avoid the embarrassment of having to tell Don Pedro that the match is off.

para mostrar cuánto estoy
ufano de merecer...

DON LUIS   Señor Don Pedro, yo soy
el que las dichas de ayer   2690
tiene por disculpas hoy.
Confieso que me atreví
a tanto empeño, y que fui
venturoso en tanto empeño,
pues ser de estas honras dueño   2695
por lo menos merecí.
Pero soy tan desdichado,
aun con las dichas, señor,
que para tomar estado,
un nuevo empeño de honor   2700
lo ha deshecho y lo ha estorbado.

DON PEDRO   ¿De honor empeño ([ap.] ¡ay de mí!)
os retira de esto?

DON LUIS   Sí.

DON PEDRO   Pues ¿cómo? ¿En qué ([ap.] ¡estoy mortal!)
puede a Beatriz estar mal?   2705

DON LUIS   Que no lo entendáis así,
que de vuestro enojo ha sido
el honor mal entendido.
Vos de mis disculpas no...

DON PEDRO   ¿De qué suerte?

DON LUIS   Porque yo,   2710
señor, habiendo sabido
que su majestad (que el cielo
guarde por sol de esta esfera,
por planeta de este suelo)
con su católico celo   2715
sale aquesta primavera,
y sabiendo cómo hacía
gente un señor de quien fui
deudo, por ventura mía,
que me honrase le pedí   2720
con alguna compañía.
Hámela dado: éste ha sido

2712–16 Spain was very much involved in the Thirty Years' War (1618–1648), and,
although she eventually got the worst of it, she was still enjoying some successes at
this time. The most important recent one was the battle of Nördlingen (6 September
1634), when the Imperial troops under the King of Hungary and Philip IV's brother

	naturally, I am obliged to you, and to show you how proud I am to have deserved...
DON LUIS	Don Pedro, I am a man for whom yesterday's rejoicing has become today's regret.

I confess I dared to entertain such hopes, and therein met with some success, and that indeed I deem myself worthy of such a privilege.

But such is my misfortune that, in the midst of my rejoicing, a matter of honour has arisen which quite rules out the possibility of my contracting marriage.

DON PEDRO	You are withdrawing (Heavens above!) because of a matter of honour?
DON LUIS	Yes.
DON PEDRO	What's that? (*Aside.* Oh, I shall die!) How can such a question touch Beatriz?
DON LUIS	Do not interpret it so! Your anger has caused you to misunderstand my reference to honour. My excuses are not...
DON PEDRO	What do you mean?
DON LUIS	Learning, sir, that His Majesty (whom God preserve as the sun of this sphere and the planet of this earth) proposes to set forth this spring in Catholic zeal, and knowing that a gentleman who happily is a relative of mine was raising a troop, I asked to be honoured with a company.

He has given me one, and it is for this

Ferdinand won a notable victory. Philip himself did not set forth in 1634 or 1635, merely his armies.

2720–1 **honoured with a company**: that is, made a captain. In the days before professional standing armies were set up, any young nobleman, experienced or not, could expect to become an officer.

el empeño que he tenido
para no tomar estado,
que el que es marido y soldado,   2725
no es soldado o no es marido.
Si yo volviese, señor,
entonces con más valor
me podéis hacer feliz,
porque hoy casar con Beatriz   2730
no le está bien a mi honor.

Vanse los dos

DON PEDRO   'Porque hoy casar con Beatriz...'
¡Válgame el cielo! ¿Qué ha sido
lo que he visto, lo que he oído?
Poco siento, ¡ay infeliz!   2735
No me deja mi sentido...
Pero afligirme es error:
si en aquel caso consiste
su honor, miente mi temor,
que en fin, cuanto piensa un triste   2740
siempre ha de ser lo peor.

Vase. Salen Beatriz e Inés.

BEATRIZ   Inés, ¿cómo el papel tomaste?

INÉS   Como
todo cuanto me dan, señora, tomo.

BEATRIZ   Sin duda le dirías
que de mi parte ibas.

INÉS   Desconfías   2745
de mí sin causa, porque yo he callado
que era tuya la banda, y el recado
callé por tu respeto,
como suelo callar cualquier secreto.

BEATRIZ   Pues, Inés, ¿a qué efeto,   2750
si es así, me has traído
papel?

INÉS   ([*Ap.*] ¡Vive el Señor, que me ha cogido!
Mas yo me soltaré.) Que le trajera,
me dijo, y que si acaso hallar pudiera
ocasión, te le diese.   2755

2730–1   It is not clear whether Don Luis really has enlisted. If he has enlisted, it
is in order to have an excuse for not marrying Beatriz, because he believes he has
had a rival who may have captured her affections. The hint that he may have another

reason I cannot consider matrimony, for a man who is both husband and soldier is neither soldier nor husband.

Should I return, sir, you will then have better occasion to make me a happy man; however, to marry Beatriz at present is not compatible with my honour.

Exeunt Don Diego and Don Luis

DON PEDRO   'To marry Beatriz at present...'
By Heavens! What is this I'm hearing? What is this I'm seeing?
I am stunned. My sorrow will not let me...
But I must not torment myself. If that is the only threat to his honour, I need have no fear. Besides, worries always make one think the worst.

Exit. Enter Beatriz and Inés.

BEATRIZ   How did you get the note?
INÉS   The way I get everything!

BEATRIZ   I suppose you told him I sent you.

INÉS   You needn't be so suspicious of me! I didn't tell him the ribbon was yours. And, out of respect for you, I also kept your message to myself, the way I keep all secrets.

BEATRIZ   In that case, how have you brought me a note?

INÉS   (*Aside.* Oh, Lord! She has trapped me! But I'll wriggle out of it!) He asked me to bring it, and to give it to you if I got

---

reason besides his alleged enlistment is strong enough to fill Don Pedro with anxiety. The thought of having a daughter whose reputation had been 'compromised' was supposed, at least in literature, to fill fathers with dread.
2741+   ***Exit...*** : the final scene-change, back to a room in Don Pedro's house.

Yo le tomé porque de mí creyese
cuán de su parte estaba,
que, puesto que una banda le llevaba
hurtada, que era tuya, bien creería
que un papel, que es más fácil, te traería.   2760

BEATRIZ   Esta satisfacción algo me agrada.

INÉS   ([*Ap.*] Aqueso es dar satisfacción honrada.)
Leonor, señora, viene.

Sale Leonor

BEATRIZ   Pues, que el papel me vea, no conviene.

LEONOR   Bien pudiera yo agora   2765
decir con mayor causa (¿quién lo ignora?),
¿qué idioma fue misivo el que en lineado
papel ocultas en tu manga ajado?

BEATRIZ   Y yo también pudiera
decir que en vano preguntarlo fuera,   2770
pues quien saber no quiere
lo que quiero decir, saber no espere
lo que callarlo quiero.   *Vase*

LEONOR   ¡Inés, Inés!

INÉS   ¿Pues no por hablar muero?

LEONOR   Inés, oyes, ¿qué ha sido   2775
este papel?

INÉS   ¡Qué poco te he debido!
¿No aguardaras siquiera
a que sin preguntar te lo dijera?
Que se me hace conciencia, te prometo,
la pregunta llevar, pero ¡un secreto!   2780

Al paño Beatriz

BEATRIZ [*ap.*]   Mal segura, escuchar desde aquí quiero
qué hablan las dos.

INÉS   Fui a verle, y lo primero
le dije que Beatriz me lo mandaba.

LEONOR   Bien hiciste.

BEATRIZ [*ap.*]   Yo mal, pues me fiaba
de crïada. ¡Ay, Leonor, que en ellas anda!   2785

INÉS   Lo segundo, en su nombre di la banda.

2767–73 Leonor recalls the words her sister used in lines 866–7; Beatriz in turn echoes
what Leonor said in lines 876–83.

2785 we retain D's *en ellas*, which other editors reject. See Lope de Vega, *La dama*

| | a chance. I accepted it so he'd think I was on his side. I suppose he thought that if I took him a stolen ribbon belonging to you, I'd find it even easier to bring you a note from him. |

BEATRIZ I am satisfied with this explanation.

INÉS (*Aside.* Then I've given honest satisfaction.) Madam, Leonor is coming.

Enter Leonor

BEATRIZ She must not see me with this note!

LEONOR Now it's my turn to say, with even greater justification (can you guess?): what verbal missive is this on lineated paper that you crumple and secrete in your sleeve?

BEATRIZ And it's my turn to say that the question would be pointless, for someone who will not listen to what I do wish to say cannot expect to hear what I don't wish to say.   *Exit*

LEONOR Inés, Inés!

INÉS I'm just dying to speak!

LEONOR Listen, Inés, what note was that?

INÉS How little you know me!
    Couldn't you even wait for me to tell without being asked?
    It hurts my conscience, I can tell you, to hold on to a question, let alone a secret!

Beatriz at the backcloth

BEATRIZ (*aside*) I suspect some mischief, so I shall eavesdrop on them from here.

INÉS I went to see him, and the first thing I did was to tell him Beatriz had sent me.

LEONOR You did right.

BEATRIZ (*aside*) And I did wrong to trust a servant. Woe to you, Leonor, if you consort with them!

INÉS Next, I gave him the ribbon in her name.

---

boba (*The foolish lady*), lines 401–2: 'A nadie quiere / más, en todas las criadas' ('Of all the servants, she's fondest of her'). See also the note on this line in A. Zamora Vicente's edition of the play (Madrid, 1963).

BEATRIZ [ap.]	¡Ay infeliz! ¿Qué he oído?	
LEONOR	En esa cuadra hay ruido.	
INÉS	Don Juan es el que ha entrado.	
LEONOR	Pues, ¿cómo, si de aquí se fue enojado,	2790
	diciendo que en su vida no me había	
	de ver?	
INÉS	¡Que estés tan nueva todavía	
	que no sepas que cuando está un amante	
	diciendo más furioso y arrogante	
	'No he de volver a verte, ingrata bella',	2795
	es cuando muere por volver a ella!	
BEATRIZ [ap.]	Ya que a escuchar mis penas he empezado,	
	acabe de escucharlas mi cuidado.	

Salen Don Juan, Don Alonso [y] Moscatel

DON JUAN	Pensarás que me han traído	
	a verte, Leonor, y hablarte	2800
	mis celos, porque los celos	
	(perdona el civil lenguaje)	
	son ordinarios de amor,	
	que así llevan como traen.	
	Pues no, Leonor, no he venido	2805
	para que me desengañes,	
	porque el desaire de amor	
	es hablar en el desaire.	
	Con otra ocasión he vuelto	
	a pisar estos umbrales,	2810
	porque nunca les faltó	
	ocasión a los pesares.	
	Don Alonso, a quien tú hiciste	
	de Beatriz fingido amante,	
	desairado de tu casa	2815
	salió con el primer lance,	
	tanto, que porque no piensen	
	de Beatriz las vanidades	
	que el no volver aquí es	
	de escarmentado y cobarde,	2820
	me ha pedido que le traiga	
	a verla. ¿Cómo negarle	
	puedo yo lo mismo a él,	
	que él no me negó a mí antes?	

2802 **plainly**: *civil*, which now means 'civil', 'polite', then meant the opposite: 'coarse,

BEATRIZ (*aside*)	Oh, misery! What am I hearing?
LEONOR	There's some sound from that room.
INÉS	Don Juan has just come in.
LEONOR	But, is that possible? He left here saying he would never see me again.
INÉS	You're still very green if you don't realise that, when a lover is at his most arrogant and furious, saying 'I shall never see you again, beauteous traitor!', it's precisely then that he's dying to run back to you.
BEATRIZ (*aside*)	Now that I have started to hear the tale of my woes, let my sorrow hear it out.

Enter Don Juan, Don Alonso and Moscatel

DON JUAN	You will no doubt think, Leonor, that it is jealousy that brings me here to see you and to speak to you, because jealousy (to put it plainly) acts as Love's courier, fetching hither and carrying thither.

But no, Leonor, I have not come to seek reassurances, for love is slighted by talk of being slighted.

It is for a different reason (misery will always find a way!) that I have crossed this threshold once again.

Don Alonso, whom you enlisted as Beatriz's feigned lover, left your house in some indignity after his first visit.

In case Beatriz might be vain enough to think he had failed to return because he felt abashed or afraid, he has asked me to escort him here to see her.

How could I refuse to do for him what he had earlier not refused to do for me?

---

crude, belonging to the lower orders of society'.

2803 **courier:** strictly speaking, the *ordinario* was a 'carrier', in the sense of 'a person who took goods (or sometimes letters or dispatches) from one place to another'. *OED* records *ordinary* (s.v., item 6) in the sense of 'courier'.

BEATRIZ [*ap.*]	¡En notable obligación	2825
	estoy, cierto, a estos galanes!	
DON JUAN	Él viene, Leonor, a esto;	
	y porque en aquesta parte	
	nunca piensen mis desdichas,	
	nunca sospechen mis males,	2830
	nunca imaginen mis penas	
	que fue gana de buscarte,	
	en la calle me estaré	
	en tanto que a Beatriz hable	
	y de este escrúpulo leve,	2835
	y de esta malicia fácil	
	desempeñe su opinión,	
	su crédito desengañe.	
	—Don Alonso, entrad, y pues	
	ya el sol, helado cadáver,	2840
	agonizando entre sombras,	
	en brazos de noche yace,	
	hablad a Beatriz, y ved	
	que aquí Don Pedro no os halle.	
LEONOR	Aguarda, Don Juan, espera.	2845
DON JUAN	¿Qué quieres, Leonor, que aguarde?	
LEONOR	Desengaños.	
DON JUAN	Son en vano.	
LEONOR	Disculpas.	
DON JUAN	Serán en balde. [*Vase*]	
LEONOR	Tras él iré, Don Alonso;	
	luego vuelvo. Perdonadme,	2850
	pues en cualquiera suceso,	
	todo lo que es me era antes. *Vase*	
DON ALONSO	¿Mas que me voy sin hablar	
	a Beatriz?	
MOSCATEL	¿No dirás mas que	
	nos vemos en otro aprieto	2855
	al pasado semejante?	
DON ALONSO	Inés, dime dónde está,	
	para que entretanto le hable,	
	Beatriz.	

2836 **baseless**: *fácil* now means 'easy', but in classical Spanish the word also meant 'fragile, weak and insubstantial' (*Autoridades*).

2854 **surely what you mean is**: the metre of the original, demanding assonance in

BEATRIZ (*aside*)   I must say, I am deeply obliged to these fine
gentlemen!

DON JUAN   That is why he has come, Leonor.

Lest it should be thought or suspected
or imagined, that it was my unhappiness
or my misery or my woes, that drove me
here to seek you out, I shall wait below
in the street while he talks to Beatriz and
clears his good name and rids his reputation
of this wisp of suspicion and this baseless
imputation.

Come in, Don Alonso. As the sun is
already but a frozen corpse expiring among
shadows in the arms of night, speak now
to Beatriz, and be sure her father doesn't
catch you!

LEONOR   Wait, Don Juan, don't go!

DON JUAN   Wait for what, Leonor?

LEONOR   For explanations.

DON JUAN   They are in vain.

LEONOR   For apologies.

DON JUAN   They will be of no avail.   *Exit*

LEONOR   I'm going to follow him, Don Alonso. I'll
return shortly. Forgive me, but he means
as much to me as ever.   *Exit*

DON ALONSO   Now I suppose I'll have to leave without
speaking to Beatriz?

MOSCATEL   Surely what you mean is that we've landed
in the same pickle as last time?

DON ALONSO   Inés, tell me where Beatriz is, so I may
speak to her.

---

a-e, would be sound if *mas que* were a single word (which is not the case). However,
comic servants are often permitted to take liberties with metre, and there is no
obvious way of retaining good sense by tinkering with this line alone.

Sale Beatriz

BEATRIZ   Aquí está Beatriz,
                escuchando los ultrajes   2860
                de una vil hermana, de un
                falso amigo, de un infame
                criado, una criada aleve,
                y de un cauteloso amante,
                porque entre Leonor, Don Juan,   2865
                Inés y Moscatel halle,
                si no consuelo a mis penas,
                disculpa a mis disparates.
                Y aunque pudiera de tantos
                agravios, tantos pesares,   2870
                tantas ofensas y tantas
                bajezas vuestras quejarme,
                viendo que contra mí todos
                el falso motín firmasteis,
                porque en la corte del alma,   2875
                donde en pacíficas paces
                reina el desdén, nunca tiene
                el amor comunidades,
                sólo en esta parte intento,
                sólo quiero en esta parte,   2880
                como quejosa, ofenderme,
                como ofendida, quejarme
                del mayor de mis agravios
                y no el menor de mis males;
                porque en las mujeres es   2885
                el más sensible desaire
                que las ame la mentira
                y no la verdad las ame.
                ¿Tan pocas las partes son
                de mi hacienda y de mi sangre?   2890
                ¿Tan pocas de mi persona
                (decirlo tengo), las partes
                que hay, que si un hombre hubiera
                que atrevido me mirase,
                fuese con fingido amor?   2895
                ¡Quererme a mí por burlarme,
                a mí por...!

DON ALONSO   Beatriz hermosa,
                si de todos tus pesares
                sales tan airosa como

Enter Beatriz

BEATRIZ

Beatriz is here, listening to the slanders of a vile sister, of a false friend, of a shameless manservant and a treacherous maid, and of a deceitful lover. The behaviour of Leonor and Don Juan, of Inés and Moscatel, may not console me in my grief, but at least it may explain my foolishness.

Though I might well protest against your many mean, injurious, hurtful and offensive deeds, and though I see that you have all deceitfully conspired against me, I realise that, in the palace of the soul, disdain reigns in perfect peace and love brooks no rebellion: and so, my only wish, my one intention, is complainingly to take offense and offendedly to make complaint about that which was the gravest of my injuries and not the smallest of my woes; for women's greatest problem is that lies make them fall in love when truth will not.

Are my station and my breeding worth so little? Is my person of such small account that, if some man dared look upon me, he could not feel love but only feign it?

To think that a man should court me just to mock me, just to...!

DON ALONSO

Oh, my lovely Beatriz! If you emerge so radiant from all your tribulations as you do

	de ése, que más sientes, sales,	2900
	fácil es el desengaño.	
BEATRIZ	¿Cómo el desengaño es fácil,	
	cuando el quererme es por burla?	
DON ALONSO	Si atiendes, con escucharme.	
	Tal vez por burla se atreve	2905
	uno al mar, sin que presuma,	
	viéndole jardín de espuma,	
	viéndole selva de nieve,	
	que hay peligro en él; y, en breve,	
	selva y jardín son horror.	2910
	Mar es amor en rigor;	
	luego en placer y en pesar,	
	si no hay burlas con el mar,	
	no hay burlas con el amor.	
	Tal vez, por burla o ensayo,	2915
	polvorista artificial	
	hace un rayo material,	
	y forja contra sí el rayo,	
	cuando con mortal desmayo	
	muere a su violento ardor.	2920
	Rayo es amor en rigor	
	contra su artífice; luego,	
	si no hay burlas con el fuego,	
	no hay burlas con el amor.	
	Tal vez desnuda un amigo	2925
	la espada para esgrimir	
	con otro, y le viene a herir	
	como si fuera enemigo;	
	su destreza es su castigo,	
	y así, usar de ella es error.	2930
	Espada amor en rigor	
	es; luego, desenvainada,	
	si no hay burlas con la espada,	
	no hay burlas con el amor.	
	Tal vez por burla, mirando	2935
	doméstica y mansa ya	
	una fiera, un hombre está	
	con ella, Beatriz, jugando;	
	cuando más la halaga blando,	
	volver suele a su furor.	2940
	Fiera es amor, en rigor;	

now from these that you have felt so deeply,
there is a very simple remedy.

BEATRIZ   How can there be a simple remedy when
your love for me was just a joke?

DON ALONSO If you listen, you shall learn.

For a joke, a man may brave the sea, not
realising, when he observes it like a garden
of foam or a forest of snow, that there could
be any danger in it. But then forest and
garden turn horrendous.

Love is a sea. Just as the sea, whether
rough or smooth, must not be trifled with,
likewise love must not be trifled with.

As a joke, or perhaps as an experiment, a
firework artist may make a real thunderbolt, only to find, as he swoons beneath
its deadly heat, that he has turned it on
himself.

Love is a thunderbolt turned on its own
creator. Just as fire must not be trifled
with, likewise love must not be trifled with.

A man may unsheathe his sword to fence
with a friend, and then wound him as if he
were an enemy.

He is punished by his own dexterity.
Therefore it is foolish to use it.

Love is a sword. Just as an unsheathed
sword must not be trifled with, likewise love
must not be trifled with.

A man may amuse himself by playing
with a savage beast which he thinks is tame
and domesticated. While he is caressing it
most fondly, the beast reverts to its native
ferocity.

Love is a wild beast.

luego, si ya lisonjera,
no hay burlas con una fiera,
no hay burlas con el amor.
Por burla al mar me entregué,   2945
por burla el rayo encendí,
con blanca espada esgrimí,
con brava fiera jugué;
y así, en el mar me anegué,
del rayo sentí el ardor,   2950
de acero y fiera el furor:
luego, si saben matar
fiera, acero, rayo y mar,
no hay burlas con el amor.

BEATRIZ   A ese argumento...

Sale Inés de prisa, alborotada, y Leonor

LEONOR   ¡Ay de mí!   2955
Huyendo salió a la calle
Don Juan, y cuando le daba
voces, vi entrar a mi padre.
Esconder me importa agora...

BEATRIZ   No, Leonor, porque ya es tarde;...   2960

LEONOR   ...a Don Alonso.

BEATRIZ   ...que hoy
ha de saber cuanto pase
mi padre, pues tus engaños
se han de saber.

LEONOR   Cuando trates
tú decirlo, yo sabré   2965
culparte a ti, y disculparme;
y así, puesto que las dos
corremos el riesgo iguales,
iguales, Beatriz, busquemos
el remedio.

BEATRIZ   Por mostrarte   2970
a proceder bien, lo haré,
que es fuerza estar de tu parte.

MOSCATEL   Alacena, como iglesia,
pido.

2973–4 **sanctuary**: *pedir iglesia* (literally, 'to ask for church') means 'to ask for sanctuary (in a religious establishment)'. In the collaboration play *Polifemo y Circe*
(*Polyphemus and Circe*), written in 1630 by Calderón and others, the comic servant,

> Just as a beast, however gentle, must not
> be trifled with, likewise love must not be
> trifled with.
>
> As a joke I launched upon the sea; as a
> joke I lit a thunderbolt; as a joke I bore a
> sword and played with a savage beast.
>
> And so I perished in the sea; I was
> scorched by the thunderbolt; I felt the fury
> of steel and beast.
> If, then, beast and steel and bolt and sea
> can kill a man, love must not be trifled with.

BEATRIZ   To that argument...

Enter Inés, hurrying and very upset, with Leonor

LEONOR   Oh dear! Don Juan rushed into the street,
                   but when I shouted after him I saw my
                   father coming in.
                   I must hide...

BEATRIZ   Too late, Leonor,...

LEONOR   ...Don Alonso.

BEATRIZ   ...for today my father shall know everything
                   that is going on, and all your lies will be
                   discovered.

LEONOR   If you try and tell him, I'll find a way
                   to throw the blame on you and exonerate
                   myself.
                   Since we're both in the same predica-
                   ment, let us both seek a way out.

BEATRIZ   Just to show you how to behave properly,
                   I'll do so. Besides, I have no choice but to
                   take your side.

MOSCATEL   The cupboard! I demand the sanctuary of
                   the cupboard!

---

who had earlier hidden in a cave, when faced with danger cries 'Cueva pido otra vez',
'I demand [the sanctuary of] the cave again' (BAE, XIV, 425b). Similarly, the comic
servant Chacón in *El maestro de danzar* (*The dancing-master*) says: 'Guitarra pido,
/ como iglesia', Aguilar II, 1565; that is, fearing discovery by an irate father, he calls
for the guitar he had used to pass himself off as the dancing-master's assistant.

DON ALONSO	Eso no haré, que es antes...	
INÉS	Él entra ya.	
BEATRIZ	Este aposento	2975
	hoy de su vista te guarde.	
MOSCATEL	¡Y a mí me guarde también!	
DON ALONSO [ap.]	¡Qué pesados son los lances	
	de amor hijo de familias!	
MOSCATEL	Inés, avisa en la calle	2980
	que ya estamos escondidos:	
	que haya quien nos descalabre.	

Escóndense los dos, y sale Don Pedro

DON PEDRO	¿Tan tarde, y no han encendido?	
	Haz tú que unas luces saquen.	
INÉS	Ya las tengo prevenidas.	2985
DON PEDRO [ap.]	¡En mi casa tal desaire!	
	¡A mis ojos tal afrenta!	
	Cielos piadosos, o dadme	
	paciencia, o dadme la muerte.	
BEATRIZ	Señor, ¿qué tienes?	
LEONOR	¿Qué traes?	2990
DON PEDRO	Tengo honor, y traigo agravios...	
	aunque miento en esta parte,	
	puesto que yo no los traigo:	
	ellos vienen a buscarme	
	dentro de mi misma casa.	2995
LEONOR [ap.]	¡Ay de mí!	
INÉS [ap.]	Todo se sabe.	
BEATRIZ	Pues, señor, ¿no me dirás	
	de qué estos extremos nacen?	
DON PEDRO	De tus locuras, Beatriz;	
	que ya es fuerza declararme,	3000
	viendo que por ti se atreve	
	hoy un mozuelo arrogante	
	al honor de aquesta casa.	
LEONOR [ap.]	Ya no hay cosa que no alcance.	
BEATRIZ	¿Yo, señor?	
MOSCATEL [ap., al paño]	Malo va esto.	3005

2980–2 As events repeat themselves, Moscatel implies that hiding will again be followed by a leap from the balcony and an attack in the street.

DON ALONSO	Ah, no! Not that again! I'd rather...
INÉS	He's almost here!
BEATRIZ	Let this room preserve you from his gaze.
MOSCATEL	Let it preserve me, too!
DON ALONSO	How tiresome these family affairs are!
MOSCATEL	Inés, send word down to the street that we're in hiding, so that somebody can come along later and beat us up.

They both hide, and enter Don Pedro

DON PEDRO	So late, and no lamps lit yet! Send for lights!
INÉS	I have them ready.
DON PEDRO (*aside*)	Such aspersions on my house! Such insults to my face! Merciful Heaven, give me patience or give me death!
BEATRIZ	What is the matter, sir?
LEONOR	What's wrong?
DON PEDRO	What is the matter is that I have honour. What's wrong is that I have met insults, though it might be truer to say insults have come calling on me in my house.
LEONOR (*aside*)	Oh dear!
INÉS (*aside*)	He knows everything!
BEATRIZ	But, will you not tell me, sir, from whence these sorrows spring?
DON PEDRO	They spring from your foolishness, Beatriz. I must now speak plainly. Because of you, an arrogant young pup today had the effrontery to impugn the honour of this house.
LEONOR (*aside*)	Nothing will escape him now!
BEATRIZ	Because of me, sir?
MOSCATEL (*aside, at the backcloth*)	This is going very badly.

2986–95 Don Pedro is still smarting with the slight to his honour implied by Don Luis's refusal to marry Beatriz.

Don Pedro	Sí, pues por ti Don Luis hace desprecios de ella, y de mí.
Beatriz [ap.]	Convaleciendo va el lance.
Leonor [ap.]	Eso bien, cobre mi aliento.

Sale Don Juan

Don Juan	([Ap.] Un caso bien puede errarse	3010
	de una vez, pero de dos	
	la una no le yerra nadie.	
	No he de esperar a que cierren	
	las puertas, y después baje	
	por el balcón Don Alonso:	3015
	remediarlo pienso antes.)	
	Señor Don Pedro, si en vos	
	hoy la amistad de mis padres,	
	heredada obligación	
	de mi casa y de mi sangre...	3020
Leonor [ap.]	¿Qué es lo que intenta Don Juan?	
Beatriz [ap.]	Muerta estoy hasta escucharle.	
Don Juan	...os obliga en un aprieto	
	a valerme y ampararme,	
	de vuestra casa a las puertas	3025
	me ha sucedido un desaire	
	con tres hombres, y me importa	
	no volver solo a buscarles.	
	Muy bien sé que puedo a vos	
	atreverme y declararme,	3030
	porque sé que es vuestro pecho	
	el Etna que dentro arde,	
	aunque cubierto de nieve.	
Don Pedro	No paséis más adelante;	
	que ya sé que es ley precisa	3035
	de mi honor y de mi sangre	
	en esta edad no dejar	
	a hombre que de mí se vale.	
	Vamos.	

3008-9   Both Beatriz and Leonor (and all the others, for that matter) had supposed that Don Pedro had somehow found out about Don Juan's and Don Alonso's
courtship of his daughters, and perhaps even about Don Alonso's presence in the
house; so they are relieved that his anger is inspired only by Don Luis.

3017-28   Once again, Don Juan makes an appeal in the name of the friendship which
puts nobles under an obligation to each other. It may be noted that he invents an
extra enemy, to increase the odds against him and so to increase the sense of duty

DON PEDRO

Yes. Because of you Don Luis insults both my house and me.

BEATRIZ (*aside*)

Not as bad as I thought!

LEONOR (*aside*)

That's all right. I can breathe again!

Enter Don Juan

DON JUAN

(*Aside*. It's reasonable to make a mistake once, but no one can afford to make the same mistake twice.

I shan't wait for them to close the doors and for Don Alonso to drop from the balcony. This time I'll move first.)

Don Pedro, if your friendship for my parents, a bond which I inherited with my house and with my blood...

LEONOR (*aside*)

What is Don Juan trying to do?

BEATRIZ (*aside*)

I'm on tenterhooks to hear what he'll say next.

DON JUAN

...obliges you to assist me in time of need, know that my honour was impugned by three men at the very door of your house, and I am reluctant to pursue them on my own.

I believe I can turn to you and call upon your valour, in the knowledge that your heart is like Mount Etna, ablaze within though outside capped in snow.

DON PEDRO

Say no more! I know I am bound by my honour and my blood, in this day and age, to assist any man who turns to me for help. Let us go!

---

which Don Pedro will feel.

3029–33 Mount Etna (Sicily) is over 10,000 feet high, and there is often snow on the summit. Calderón (and Lope de Vega before him) often made use of the fire/ice contrast of the snow-covered volcano. Silius Italicus has just such a contrast in his *Punica* (XIV, 66–9), and so do other Classical authors. Here the 'cap of snow' is Don Pedro's white hair. It may be that Calderón wrote this part with Antonio de Prado in mind: in 1635 Prado was fortyish and plump, but we do not know if he was greying.

DON JUAN	En fin, sois quien sois.
	[*Ap. a ella*] En llevando yo a tu padre, 3040
	Leonor, echa a Don Alonso.
DON ALONSO [*ap.*	Éstos son los que matarme
al paño]	quisieron. No me está bien
	ir con ellos ni quedarme.
DON PEDRO	Esperad, que ya es de noche, 3045
	que de aquesa sala saque
	un broquel, prenda olvidada
	de mi mocedad.
DON JUAN	Sacadle
	presto.
BEATRIZ [*ap.*]	Él se ha empeñado más
	por donde pensó librarse. 3050
DON PEDRO	¿Quién está aquí dentro?
DON ALONSO [*dentro*]	Un hombre.

[Salen Don Alonso y Moscatel]

MOSCATEL	Dice bien, porque no es nadie
	el otro que está con él.
DON PEDRO	Don Juan, pues que yo a ayudarte
	iba contra tu enemigo, 3055
	obligación es más grande
	el ayudarme tú a mí,
	cuando es la causa más grave.
	Este hombre ofende mi honor,
	y a mí me importa matarle. 3060
DON ALONSO	Don Juan, de tan grande empeño
	la obligación tuya sabes.
	Mi vida y las de estas damas
	es preciso que yo ampare.

Riñen, y Don Juan en medio

LEONOR	¡Ay de mí!
BEATRIZ	¡Infelice soy! 3065
DON JUAN	¿Quién vio empeño semejante?
DON PEDRO	¿Te suspendes?
DON ALONSO	¿Ahora dudas?

3047–8 **a buckler** is a small round shield, usually of wood with a steel rim. Gentlemen habitually wore swords at this time, but to go out with a shield was to be seen
to be looking for trouble. Young men did it, but someone of Don Pedro's supposed

DON JUAN	You are indeed a man of honour! (*Aside to Leonor.* As soon as I remove your father, get Don Alonso out of here.)
DON ALONSO (*aside, at the backcloth*)	These are the men who tried to kill me. I cannot very well join them, but I can hardly stay here either.
DON PEDRO	Wait a moment. It's dark already; let me go into this room and fetch a buckler that I haven't used since I was a young man.
DON JUAN	Get it quickly, then.
BEATRIZ (*aside*)	Don Juan's escape from the frying-pan has landed him in the fire!
DON PEDRO	Who is in here?
DON ALONSO (*offstage*)	A man.

Enter Don Alonso and Moscatel

MOSCATEL	He's right. The other one with him is nobody at all.
DON PEDRO	Don Juan, since I was going to assist you against your enemy, you are now obliged to help me in an even graver matter. This man offends my honour, and I must kill him.
DON ALONSO	Don Juan, in a predicament such as this, you know where your obligation lies. I must defend my own life and the lives of these ladies.

They fight, with Don Juan between them

LEONOR	Oh, my goodness!
BEATRIZ	Oh, woe is me!
DON JUAN	Did anyone ever see such a quandary?
DON PEDRO	What are you waiting for?
DON ALONSO	What's keeping you?

---

maturity could do so only under cover of darkness (3045).

3066–72 A favourite situation with Calderón: a hero torn two ways. Don Pedro expects Don Juan to assist him against the intruder Don Alonso; Don Alonso expects him to help protect the girls from their father's wrath (cf. notes 359–60, 379–81).

DON PEDRO   Mas soy bastante a vengarme
                       sin ti.

DON JUAN   Tente, Don Alonso.
                       Tente, señor.

DON PEDRO   Pues, ¿tú paces   3070
                       pones?

DON ALONSO   Pues, ¿tú contra mí
                       tan viles extremos haces?

Dentro DON LUIS   Cuchilladas hay en casa
                       de Don Pedro.

[*Dentro*] DON DIEGO   Más no aguardes;
                       entremos, Don Luis.

                       Salen Don Luis y Don Diego

DON LUIS   ¡Teneos!   3075
DON PEDRO   Gente viene.
DON ALONSO   ¡Duro trance!
DON LUIS   ¿Qué es esto?
DON PEDRO   Esto es, Don Luis,
                       satisfacer el ultraje
                       que te oí, pues si no está
                       bien a tu honor el casarte   3080
                       con Beatriz, al mío está bien
                       satisfacer y vengarme.

DON LUIS   Ahí verás que no sin causa
                       traté yo de disculparme,
                       que ya, por haber tenido   3085
                       algún empeño en la calle...

DON ALONSO   Sin duda que tú me heriste.
DON LUIS   Es verdad.
DON ALONSO   Yo he de vengarme.
DON JUAN   Pues quiere el cielo que así
                       hoy mis celos desengañen,   3090
                       viva Leonor en mi pecho.
                       [*A Don Pedro*] Ya es forzoso que la guarde
                       contra ti.

DON PEDRO   Don Juan, Don Juan,
                       en aquesta casa nadie

3090 **jealousy . . . unfounded**: that is, Don Juan realises Don Luis was paying court

DON PEDRO	Never mind, I can avenge myself without you.
DON JUAN	Hold on, Don Alonso. Hold on, sir.
DON PEDRO	Are you trying to play peacemaker?
DON ALONSO	How can you behave so disloyally towards me?
DON LUIS (*offstage*)	There's fighting in Don Pedro's house.
DON DIEGO (*offstage*)	Wait no longer. Let us go in, Don Luis.

Enter Don Luis and Don Diego

DON LUIS	Stop!
DON PEDRO	Someone's coming!
DON ALONSO	What a frightful dilemma!
DON LUIS	What's this?
DON PEDRO	This, Don Luis, is expunging the dishonour you spoke of. If marrying Beatriz is incompatible with *your* honour, leaving an insult unavenged is incompatible with *mine*.
DON LUIS	Now you realise that it was not for nothing I withdrew. As a result of that incident in the street...
DON ALONSO	Then *you're* the one who wounded me!
DON LUIS	I am.
DON ALONSO	I will be avenged!
DON JUAN	Thank Heaven! My jealousy turns out to be unfounded! Leonor, live forever in my heart! (*To Don Pedro*) Now I must defend her against *you*.
DON PEDRO	Don Juan, Don Juan, in this house my

---

to Beatriz, not to Leonor, and that he therefore had no rival to be jealous of.

	ha de defender mis hijas	3095
	si no es con quien ellas casen.	
Don Alonso	Esa palabra te tomo.	
Don Juan	Pues el remedio es tan fácil,	
	yo soy de Leonor.	
Don Alonso	Y yo	
	de Beatriz.	
Don Pedro	Fuerza es que calle;	3100

Don Alonso
ha de defender mis hijas 3095
si no es con quien ellas casen.

Don Alonso
Esa palabra te tomo.

Don Juan
Pues el remedio es tan fácil,
yo soy de Leonor.

Don Alonso
       Y yo
de Beatriz.

Don Pedro
       Fuerza es que calle; 3100
que, ya sucedido el daño,
nada puede remediarse.

Moscatel
En fin, el hombre más libre,
de las burlas de amor sale
herido, cojo y casado, 3105
que es el mayor de sus males.

Inés
En fin, la mujer más loca,
más vana y más arrogante,
de las burlas del amor,
contra gusto suyo, sale 3110
enamorada y casada,
que es lo peor.

Moscatel
       Inés, dame
esa mano; si ha de ser,
no lo pensemos, y acaben
burlas de amor, que son veras. 3115

Don Alonso
No se burle con él nadie,
sino escarmentad en mí:
todos del amor se guarden,
y perdonad al poeta
que humilde a esas plantas yace. 3120

FIN
De la famosa Comedia de
No hay burlas con el
amor.

	daughters shall be defended only by the men they marry.
DON ALONSO	I accept that role.
DON JUAN	Well, if the remedy is that simple, I'll belong to Leonor.
DON ALONSO	And I to Beatriz.
DON PEDRO	I must hold my tongue. Once the damage is done, it cannot be undone.
MOSCATEL	And so we see that the freest of men emerges from the game of love maimed and lamed and (worst of all disasters!) wed.
INÉS	And the silliest, vainest, haughtiest woman emerges from the game of love enamoured in spite of herself and (what's even worse!) wed.
MOSCATEL	Inés, give me your hand. If that's how it has to be, let's not waste time thinking about it, and let this be the end of the serious game of love.
DON ALONSO	And so you see that love is no laughing matter! Take a lesson from me; let everyone beware of love!
	And now forgive the poet who humbly prostrates himself at your feet.

END
of the famous play
Love is no laughing
matter.

Editorial emendations made to D (Zaragoza, 1650)

The reading before the bracket is that of our text; the reading after it is that of D.

0+ *triste*] *tristes*
10 el] al
12 a suspirar hoy así?] a suspiros? ay de mi.
47 rey de romanos] Rey Romanos
49 estoy] soy
52 afectüoso] efectuoso
54 hay para qué] ay que
55 querrás] querra
57 al] el
64 yo el galán, tú] yo en galan, y tu
139 hace] hazen
161 del] De
180 el] del
181 no da] nada
262 yace] haze
274 bellísima] bellisimo
338 explicó el] esplico al
354 temiendo] teniendo
364 disimulado y secreto] (lacking; supplied from VT1)
402 temer puedo] temer no puedo
410 no] o no
412 he] (lacking)
439 darás] da
444 éste el] este es el
450 hoguera de hielo] o guerra de nieue
475 es ejercicio] es el exercicio
491 no vive] viue
503 yo] oy
504 desvanecida] descodocida [sic]
510 a gusto en] en gusto de
520 culto, él] oculto, y el
534 el] en
539 y digo que no] y no
541 la] lo
547 lo que no llegan a verlo] (lacking; supplied from H)
566 haciendo del] Haziendo el
575+ *en él*] *en el, y Clara, y otras dos*
576 hay una fámula] ay famula
577 abstraigas] traygas
603 viene a arrojarse] viene arrojarse
610 del caos de] el caos a
613 atento] atenta
616 inficione, aliento] inficion se alienta
636 ¿qué másculo] que es Masculo
655 Áspid al] Adpizal

656+ *Beatriz*] *Beatriz, y Clara, y Sale Moscatel*
661 siguiendo] siruiendo
661+ (D's stage direction *Sale Moscatel* also serves as speaker's name for 661–4)
669 a haber] auer
677 y aunque] aunque
683 que a mi] que mi
710 que] pues
723 ¿Que no habláis?] Que hazeis? no hablais?
731 soy] si oy
734 crïado me llamo] me llamo criado
740 justa] lustre
754 está allí] està
760+ *Llega*] *Sale*
763 no sé.] no se que.
766 DON JUAN Algo di] (speaker and speech supplied by editors; in D, Moscatel says 'Bueno. / Moscatel que importa assi.', and his name appears again as speaker opposite 768. Clearly Don Juan was meant to say 767, preceded by three syllables rhyming in -í, to complete 766.)
769 hallando] he hallado
772 fui] fue
790 le] se
794–5 turbó / el] turbais de
805 DON PEDRO] (lacking)
807 Venid] venir
861 Dices] Dezis
873 ansarino] en seruicio
882 querer] querrê
884 fraternidad no atiende] fraternid no entiende
892+ *las*] *los*
895–6 por fuerza verle, tirana, poco podré o no] verle, no
903 abstraes] atraes
904 fragmento] fracmentos [sic]
905 referirá] preferirâ
912 BEATRIZ ¿Yo?] (D omits speaker's name, adds 'yo' to Leonor's speech)
912 verme] verle
929 me construyó] construiô
940 mal tan] combate

948 acosado] acosada
949 cercado] cercana
957 (D adds '*Leo*. Yo, señor?' after Beatriz's speech)
960 mentil] mental
969 El] Al
970 es] en
987 el] en
988 contiene] contienes
989+ *Lee*] *Leo*. (as if speaker's name)
1041 estelionato] este tronato
1078 refrena] afrena
1107 Para] Ha
1111 quiera] querrâ
1119 Oye] (lacking)
1132 si entraba] ò estaua
1167 queréis] quieres
1168 Que aquí no] Que no
1173 Decís] Dizes
1184 vais] vayas
1209 ¡Ay, dulce hechizo del alma,] (lacking, supplied from VT1)
1218 pluguiera] plegue
1252 esa] la
1255 tal] tanta
1286+ (D lacks any indication for Inés to go off stage here; but if 1287–1477 take place inside Don Pedro's house, as seems almost certain, she should follow convention and do so, indicating that the scene has changed from street to inside)
1289 tuyo] suyo
1293 evidencia] obediencia
1294 en] (lacking)
1297 entrambas] entrãbos
1313 convenía] conuiniera
1328 he] (lacking)
1330 por] para
1357 nombre] nube
1361 error] orror
1372 ¿Tú no fuiste] (lacking in D; four syllables ending in -iste are needed, and Hartzenbusch offers the solution which is most elegant and most in keeping with 1371 and 1376)
1391 yo muero] y muero
1394 error] horror
1417–23 (a *décima* with only seven lines)
1439 quede] quedes
1466 relevante] reuelante
1470 evidencia] obediẽcia

1472 queriendo con su injusticia] (lacking in D; supplied from VT1)
1474 Beatriz, el vicio] el juyzio Beatriz
1476 tu] su
1482 dijo] digo
1505 dijo] digo
1514 mejor es] mugeres
1523 media] medio
1526 al] a
1534 finca] fiança
1546 lo] la
1617 ande] anda
1633 mi] a mi
1639 haciéndola] haziendome
1666 finjas] finja
1705 a un hombre amores] vn hõbre anoche
1707 entró] entrê
1708 el] al
1709 son] sin
1710 aun a pensar] aun pensar
1711 así] si
1720 parangón] parangel
1721 no me ha de ver la cara,] (lacking in D; supplied from VT2)
1732 viera] diera
1765–8 (the rhyme and versification of these lines is defective, but the sense is good, so we have left them alone)
1773 huïdas] vidas
1799 Sirtes] fletes
1800 Escilas] encinas (D's 'en caribdes' in the next line persuades us that this is meant to be a reference to Scylla, made plural)
1816 salto] falto
1817 golfo navegue] golfe naue, que
1821 pude] pudo
1829 mustio al] mostrò el
1831 entre] antes
1837 este alboroto] tanto absurdo
1844 que] (lacking in D)
1853 tuyo] suyo
1854 le] lo
1894 (lacking in D; supplied by the editors)
1901 gente] tente
1971 Quedá adiós] quedaos con Dios
1975 habrá] auia
1990 haz al] a tal
2002 desdoblaros] despoblaros
2009 el] este

2025 arrojaos] arrojados
2026 Ea, pues] (lacking in D, two syllables assonating in -é; we supply from VT1)
2032 no] y no os
2039 (D begins the act with our present line 2049, followed by our 2039 and 2041, both said by Beatriz: i.e., a single unattached line, followed by a *décima* with only nine lines. Our intervention restores the metre and improves the sense.)
2054 copla que por ti] coxo que partió
2063 es claudicante] es ser claudicante
2064 perder vicio] perder ese vicio
2075 ¡Qué ultraje!] que le traxo
2077 un] en
2086 fiera] si ve
2114 pueda] puede
2115 suya] tuya
2118 a agradecer] agradecer
2119 señora] ya
2124 has] he
2140 yo] y
2144 fiel...intente] si el...intento
2145 consiente] consiento
2155 tú la ladrona] tu ladrona
2157 tan bien] tambien
2171–2 vuestra diligencia / en Beatriz un grande efeto] vna diligencia / grande, Beatriz de este efecto.
2189-95 (a *décima* with seven lines)
2196 Sí] (supplied by the editors; the line lacks a final syllable in -í)
2209 justo...justo] gusto...gusto
2213 y] (lacking in D)
2222 ellas] ella
2226–34 (a *décima* of nine lines; the missing one, ending in -elos—possibly '¡cielos!'—belongs between 2229 and 2230)
2231-2 así / a] ha sido, / y
2238 ese] este
2245-53 (a *décima* of nine lines; the missing one should rhyme with 2252)
2248 Pero yo] (supplied by the editors, since D needs three more syllables with a rhyme in -ó)
2256 tenerle] tenerlo
2270 aquésta] esta

2272–3 (D has only one line here, 'querida tanta priuança'. Although this has eight syllables and the right assonance, we cannot fit its sense into the context, and believe *querida* to be a misreading of *tu erida*, i.e. *tu herida*, a reference to Don Alonso's injury. 2272 is our invention.)
2279 gusto] justo
2292 (a line with a syllable too many; but the sense is good and the error not obvious)
2313 en] a
2314 No] Yo no
2329 terció] torció
2330 se quitó] requirió
2345 y siendo] diziendo
2363-4 de aquesa dama / qué es el nombre] que desta dama / quede vn hombre
2385 y] (lacking in D)
2423 tanta] tal
2456 la] las
2467 se entra] se en entra
2469 Hircania] Arcadia
2503 esa] esta
2508 Toma] Tomo
2510 este] esse
2516–17 diablos hoy / heréticos] diablos / en critico
2519 que das] quedar
2525 dicen] dize
2548 DON JUAN] (in D, from 'q̃ ya' to 'estàs' is attributed to Alonso, and Juan says only 'Como acaba oy mi amor')
2549 estáis, como se acaba] estàs. / Como acaba
2554 amada] criada
2555 ni] (lacking in D; supplied by the editors)
2556 ni de verla] (lacking in D; supplied by the editors)
2558 hablarla] hablarle
2587 allá?] a la
2653-6 (a *quintilla* with only four lines, although the sense is good)
2655 celos] cielos
2667 hielo] zelo
2675 que] (lacking in D)

2690 que las] que a las
2693 fui] fue
2697 soy] fuy
2698 con] que
2706 entendáis] entendeis
2711 sabido] oîdo
2732–3 (D here repeats 2731, but this creates a *quintilla* with six lines, as well as a problem with rhyme)
2735 ¡ay infeliz!] poco siento [sic, repeated]
2748 callé] halla
2754 si acaso] viera si
2767 misivo el que en lineado] misero el que lineado
2779 te prometo] (lacking in D, which needs four syllables with a rhyme in -eto; we choose 'te prometo' from VT1, since these words are also used for this rhyme in line 2169)
2782 verle] verlo
2784 mal, pues me] mal me
2786 en] es, que en
2787 (this line and its speaker are lacking in D; the rhyme calls for a line in -ido, and while Beatriz's speech is not essential, it is an improvement)
2793 está un] estaua
2798+ y] (lacking in D; supplied by the editors)
2816 salió con] salieron
2819 aquí es] a que quedes
2829 piensen] piensan
2838 crédito] acredito
2859 Beatriz] a Beatriz
2871 y] (lacking in D; supplied by the editors)
2877 nunca tiene] (lacking in D; the editors have supplied four syllables which fit the sense)
2884 mis] los
2893 que si un] que vn
2898 de todos tus] de tus
2906 al mar] a amar
2910 son] sin
2911 Mar] mas
2913 el mar] amar
2930 error] honor
2951 y fiera] fiero
2958 vi entrar] mientras
2962 ha...pase] se ha...passa
2965 tú decirlo] tu de dezirlo
2970 remedio] medio
2976 su] tu
2987 A] en
2992 miento] miente
2993 puesto que] porque
2996 (in D, Inés also says 'Ay de mi!', as well as 'todo se sabe')
3002 hoy] y
3014 baje] vaya
3051 dentro] (lacking in D; first added by VT1)
3054 yo a ayudarte] yo aiudarte
3058 grave] grande
3067 Te] Aora te
3068 Mas soy] Mas yo soy
3070–1 paces / pones] pones pazes (D omits 'Pues' in 3071)
3079 te] os
3089 así] casi
3092 Ya] y
3099 Y yo] Yo
3101 sucedido] sucedio
3110 sale] salen
3114 y acaben] (lacking in D; supplied from H)
3120 esas] sus

LOVE IS NO LAUGHING MATTER

NO HAY BURLAS CON EL AMOR

The stage of the theatre in Almagro (Ciudad Real), seen from a balcony.
Most public theatres in Calderón's time were simple and intimate like this.
(Courtesy of Professor J.E. Varey, London)